T0271228

Historically, enterprises were an important delivery vehicle for the administration and financing of many programmes of social protection in the economies of Central and Eastern Europe and the former Soviet Union. In most cases this was through systems mandated by the state. When the Central and East European countries began their reforms many expected enterprises quickly to eliminate the benefits they had provided to workers once freed from the encumbrance of state control.

This volume is the first to investigate the size of these benefits and the forces producing changes in them. Each chapter covers a specific country, exploring the scope, scale and change of benefits in the respective countries, and investigates their determinants. Surprisingly, they find only modest declines and even some increases in aggregate benefits, rather than rapid change. Change is more visible in the details. This volume examines new social functions, like early retirement, in both established and newly privatized enterprises.

Enterprise and social benefits after communism

Institut für Höhere Studien (IHS), Wien
Institute for Advanced Studies, Vienna

The Institute for Advanced Studies (IHS) was established in 1963 on the initiative of Paul F. Lazarsfeld and Oskar Morgenstern with the help of the Ford Foundation. It is a postgraduate research and education institution which trains highly qualified young scientists and managers. Young graduates can obtain further qualifications in economics and the social sciences from internationally renowned visiting professors. The special feature of the Institute for Advanced Studies is its combination of research and education.

The Institute is divided into four departments:

Mathematical Methods and Computer Science
Economics
Political Science
Sociology

It has approximately 45 scientific employees and 17 administrative employees. There are about 70 students.

Director   Professor Dr Bernhard Felderer

Centre for Economic Policy Research

The Centre for Economic Policy Research is a network of over 350 Research Fellows, based primarily in European universities. The Centre coordinates its Fellows' research activities and communicates their results to the public and private sectors. CEPR is an entrepreneur, developing research initiatives with the producers, consumers and sponsors of research. Established in 1983, CEPR is a European economics research organization with uniquely wide-ranging scope and activities.

CEPR is a registered educational charity. Institutional (core) finance for the Centre is provided by major grants from the Economic and Social Research Council, under which an ESRC Resource Centre operates within CEPR; the Esmée Fairbairn Charitable Trust; the Bank of England; the European Monetary Institute and the Bank for International Settlements; 21 national central banks; and 42 companies. None of these organisations gives prior review to the Centre's publications, nor do they necessarily endorse the views expressed therein.

The Centre is pluralist and non-partisan, bringing economic research to bear on the analysis of medium- and long-run policy questions. CEPR research may include views on policy, but the Executive Committee of the Centre does not give prior review to its publications, and the Centre takes no institutional policy positions. The opinions expressed in this volume are those of the authors and not those of the Centre for Economic Policy Research.

Enterprise and social benefits after communism

Edited by

MARTIN REIN,

BARRY L. FRIEDMAN

and

ANDREAS WÖRGÖTTER

CAMBRIDGE
UNIVERSITY PRESS

CAMBRIDGE UNIVERSITY PRESS
Cambridge, New York, Melbourne, Madrid, Cape Town,
Singapore, São Paulo, Delhi, Tokyo, Mexico City

Cambridge University Press
The Edinburgh Building, Cambridge CB2 8RU, UK

Published in the United States of America by
Cambridge University Press, New York

www.cambridge.org
Information on this title: www.cambridge.org/9780521584036

First published 1997

A catalogue record for this publication is available from the British Library

Library of Congress Cataloguing in Publication data
Enterprise and social benefits after communism / edited by Martin Rein, Barry L. Friedman, and
Andreas Worgotter
    p. cm. Includes index.
ISBN 0 521 58403 5 (hardback)
1. Employee fringe benefits – Europe, Eastern.
2. Employee fringe benefits – Former Soviet republics.
3. Privatization – Europe, Eastern.
4. Privatization – Former Soviet republics.
5. Public welfare – Europe, Eastern.
6. Public welfare – Former Soviet republics.
I. Rein, Martin, 1928– . II. Friedman, Barry L. III. Wörgötter, Andreas.
HD4928.N6E57 1997
331.25′5′0947– dc21   96–48932   CIP

ISBN 978-0-521-58403-6 Hardback

Contents

Figures

Tables

Preface

There is a dominant view that within the framework of economic stabilization one of the main goals of policy in the economic transition should be the rapid privatization of enterprises. Yet, even when privatization has occurred, the expectation that enterprises would be radically transformed has not always been realized. In particular, the assumption that ownership matters and is the decisive determinant of how much enterprises spend on social benefits may be too strong. We feel that, with several years having passed since the beginning of the transition, it is time to start looking not only at the theory but at the details of what was actually happening within the enterprises. One of the areas of detail that has not yet received much systematic attention is that of changes in the level and composition of enterprise social benefits that had been a major feature of the old system. We began hearing accounts of how these social benefits had been declining, but other stories also made it clear that these benefits were not disappearing at all and were perhaps even growing. Of course, both accounts could be true, as several chapters of this volume consider in detail.

On one side, analysts take the view that there is so much unemployment, poverty, hardship, and severe erosion of living standards, and an astonishing decline in the longevity of mature adults that dealing with these urgent social issues should be the prime goal of policy. But even if the need to respond to this urgent agenda is acknowledged, there is still the question of what are the available tools for doing so. Were these benefits still being used as a tool, or were the changes in the benefits undermining social well-being? Again, this called attention to the need to examine what was actually happening in practice.

Martin Rein used the occasion of a sabbatical year in 1993–4 from MIT, the financial support of the International Institute of Applied Systems Analysis (IIASA), and the encouragement of its Director, Peter de Janosi, to pursue this topic. His affiliation as a member of the External

Faculty of the European Center in Vienna helped bring this project to its successful outcome. During that sabbatical year in Vienna, the Institute for Advanced Studies (IHS) had its thirtieth anniversary, at which Richard Portes spoke. As Director of the Centre for Economic Policy Research (CEPR), he discussed issues concerning social protection in East European enterprises with the Director of IHS, Bernhard Felderer, and they agreed to sponsor a joint conference on this subject. This project would never have been realized without the support of the directors of all three institutions. Indeed, Andreas Wörgötter, the Head of the Economics Department at IHS, became sufficiently enthusiastic about the project to be a co-editor and a contributor to several chapters of the book. Nor could the work have been produced without the financial support provided by the studies programme of the Directorate-General for Economic and Financial Affairs (DG II) of the European Commission. The papers in this volume were commissioned under a contract from the Commission of the European Communities entitled 'Study of enterprises as a source of social protection in transitional economies'.

The ideas that Martin Rein brought to this project had originated before the sabbatical year and were the outcome of two joint papers written with Barry Friedman. Friedman is currently an economist at the Florence Heller School of Social Welfare at Brandeis University with a primary interest in the social policy of enterprise in China.

The conference was held at IHS in Vienna on 25–26 March 1994. The smooth running of the conference could not have been possible without the skill, cheerfulness, and even disposition of Beatrix Krones in the face of all the usual frustrations of organizing an international conference. The conference papers led to the present volume. The timely publication of this volume was made possible by the highly professional performance of the Publications Department at CEPR in London: in particular the work of Kate Millward, Publications Manager, and James MacGregor, Publications Assistant. Martin Rein owes a special debt to Debby Kunz, secretary at MIT, for her unflagging and energetic support before and after the conference. Liz Paton, the copyeditor, insisted on high standards, and for this we are enormously in her debt.

Martin Rein
Barry L Friedman
Andreas Wörgötter

Conference participants

Fabrizio Coricelli *University of Siena and CEPR*
John Earle *Prague CEU Foundation*
Gáspár Fajth *UNICEF, Florence*
Barry L. Friedman *Brandeis University*
János Gács *International Institute for Applied Systems Analysis, Laxenburg*
Paul G. Hare *Heriot-Watt University*
Georg Heinrich *University of Vienna*
Eduard Hochreiter *Austrian National Bank*
Robert Holzmann *Europa Institut, Universität des Saarlandes*
Zuliu Hu *International Monetary Fund*
Richard Jackman *London School of Economics*
Martin Kohli *Freie Universität Berlin*
Judit Lakatos *Central Statistical Office, Budapest*
Jan Mládek *CERGE, Prague*
Mitchell Orenstein *Institute for EastWest Studies, Prague*
Joan Pearce *Commission of the European Communities*
Karl Pichelmann *Institute for Advanced Studies, Vienna*
Ján Plánovský *CERGE, Prague*
Richard Portes *CEPR and London Business School*
Martin Rein *MIT and Institute for Advanced Studies, Vienna*
Gérard Roland *ECARE, Université Libre de Bruxelles, and CEPR*
Peter Rosner *University of Vienna*
Mark E. Schaffer *London School of Economics*
Winifred Schmähl *Zentrum für Sozialpolitik, Universität Bremen*
Viktor Steiner *ZEW, Mannheim*
Jan Svejnar *University of Pittsburgh and CERGE, Prague*
Georg Winckler *University of Vienna*
Andreas Wörgötter *Institute for Advanced Studies, Vienna, and CEPR*

Foreword

The Centre for Economic Policy Research and the Institute for Advanced Studies have compiled a wide-ranging set of papers from authors in both the European Union and Central and Eastern Europe to address a central issue of the process of economic transition. Reallocating the responsibilities that state-owned enterprises assumed under central planning for providing social protection impinges on several of the key challenges of transition: restructuring enterprises; adapting labour markets; reforming tax and social security systems; and maintaining social consensus in support of the reform process. Those countries that are preparing for accession to the European Union will have to meet these challenges in order to comply with the economic criteria that have been set out for membership: functioning market economy; ability to cope with competitive pressures; and ability to assume the obligations of economic and monetary union.

Despite a shared history of central planning, the experience and practice of the countries covered in this volume have been quite diverse, in this as in other aspects of their economies. For a number of countries, the desire to join the European Union has brought about some uniformity of approach in certain areas. For example, the broad design features of their tax systems have been largely shaped to be compatible with EU membership. The system of expenditure and transfers, by contrast, is not subject to any specific requirements. Member states are entirely free to organize their social security as they wish, and within the EU a variety of different models exist.

In the papers in this volume two aspects of social protection can be distinguished: social insurance and benefits in kind. Social insurance, as in most market economies, was mainly the responsibility of government. Furthermore, the range of benefits in kind provided by enterprises under central planning was not markedly different from those provided by enterprises in market economies. There were two main differences: first, enterprises were often the principal providers, whereas in market economies they more typically supplement state or private provision; and, second, benefits tended to take the form of fixed assets, such as houses, schools, or clinics, rather than financial support, such as mortgage subsidies, scholarships, or health insurance.

Under central planning the countries of Central and Eastern Europe had comprehensive social insurance systems. Enterprises paid a payroll tax which entitled their workers to benefits. One important and costly, albeit hidden, benefit, however, was provided directly by enterprises: protection against loss of income through unemployment – redundant workers were kept on the payroll. This benefit was all the more valuable in view of the access that employment gave to a wide range of benefits in kind. Furthermore, it relieved the state of the obligation to provide some types of social insurance: there were no unemployment benefits or employment offices and no social assistance cash benefits. This system resulted in very high rates of participation in the workforce in centrally planned economies.

The steep fall in output that occurred in the first few years after the change of regime, together with the labour shedding by enterprises seeking to become competitive, led to a sharp rise in unemployment. Now that the fall in output has been reversed and most economies are growing strongly, unemployment has begun slowly to decline. Lower participation rates have also contributed to this improvement. None the less, for the time being new or restructured enterprises are able to absorb only a part of the workers released from the old enterprises.

The countries of Central and Eastern Europe moved quickly to set up new benefits and systems of administration for unemployment and poverty. As GDP contracted and as more people became unemployed or withdrew from the labour force, spending on social insurance as a proportion of GDP rose. Because of the acute fiscal problems faced by several countries, policy in this area tends to be treated primarily as a matter of achieving short-term cost reductions. Less attention has been given to undertaking fundamental reform of social security systems. Some steps have been taken, such as better targeting of benefits on needy groups and curbing previous social privileges, notably the right to early retirement. But much remains to be done, particularly with regard to pensions and health services.

The prospect in most countries that, despite rapid growth, unemployment will decline only gradually and will remain relatively high for some time to come has prompted governments in Central and Eastern Europe to develop active labour market policies. In view of the high proportion of long-term jobless and young people among the unemployed, it will be necessary to maintain and where possible extend these policies to avoid this part of the labour force becoming marginalized.

Enterprises, in endeavouring to restructure so as to become competitive, have not only laid off workers but also cut back on the benefits in kind they provide for the workers whom they continue to employ. In particular, they have withdrawn those benefits that involve fixed assets. This is a positive shift in that it helps make the labour market more flexible; in the past, provision of houses, schools, and clinics tended to induce the worker to stay in the place where the enterprise was located. Nevertheless, the effect of enterprise restructuring has been to deprive workers of all or some of their entitlement to benefits in kind, either through unemployment or through curtailing of benefits.

Although some of these benefits will be replaced by private provision, it will mostly fall to the state to make good others, notably health and education. This imposes additional spending obligations on budgets that are already under pressure. Central and East European countries face the delicate task of setting fiscal targets that ensure adequate discipline without postponing the transfer of social functions from the state enterprises to government.

Changes in the social protection provided by enterprises are essential if the countries of Central and Eastern Europe are to be functioning market economies able to compete on an equal footing within the European Union and to assume the obligations of economic and monetary union. At the same time it is important to make appropriate provision for those people who are most disadvantaged by the changes. These two objectives are interdependent: if the economies of Central and Eastern Europe do not achieve rapid and sustainable growth, they will not be able to afford adequate social protection; if a significant part of the population feels that the costs of reform are too great or too inequitable, the social consensus that is essential to the success of transition to a market economy risks breaking down.

The Directorate-General for Economic and Financial Affairs commends the papers in this volume to policy-makers who are dealing with an area of policy that is important both for completing the transition to a market economy and for preparing accession to the European Union.

Giovanni Ravasio
Director-General,
Directorate-General for
Economic and Financial Affairs,
European Commission

1   Introduction

MARTIN REIN, BARRY L. FRIEDMAN and
ANDREAS WÖRGÖTTER

When the reforms began in Eastern Europe, there were expectations of rapid change. In particular, enterprises freed of the encumbrance of state control were expected to become more efficient quickly, especially if they were privatized. One of the characteristics of the old enterprises was their practice of providing a variety of benefits to their workers in addition to wages. If these were imposed on enterprises by mandate of the state, they might be a source of unnecessary cost and inefficiency that could be quickly eliminated by privatized enterprises. It was possible at the start of the reforms to assemble a series of arguments leading to the prediction of rapid change in enterprise benefits – specifically rapid decline. The papers in this volume suggest, however, that in many cases the outcome has looked more like stability than change. There has, indeed, been change, but it has generally been gradual. None the less, a story of stability, if carried too far, would also be misleading. In the aggregate, the tendency has been toward modest declines in aggregate benefits in some countries, but also a modest increase in some. According to some of the studies, privatized enterprises, rather than curtailing benefits, have reduced them only slightly faster than have the still state-owned enterprises. Change is more visible in the details. New private enterprises do differ in their benefits from either state-owned or privatized enterprises, according to some of the studies, but they do give benefits. Considering particular benefits, there have been sharp reductions in some, but large increases in others. The apparent stability in the aggregate may be a matter of offsetting changes. It may be that enterprises freed of the old controls are redesigning – but not abandoning – their benefit packages. Moreover, government has not withdrawn from the picture in spite of the reforms. Governments still regulate and provide incentives, but the patterns of regulation have changed. It is possible that some of the changes in benefits, both increases and decreases, result from the changing policies of government.

Existing knowledge about the benefits in East European enterprises is rather slight. Prior to the studies in this volume, little was known about the size of benefits. Even less was known about the forces producing changes in them. The papers in this volume, each covering a specific country, provide a first step in understanding the non-wage compensation systems in Eastern Europe during the period of transition. Yet the importance of the subject is not just a matter of curiosity about a gap in knowledge. The enterprise benefit system may have important consequences for the efficiency of enterprises, for labour supply, and for the welfare of society. The impacts of enterprise benefits on these are complex and cannot be assessed without evidence.

Benefits may affect enterprise efficiency, but the direction of effect could go either way. Benefits may add to enterprise costs, reducing competitiveness. This could be true particularly when the benefits are mandatory and would not be voluntarily provided. Expensive benefits could also complicate the process of restructuring and privatization by reducing the value of the enterprise to potential investors. On the other hand, benefits are often used by enterprises to attract the desired kind of worker, to increase the loyalty of existing workers, and to enhance productivity. Enterprises voluntarily provide benefits because there are situations in which the benefits are expected to contribute to profitability. Moreover, enterprises respond to incentives from government. It might be profitable for enterprises to provide a benefit that is subsidized. Overall, it is possible that some benefits would reduce enterprise efficiency while others would increase it, and the outcomes would differ across different types of enterprises. In other words, a blanket judgement about the effects of benefits on the providing enterprises is not possible. Empirical evidence is needed on whether a benefit contributes to profitability, and for which kinds of enterprises.

Benefits also affect the prospects for restructuring through their effects on labour supply, but the effects can go in more than one direction. Enterprise-provided benefits can be a barrier to mobility. Workers receiving valued benefits may hesitate to seek a different job knowing that they will lose the benefits. But mobility may be an essential part of restructuring in that it shifts workers to new areas where they could be more productive. On the other hand, to the extent that benefits are conditional on employment, they could stimulate labour supply. Again there will be differences across firms since some are seeking while others are shedding workers. Evidence is needed both on the effects of benefits on labour supply and on the way firms make use of labour supply responses in designing benefit packages to meet their own needs. Given the various possibilities, one could imagine a scenario in which the effects of benefits on enterprises were primarily adverse and in which enterprises would seek quickly to drop benefits – a scenario of rapid change. One could also imagine a scenario in which the old benefits were largely productive and enterprises would seek to preserve them – a scenario of stability. The likeliest story, however, is one of diversity. Diversity is likely across benefit types, some being productive and others simply driving up costs. Diversity is also likely across enterprises, the same benefit being productive in one firm and not in another. The studies in this volume provide evidence on the determinants of benefits, and in so doing provide evidence on the factors that contribute to the diversity.

There is a convention in both East and West of referring to non-wage compensation as the 'social benefits' provided by enterprises. The presumption is that these benefits have consequences that somehow serve social ends. As a matter of terminology, we will follow this convention and sometimes refer to non-wage compensation or portions of it as 'social benefits' or 'social benefits provided by enterprises'. In fact, the language is not very precise because benefit packages include elements that serve only the business interests of the enterprise and not any social functions that go beyond these. There are, however, benefits that are provided by enterprises in East European countries that in the West are more likely to be provided by local governments or non-profit organizations. These include benefits such as hospitals, kindergartens, and crèches, and even housing. Suppose enterprises were to suspend benefits in these areas based on their calculations that they diminish profitability. Would these private actions have social consequences deserving public intervention? Again, the argument could be made both ways. It could be argued that some or all of these benefits are not matters of social interest. In all of these areas, there are instances in other countries where the service is delivered through the market. These are not suitable responsibilities for enterprises, but should be devolved to the market. An alternative line of argument focuses on the alternatives to enterprise provision. If the enterprise chooses to give up a service, is there an alternative source of supply? Assume, for example, that the local government seems a preferable provider. In some East European countries, local governments have little revenue or capacity to administer such programmes, and there is little revenue sharing among governmental units in a country such as Russia. Even if the market is the best place to deliver a service such as housing, there are problems in making a housing market function, and the transition might at least take time. This line of argument suggests that, even if the enterprise is not the suitable agent for delivering the service, there are problems in transition, and enterprise reform should be evaluated in terms of its social consequences as well as its effects on enterprise efficiency. The evaluation of the social consequences of enterprise benefits gets into normative issues, which generally are avoided by the papers in this volume. However, some of the papers do try to assess the transition problems that might be incurred if responsibility for social benefits were transferred out of enterprises to other agents.

There are many ways to approach the subject of enterprise social benefits. The papers in this book vary in the questions asked and in the answers provided. The papers explore the scope and scale of benefits in the respective countries and how these have changed since the reforms began. The papers explore the determinants of non-wage compensation, either as a whole or specific types of benefits; again, the papers vary in the hypotheses examined. This introduction highlights the questions asked in the country-study papers and the answers suggested in an effort to reveal some of the many approaches possible and the variety of questions that can help illuminate the subject. Before turning to this, however, we consider the ways countries have divided the responsibilities for benefits between enterprises and government. This discussion can also help identify the ways in which the term 'social' has been used.

'Social benefits' and the division of responsibilities between enterprises and government

The term 'social benefits' seems to imply that employer-provided benefits are inherently social. There is rarely complete agreement on what 'social' means, and we will not attempt to impose our own definition. We will instead explore common usages of the term. It is useful to consider different kinds of benefits separately, since all may not have an equal claim to being social, in spite of the conventional terminology. As a starting point, it should be recognized that many of the benefits provided by enterprises are also provided publicly, either in the same country or in different countries. Moreover, within countries, there are occasional shifts in responsibility from one sector to another. If a benefit is social by virtue of having been made into a public programme, would it have a similar claim to be social if it were an enterprise-provided benefit? The case for treating both a public and a corresponding employer-provided benefit as social is that both serve the same function. On the other hand, even when the function is the same, there is generally a distributional difference between public and enterprise benefits. Enterprises provide benefits only to their own workers whereas government benefits can be universal. One view is that the distributional factor is so important that enterprise benefits are not social no matter what their function. In contrast, when the emphasis is on function, enterprise counterparts to public benefits might be considered social. Moreover, even when benefits are provided by enterprises, there are possibilities of changing the distribution of benefits. Coverage can be mandated, which could make the enterprise-provided benefit universal for workers. Or enterprise 'social' facilities can be used by the community as a whole and not just by workers, as was the case in Eastern countries such as East Germany (although not in Hungary).

To move beyond such comparisons in function, we consider the following categories of benefits that have been provided by enterprises: social protection benefits; social, cultural, and recreational services; commodity subsidies; and paid leave. There is some country in which each of these has been considered social. There are, of course, enterprise benefits outside of these categories and which may not be considered social anywhere.

Social protection benefits

Social protection programmes protect people from the risk of income loss from certain specific sources such as retirement, unemployment, sickness, and disability. Governments have programmes in these areas, but in many countries enterprises also offer similar benefits to their own workers. The employer-provided benefits serve the same function as public programmes in that they provide protection against the risk of income loss. If the function of protection against the risks of the specified income losses is a matter of social concern, then the employer programmes may be considered a form of social protection. Although the designation as 'social' may be controversial because of distributional issues, it has become common to refer to enterprise as well as government benefits that reduce the risk of income loss as social protection.

Whereas enterprise social protection benefits are common in some Western countries, they were not a major feature in Eastern Europe. Governments tended to assume full responsibility for social protection. Although enterprises provided many benefits, generally they were not social protection against the risk of income loss. There was one major country exception in the old socialist world – China. There the government mandated that enterprises provide social protection benefits to their workers. The government itself was not a direct provider of benefits, and enterprises became the main providers of social protection benefits to urban workers. There was also one major benefit that was a protection against the risk of income loss and that was provided by enterprises in Eastern Europe: enterprises in most socialist countries provided a significant, although varying, degree of job security. Workers were often retained and paid even if they were redundant. Workers were in effect protected against the risk of income loss not after the fact, but on a preventive basis: the income loss was not allowed to take place. It was a form of social protection that was costly to enterprises, but the cost was not visible, not measured, and not included in lists of social protection costs.

As the reforms have proceeded in Eastern Europe, governments have begun to consider the possibility of transferring some of their social protection responsibilities to enterprises. So far, however, such efforts have been limited to protection for dismissed workers. In Hungary, for example, enterprises have been providing severance pay and have been contributing to early retirement pensions for older dismissed workers. In other words, the old enterprise benefit of job security for redundant workers is being transformed into the new benefit of protection for redundant workers after they are dismissed.

As one consequence of the near absence of social protection among measured enterprise benefits, caution is needed in comparing the magnitudes of social benefits in the East and in those Western countries where enterprise social protection benefits are prominent. In the United States, for example, enterprise benefits (other than legally required contributions to public programmes) amounted to 19.1 per cent of total compensation in private industry in 1992 (Braden and Hyland, 1993). However, social protection in the form of pensions and various forms of insurance came to 9.2 per cent of compensation. This leaves other social benefits amounting to only 9.9 per cent. But this is the figure to compare with the social benefits of the East. Enterprise benefits in the East should be compared not with the Western total but with Western enterprise benefits exclusive of social protection.

Social, cultural, and recreational services

Enterprises in the East provide many services that are often considered social, but similar services in the West are more likely to be provided by local governments, non-profit organizations, and even for-profit organizations that specialize in such services. Of course, individual enterprises in the West do choose to provide similar benefits. There are enterprises, for example, that provide daycare centres in house, but many others offer financial support without delivering the service directly. In many Eastern countries, in contrast, there was a general expectation that each enterprise would provide kindergartens. Similarly, health clinics are common in Western enterprises, particularly to treat work-related problems. It is much less likely that enterprises provide comprehensive health care to their workers. In contrast, Eastern enterprises were more likely to have general service clinics. In East Germany, these enterprise clinics even offered services to the general community outside the enterprise. One feature of these service activities is that they often require substantial physical infrastructure. A common trend in the transition has been a tendency for enterprises to divest themselves of these investments, although there are market and legal constraints on the speed of this adjustment. In any case, conventional terminology in the East labels these benefits as social.

Commodity subsidies

Commodity subsidies are an important part of enterprise benefits, although their social value is questionable. In the West, there are governments that have provided subsidies for food or housing or heating fuel. Economists have argued that outright income subsidies might be more efficient, but there seems to be considerable appeal to commodity subsidies as a tool of public policy. In the socialist economies, there was an additional social justification. Because markets did not work, shortages were frequent, and enterprise-provided goods were a way to make goods available outside of markets. In market economies, some enterprises do choose voluntarily to provide subsidized goods, but the motivation is generally private: they believe it would help attract and retain the desired kind of worker. The reforms in the East are allowing enterprises more discretion in designing benefits. However, the commodity subsidies are not going away, although they are often changing in form. Perhaps the old enterprise social benefits are becoming more private, but this transition is not yet reflected in the language, which still refers to them as social.

Paid non-work

In virtually every country, some form of paid leave is included in enterprise benefits. Benefits include vacations, maternity leave, and sick leave. Moreover, government is generally involved in regulating and even subsidising the leaves. At least some people see these benefits as social. There has been a change in some East European countries – a tendency for governments to pass on some of the cost of leaves to enterprises. However, as with other benefits, the change in behaviour is not yet reflected in a change in language.

There is ample precedent for calling the above benefits social. What they are called, however, is less important than who provides them. At this level, the old benefit system in Eastern Europe had distinctive features, and the division of responsibilities between government and enterprises has been changing. In the East, social protection is the responsibility of government except for the unmeasured enterprise benefit of job security. In the West there are varying degrees of enterprise involvement in social protection, depending on the country. For local services – social, cultural, recreational – enterprises in the East may be more regularly involved, although there are variations by enterprise in both East and West. Commodity subsidies for food, clothing, and housing are a major part of benefits in the East. Paid leave is common in both, and both government and enterprises may be involved in paying for some of the benefits such as maternity leave and sick pay. As the reforms proceed, both government and enterprises are rethinking their roles as providers of benefits. In some countries, there is interest on the part of governments in passing social protection responsibilities on to enterprises. On the other side, restructuring enterprises are tending to cut back on some of their social and recreational services. The process so far has generally been slow. It is still too early to predict the ultimate shape of the benefits system in Eastern Europe, but we can examine the current situation in more detail.

An overview of issues and results

Before reviewing the country studies in this volume individually, we will identify a number of themes – questions asked and answers presented on issues that cut across the countries. The issues fall into two main categories: the scope and magnitude of enterprise social benefits; and the determinants of benefits. In this overview, the studies will be identified by country only, except where there is more than one study of the same country.

The scope and magnitude of enterprise social benefits

Social protection is generally the responsibility of government in Eastern Europe, but is financed by contributions from enterprises and more recently from workers. The mandatory contributions of enterprises to government programmes are considerably larger than the enterprise-provided benefits in most countries. In two countries the mandatory contributions are more than 40 per cent of total labour costs. In Slovakia, for example, contributions are 50 per cent of the gross wage, 38 per cent from employers and 12 per cent from workers. In Slovenia, mandatory contributions in 1994 were 45.3 per cent of labour costs, divided almost equally between workers and employers, and down from 58 per cent in 1991. In other countries the contribution rate was more modest, for example 29 per cent in Hungary (Fajth and Lakatos), 25 per cent in the Czech Republic, and 17 per cent in Albania.

Turning to the enterprise-provided social benefits, the same kinds of benefits recur repeatedly across countries. Cafeterias, health clinics, kindergartens and crèches, recreation facilities, clothing subsidies (for work clothes), and housing are common, although the importance of housing varied considerably across countries. Several of the papers analyse samples of enterprises in their respective countries. These studies show considerable variation across enterprises and no one benefit was provided by all enterprises. For housing in particular, 28 per cent of the labour force in the overall Russian sample of enterprises lived in enterprise housing, but the figure was as much as 75 per cent in some larger enterprises. In some other countries, enterprises gave only minor housing subsidies to some workers and were trying to reduce their ownership. In the Czech Republic, for example, enterprise housing was being converted into cooperatives. Indeed, 40 per cent of tenants in enterprise-owned flats were not employees. In Hungary (Rein and Friedman), much of the enterprise housing had been used for migrants from rural areas, but, with fewer being hired, there was no longer a need for the enterprises to keep it as subsidized housing.

The prominence of housing as a benefit in Russia is largely responsible for the high overall percentage of social benefits in labour costs – 35 per cent in the sample of enterprises studied. The proportion is far smaller in every other country. Typical figures are 16 per cent in the Czech Republic and either 14 per cent (Fajth and Lakatos) or 10 per cent (Rein and Friedman) in Hungary, the latter based on an estimate that excludes some benefits as not social. The Polish study reported that in the 1980s the expenditures of the housing and social funds amounted to just 5 per cent of gross wage costs. The typical benefit proportions are considerably higher than the 9.9 per cent rate reported above for benefits in the USA exclusive of social protection. Moreover, job security for redundant workers, to the extent that it is still present, is not measured and thus is not included.

One interpretation of these figures is that the social benefits in many countries are fairly extensive, given that enterprises in the East do not provide social protection benefits. On the other hand, some papers express surprise that benefits in Eastern Europe were not larger, and there is some discussion of possible errors or distortions in the data. One possibility is that not all benefits are included in the measurement. The low figure for Poland, for example, seems to result from its restriction to the housing and social funds. It seems not to include items, such as paid leave, that are prominent in other countries. Another possibility is that the current monetary costs of enterprise benefits are genuinely low, but that their value to workers is higher. One possible reason relates to the fact that many of the services provided by enterprises in East European countries have depended on extensive physical infrastructure. If this infrastructure involves high fixed costs and the investments were largely made in the past, the current costs could be low. To test the possibility that the value of benefits to workers is greater than the cost to enterprises, Earle estimated hedonic wage functions for Romania using industry data. Although the data were not ideal for the purpose, he found no evidence that the value of social benefits exceeds the reported costs.

The determinants of enterprise social benefits

The papers suggest many hypotheses concerning the determinants of enterprise benefits, and some are tested. Several papers examine the influence of government on employer benefits. Several tested hypotheses that social benefits are related to the type of enterprise, the size of the enterprise, its average wage, and the extent of trade union involvement. Some looked at the effects of institutional features such as the accounting system and rules governing the sale of infrastructure used for social purposes. In addition, hypotheses were presented that, although interesting, were not tested. These included:

- Enterprises will increase benefits relative to wages because benefits are not subject to the high social insurance and income tax rates on wages.
- In a tight labour market (Czech Republic) employers have a better chance of retaining valuable workers by designing an attractive benefit package.
- Wage controls in some countries penalize wage increases but not benefit increases.

The conditions in these hypotheses appear to hold in particular countries, but the studies did not test the impacts of these conditions on enterprise benefit structures.

The influence of government on enterprise benefits

Although the benefits are provided by enterprises, government plays an active role. The Rein and Friedman paper describes the various ways government has been involved in Hungary. Some benefits are mandated, such as sick leave and enterprise coverage for a portion of travel costs for those who commute from outside the city. Some are stimulated by means of incentives, such as those to enterprises that give food and clothing subsidies. Moreover, whether the government mandates or gives incentives, it regulates the provision of benefits in some way. There has been a tendency for government to move away from mandating and toward incentives during the period of transition. As in the West, however, because the government is involved in some way in so many benefits, it would be misleading to think of enterprise benefits as reflecting enterprise policy alone.

Rein and Friedman hypothesize that the transition from mandates to incentives should increase the variations across firms in the kinds and extent of benefits offered. They do find evidence of considerable current variation in Hungary. However, the paper on the Czech Republic points out that, even when benefits in that country were mandated, there was still significant variation. The government mandated the benefit, but trade unions had the responsibility of controlling the quality and efficiency of delivery of the service. It appears that there was substantial variability in the way benefits were distributed even in the socialist era. Both trade unions and the Communist Party used benefit distribution as a way to motivate workers, but it appears that there was enough latitude in the system for those who controlled the distribution also to achieve political and personal goals.

Type and size of enterprise
Several papers present evidence that benefits are related to enterprise type and size. For example, in a sample of 25 enterprises in Albania, the private enterprises and joint ventures paid higher wages, but benefits were a slightly larger proportion of total compensation in state-owned enterprises. Fajth and Lakatos present results from a comprehensive survey in 1992 in Hungary of non-agricultural enterprises with more than 20 workers, showing that benefits varied with firm size but the direction of effect depended on the kind of benefit. The benefits related to worker dismissals were a larger proportion of labour costs in larger firms, as were welfare services. On the other hand, some of the benefits that go primarily to high-level employees were relatively more extensive in small enterprises. The analysis of three years of data from 200 enterprises in Poland found a concentration of benefits in state-owned enterprises, somewhat lesser amounts in privatized enterprises, and much fewer benefits in new private enterprises. Within the state sector, the extent of benefits was related to enterprise size, average wages, and indicators of employee power. Moreover, the study found a tendency toward a slight decline over time in the

benefits offered by state and privatized enterprises, the extent of which was related to enterprise size and profitability. At the same time, there has been growth in the benefits offered by new private enterprises. In a study of 41 firms in the Moscow area in 1992 and 1993, Commander and Jackman found that benefits, and particularly housing, are more concentrated in large enterprises. However, the larger enterprises have begun scaling back on their benefits and some have raised user fees. In a study of 19 enterprises in Slovakia, joint stock companies had a higher basic wage as a percentage of labour costs and at the same time higher housing and recreation benefits than other enterprise types. Among three enterprises in Slovenia, benefit levels were comparable but the kinds of benefits differed. The privately owned company, for example, spent more on education and more on insurance for key personnel. It seems clear that enterprise type and size do matter, but the studies also show that the effects can vary depending on the kind of benefit.

The role of trade unions
The effects of trade unions varied across countries. In Albania, new trade unions were set up to replace the old Communist unions but, in the presence of high unemployment, they appear weak. In contrast, unions are prominent in Poland and a high proportion of workers are members, although not in newly established private firms. Whereas the extent of unionization itself was not quite significant, a variable indicating the importance of employee preferences in decision-making was. In Slovakia, trade unions are a legal partner in negotiations and claim 90 per cent membership in state enterprises, but they appear weak in private enterprises. Trade unions have established legal roles in a number of countries, with responsibilities for benefits. What is less clear is the empirical impact of the unions on the extent of benefits.

Unemployment and benefits
Many of the countries in Eastern Europe have experienced substantial falls in employment. For example, Earle's data show a fall in the average number of workers in Romania of 17 per cent between 1989 and 1992, while Rein and Friedman report a decline of 13 per cent in Hungary during the same period. This decline in employment might reflect an erosion in the old benefit of job security. Earle shows that in Romania the fall in employment began in 1991 and accelerated in 1992 after a temporary rise in 1990. The reduction was achieved in part by a dramatic fall in the hiring rate. In terms of separations, there was a large decline in quits. Layoffs increased only slightly in 1991, then by somewhat more in 1992. Apparently, enterprises tried at first to reduce employment through

voluntary attrition and turned to layoffs only later. Indeed, there was a temporary reduction in the retirement age in 1990 in an attempt to encourage voluntary retirement. A second mechanism for preserving employment is work sharing, in which hours of work are reduced as an alternative to layoffs. Earle presents data on changes in hours and in employment by industry in Romania. These show that some industries did rely mainly on reductions in hours and were able to hold down job losses. However, many industries with large reductions in hours also had significant losses in employment. Earle concludes that there was more to hours and employment decisions than simply the desire to replace layoffs with work sharing, although his attempt to isolate these other factors statistically was not wholly conclusive. Finally, it appears that there was a significant distributional aspect to dismissals. According to Kohli, in the former East Germany dismissals were concentrated among a combination of older workers, females, and the less-skilled.

In addition to the loss in job security, it appears that the reductions in employment have been associated with other changes in benefits. In particular, new benefits have emerged for those who are dismissed. Of course, countries have encouraged early retirement, which uses the pension system as a means of support for older workers separated from employment. But countries have also created new benefits. Some of the benefits have originated in government, although enterprises have responded. In Hungary, for example, the government has required severance pay. In addition, it has allowed workers who retire early to qualify for a pension. However, unlike the old system where pensions were paid by government, employers who make use of the early retirement provision must now share the cost of the early pension with government. Thus, through political channels, the decline in employment may have stimulated an expansion of benefits to those who are dismissed. Kohli also points to a new kind of organization that has emerged in the former East Germany to absorb dismissed workers. These organizations are subsidized and employ dismissed workers in 'social' activities such as environmental clean-ups, social services, or cultural work. However, they are not governmental organizations. Rather, they are set up cooperatively by governments, non-profit organizations, and enterprises in local communities. Although not large, they have become a mechanism of at least temporary support for some of those who suffer job losses.

Infrastructure and benefits
A number of the benefits traditionally provided by enterprises in Eastern Europe depend on significant investments in physical infrastructure. This is true of housing, recreation facilities, health clinics, and even food

subsidies when provided through a company cafeteria. It has been argued that the heavy investments in infrastructure may somehow influence the design of benefits. One possibility is that, even now that enterprises have more latitude in designing their own benefit packages, they may choose to continue uneconomic benefits because of faulty accounting procedures. The infrastructure was built in the past, and no depreciation charges are made. Thus, the current cost as measured by enterprises includes only the variable costs, which may be small relative to total costs. Enterprises may choose to continue a benefit because of its seemingly low measured cost even though this understates the true economic cost. Another possibility produces the same outcome for a different reason. Enterprises do want to divest their infrastructure capital, but are unable to do so because of the undeveloped state of the markets for these assets. The sale prices under current conditions would be less than the value of the stream of services from continuing the asset in its current use.

A look at actual practices suggests that enterprises may be more responsive to current economic circumstances and more flexible than these arguments predict. Results of several industry case-studies in Hungary presented by Rein and Friedman suggest flexibility in the transformation of infrastructure, but the mechanisms differ by type of benefit. For example, much of the dormitory housing of enterprises was used for unskilled rural workers. Now that the enterprises no longer need such workers they have had no hesitation in either selling the dormitories or converting them to other uses. Enterprise-owned vacation homes seem to be a case where enterprises wanted to sell, but the undeveloped state of the market made quick sales difficult. This, however, was not a barrier to revising benefit policy. Enterprises retained the facilities, but converted them to other uses that brought a higher return. As for vacation benefits, some enterprises began substituting cash subsidies for the subsidized use of the company vacation centre. To the extent that there is a barrier to changing old infrastructure-based benefits, it may come more from local governments than from the enterprises themselves. These governments regulate certain facilities and may be reluctant to permit a change in use. For example, the recreation facilities of a hotel had been open to the general community. The government would not allow a change in use that would exclude the community or take away the facilities. It appears that infrastructure alone need not be a barrier to change in benefit policies.

The country studies

We divide the papers into two categories, those that give substantial institutional background and those that formulate distinctive behavioural hypotheses about the determinants of benefits. Since papers may do some of both, the division is somewhat arbitrary, but it is convenient for describing the different approaches of the papers.

Distinctive analytic frameworks

The papers in Part I all explore in some way the determinants of enterprise benefits. Each has some data source, often more than one, and uses it to test hypotheses about behaviour. All deal in some way with the large demand shocks that have affected enterprises throughout the region. All deal with variations across enterprises such as size or degree of state control as determinants of benefits. In spite of the general similarities, each is distinctive in the way it formulates and tests hypotheses, reflecting the availability of data as well as the resourcefulness of the authors.

The paper by Estrin, Schaffer, and Singh on Poland has the most extensive data set and uses it to test hypotheses on the determinants of the number of benefits provided by firms and the change in benefits. The authors have data on a sample of 200 firms over the three years from 1991 to 1993. They also use this data set to explore a number of relationships. They find benefits concentrated in state-owned firms and privatized firms, but much less in new private firms. There is considerable variety in the form of benefits. The majority of firms offered holiday subsidies, health care, and a housing subsidy; many also provided childcare facilities and food subsidies; many other benefits were provided by just a few firms. To test the extent of benefits statistically, the authors focus on the number of benefits provided by each firm. They use an ordered logit procedure in which the probability of the number of benefits is estimated as a linear function of a set of independent variables. They conclude that the extent of benefits depended significantly on ownership structure, the size of the enterprise, and a measure of employee power, and varied positively with wages. They also examine the social-assets used to provide benefits such as holiday homes and housing and find these concentrated in the state-owned enterprises. New private firms did provide benefits, but did not invest in social assets. To test the determinants of benefits, they focus on a four-category scale indicating the rate of decrease or increase in the extent of benefits over the three years from 1991 to 1993. They again use an ordered logit procedure. They conclude that benefits were declining in state-owned and privatized firms, although the change tended to be small. There was, however, a modest increase in the benefits in new private firms. Firm size and profitability were also significant.

The paper by John Earle concentrates on Romania, but makes comparisons with other East European countries as well. In addition to presenting evidence on the magnitude of enterprise benefits in Romania and the Czech Republic, the paper also tests two hypotheses. First, in testing the effects of the large demand shocks occurring in the process of transformation, Earle is interested in whether firms would act to protect jobs by means such as work sharing. He finds that some industries with small reductions in employment also had considerable reductions in hours, but that the industries with the largest reductions in employment also reduced hours considerably. He concludes that the size of the demand shock must affect the outcome, but its impact in turn was likely to depend on the form of the labour cost, whether it was based on hours or number of workers, or whether it was a fixed cost. He uses a random coefficients model to test the interacting effects on hours of work and employment of the demand shock and form of compensation using a sample of 22 industries. He finds support for the idea that the form of compensation affects the form of labour adjustment to a demand shock, but the support is not strong. His second test uses a hedonic wage model to explore the hypothesis that the value of benefits to workers exceeds their costs. This test was motivated by his conclusion that in both Romania and the Czech Republic the magnitude of benefits is not that different from that in Western countries. He then wonders whether the value of benefits might be understated, perhaps because enterprise accounting procedures do not take account of the full economic costs of the fixed assets used in providing them. The question of whether benefits have greater value to workers than their measured cost would be of interest, however, even if there were no accounting problems. On the basis of a limited sample of Romanian industries, he finds no evidence that the value of benefits to workers exceeds their reported costs.

The paper by Filer, Schneider, and Svejnar on the Czech Republic explores the old system as a preliminary to examining the transition. Although the state mandated broad kinds of coverage, the specific guidelines were sufficiently vague that considerable variation and a low level of provision were possible. To study the transition, the authors had access to data from a sample of 3,500 firms. However, they had tabulations only at the industry level rather than the original data by firm. They use two-digit industry averages to explore the factors affecting the ratio of benefits relative to wages in a regression analysis. They find that industries with higher labour productivity (measured as sales per worker) had a higher ratio whereas private firms had a lower ratio. They also find that shrinking firms (measured by the percentage change in the labour force) had a larger ratio, but only when benefits included bonuses and profit sharing. They interpret this as indicating perhaps that firms further along with their restructuring made greater use of incentive compensation schemes. They use the sample for further examination of details concerning benefits. They also point out that recent government policy has begun to encourage the development of private alternatives to the traditional public benefits for pensions and health insurance, opening the possibility that enterprise involvement in these areas may also grow eventually.

Commander and Jackman used a World Bank survey of 41 firms in the Moscow area to learn about benefits in Russia. Housing seems to play a larger role in their sample than it does in the other countries; a significant minority of their sample provided housing. Their sample provides extensive information on the level and composition of benefits as well as on the attitudes of employers and workers toward benefits in the sampled firms. They use this information to focus on policy issues related to divestiture. They point out that some of the important services, such as pre-school education, health clinics, and even housing, would be provided by local governments in other countries. However, in many parts of Russia, local government finances are weak and there is no mechanism for redistributing funds across localities. Divestiture would probably result simply in higher taxes for those enterprises doing the divesting in such localities. Enterprises expressed a desire to scale back, but in fact the pace of divestiture has been slow, perhaps in part because of the constraints on finding alternative providers. There have been limited cutbacks, and users' fees have been introduced for some services. In housing, there has been a clear reduction in expenditures on new construction and maintenance. There is an interest in divesting more housing activities to the market, but only limited progress.

The paper by Kohli on East Germany is the only one to take a sociological perspective. Kohli analyses the pre-reform society as one in which there was a low level of functional differentiation between society, economy, and polity. In particular, he argues that work and social protection were fused. The importance of this fusion was heightened by the nature of employment. Labour force participation rates were considerably higher than in the West. Declining rates did set in, but later than in the West. When the transition began, however, the decline was precipitous, employment falling by about one-third between 1989 and 1993. Social protection pathways out of employment were created by enterprises, but workers were also sent into public programmes for income support. At the same time, the old fusion disintegrated. Enterprises shed social benefits by either eliminating them altogether or passing them on to other non-profit and local organizations.

The paper on Hungary by Rein and Friedman demonstrates the importance of disaggregation in identifying trends in benefits. Hungarian enterprises responded to their demand shock by shedding workers and cutting real wages per worker, but an increase in real non-wage compensation per worker offset much of the decline in wages. Considering the composition of benefits, however, there have been large increases in some, generally the more cash-like benefits, and large reductions in others, mainly those given in kind. In its effort to assess the determinants of benefits, this paper emphasizes the role of government along with the voluntary choices made by enterprises. Government policy has changed during the period of transition. There has been a clear shift away from some of the old mandatory in-kind benefits. At the same time, the government has expanded incentives to enterprises to provide cash-like benefits. The government has also become more involved in mandating and regulating benefits to dismissed workers. Drawing on case-studies of six enterprises, the paper explores in more depth the benefit policies within enterprises. Enterprises demonstrate flexibility even when there are constraints. They have cut benefits sharply in areas where there is diminished need: kindergartens and crèches have diminished along with the decline in fertility; enterprise dormitories for rural migrants have been converted to other uses as the use of migrants has diminished. Enterprises seem to have a clear desire to reduce benefits dependent on physical infrastructure; they convert it to other uses even when the market constrains outright sale. On the other hand, food benefits remain among the largest, although enterprises tailor the specific form both to take advantage of government subsidies and to appeal to the tastes of their own workforces.

Institutional analyses

Although all the papers deal in some degree with the institutional aspects of enterprise-provided benefits, some are distinctive in the degree of institutional information provided.

The paper by Fajth and Lakatos on Hungary offers the most complete discussion of the evolution of benefits before 1989, going into the political and ideological factors that helped to shape them. For the period of transition, it also presents an analysis of the political forces and legislative developments shaping the development of enterprise benefits. Drawing on the Labour Cost Surveys conducted by the Hungarian government, it presents quantitative data on the extent and composition of benefits as well as on characteristics of the providers. The quantitative presentations are supplemented by a discussion of the detailed features of the various benefit programmes along with current trends.

Four of the papers studied some of the less familiar countries of Eastern Europe using parallel approaches. These were the studies by Gavez and Letonja of Slovenia; by Plánovský and Wörgötter of Slovakia; by Tratch and Wörgötter of the Ukraine; and by Brahja, Leka, and Luniku of Albania. Each of these papers begins with an overview of government social protection programmes. To investigate enterprise benefits, each set of authors surveys a number of employers varying by size and type: the survey in Slovenia covered 3 enterprises, that in Slovakia 19, in the Ukraine 10, and in Albania 25. All four studies report high statutory contribution rates to public social insurance programmes. The combined enterprise and worker rate in Slovenia was 58 per cent of wages in 1991, although it fell to 45 per cent in 1994; in Albania it was 43 per cent; in Slovakia 50 per cent; in the Ukraine 41 per cent. In Slovenia and Slovakia there are plans to scale back public benefits to lower levels but to require individuals and enterprises to set up supplementary protection plans, leading perhaps to an expanded enterprise role in social protection. As for current enterprise-provided benefits, in Slovenia, based on the small sample of three enterprises, benefits were a higher fraction of total compensation in the private enterprise than in the others, mainly because bonuses were large in the private enterprise and were counted as part of benefits. In the sample for Albania, employer-provided benefits on average were small (5 per cent of total compensation), but ranged from less than 1 per cent to 26 per cent. The paper provides a description of the detailed benefits. The paper on Slovakia runs a regression using its sample and finds that direct social benefits were positively related to the average wage across enterprises. The paper on the Ukraine gives the most complete discussion on the complex ways of financing benefits. Within the study sample, enterprise-provided benefits ranged from 8 per cent to 38 per cent; the average was 20 per cent.

Although the book focuses on Eastern Europe, the paper by Hu on China is included because of the interesting contrast. In contrast to Eastern Europe where the government is generally responsible for social insurance programmes, in China these are provided by enterprises, although mandated by government. As a result, enterprises, particularly the state-owned ones, play a much larger role in providing benefits. Hu focuses on some of the problems arising because of the Chinese structure of social protection. The enterprise-based system creates a barrier to labour mobility because workers fear losing their benefits if they change employers. The current system is also a barrier to enterprise reform aimed at making enterprises stand on their own. Without subsidies, enterprises might not be able to afford the various benefits they now provide. The paper reviews the various reforms that have been introduced, including efforts to shift the responsibility for providing benefits from enterprises to government, but concludes that more reforms will be needed before the problems in the current system are overcome.

Conclusion: the welfare state versus the welfare society

As many of the papers in this book show, enterprise benefits may play a significant role in determining the efficiency of enterprises and may also serve social functions. Returning to the social side of benefits, the subject can be put in perspective by considering the question of what major institutions distribute welfare in all societies. Of course, the answer will partly depend on what we mean by the term 'welfare' – social transfers or social services? Different institutions are involved in the transfer society and the service society. Since the days of the Great Depression of the 1930s, the Church and other voluntary non-profit organizations and informal mutual aid networks have not played a role in the distribution of cash transfers to individuals. Moreover, the role of welfare capitalism as an active alternative to the development of a state system of social protection has more or less disappeared. Finally, it is no longer socially expected that adult children support their aged parents on a regular basis as an alternative to the provision of state benefits. Both critics and proponents of the emergence of the modern welfare state have assumed that these developments have meant that the state has 'crowded out' the enterprise and the family as significant institutional actors in the welfare society. This interpretation is mistaken. In many countries as varied as the Netherlands, Sweden, the United States, and the United Kingdom, the enterprise provides occupational pensions that supplement the state social security system. These occupational pensions account for about 25 per cent of the aggregate income of households headed by a person in the last stages of his or her working career. Moreover, in the same countries the state is under attack and pressure is increasing to reduce the scope of welfare state spending on social security. The Swedish parliament passed legislation in the summer of 1994 to shift the determination of benefit levels from the best 15 years of earning to lifetime earnings. This will surely decrease the value of the public transfer system for all individuals whose income tends to increase with age and experience. In such an environment the social aspects of markets will become even more important, and, although new forms of personal savings will expand, it also seems more than plausible to imagine an expanding role for enterprise-based social spending.

What about the role of the family? Clearly, as suggested earlier, adult children no longer regularly support their aged parents. And there is strong evidence of a growth in the number of single parents who rely upon the state as an important source of family income. Over the past 40 years the proportion of families headed by a woman has dramatically increased. In the United States this proportion is now about 35 per cent among the poorest households (*The Economist*, 1994: 20). But such trends do not imply that the family is not the primary financial support for children as they grow up. Indeed there is growing evidence that, as young adults find it difficult to enter into a working career, the stage of childhood and period of financial help from families is expanding. Parents directly help their children to go to college through payments to cover the increasing cost of college tuition, the growing burden of school loans, and the decreasing availability of state scholarship grants. Moreover, co-residence of young people with their families, at least in the United States, is quite large (*Journal of Labor Economics*, 1993: 98). In some countries, such as Japan, families spend about a quarter of their household income to help their children prepare for college examinations.

The family continues as an important financial resource as young people enter adult life. In France, about half of all families acquire their first home from bequests and cash transfers from their parents. There is good evidence in both France and Germany that aged parents provide financial aid to their adult children and grandchildren. In turn, the adult children provide a range of concrete services to their aged parents, such as transportation, housecleaning, and help when sick (Rein, 1994).

Our intention here is not to identify the main institutions providing welfare in a welfare society. Rather, our main thesis is that these welfare institutions are linked. Change in one institutional arrangement has a ripple effect on the other institutions. 'Crowding out' is one hypothesis of linkage that assumes that the entry of the state displaces the other institutions. We have tried to provide some evidence to show that the 'crowding in' hypothesis is also plausible. In this view the state encourages supplementation of benefits by building on the foundations set by the state system. Obviously, this is not the appropriate place to argue the case for or against 'crowding in' or 'crowding out'. What is relevant for the study of social benefits in economies in transition is that changes do not occur in a vacuum. The understanding of linkages is one of the most interesting aspects of the welfare society. What happens when enterprise's social role retreats? Do other institutions such as the state and the family offset the decline? Offsetting is one possibility. New institutions can also emerge – witness, for example, the tremendous increase in the number of non-profit organizations in Hungary. Of course, most of this activity is a licence to try to raise money if they can. But some do provide a direct service, and, depending on the tax rules, enterprises may find that the non-profit organization is the service vehicle for social benefits previously provided by the enterprise itself.

Of course, other linkages are also possible, such as the double decline in the role of both the state and the enterprise. When government fails to offset the retreat of enterprise, or when enterprise fails to offset the retreat of the state, the burden falls on the family. Indeed, there can be a general erosion of well-being – a triple decline as all the institutions of the welfare society retreat. Whatever the answer, locating welfare in the welfare society and not just in the activities of the state is the way to approach this question. In this context, the social role of the enterprise is both interesting and important in understanding economies in transition.

REFERENCES

Braden, R. B. and S. L. Hyland (1993), 'Cost of employee compensation in public and private sectors', *Monthly Labor Review*, May.
Economist, The (1994), 'Slicing the cake: the rights and wrongs of inequality', 5–11 November.
Journal of Labor Economics (1993), vol. 11, no. 1, January.
Rein, M. (1994), *Intergenerational Solidarity*, IAASA Working Paper, Summer.

I   Distinctive analytic frameworks

2 The provision of social benefits in state-owned, privatized, and private firms in Poland

SAUL ESTRIN, MARK E. SCHAFFER, and I. J. SINGH

Introduction

It was a standard observation in texts about socialist economies that enterprises provided extensive non-wage social benefits (Gregory and Stuart, 1989; Wiles, 1977), though the actual scale of the provision was rarely indicated. The existence of significant social benefits at the enterprise level, and the implications for restructuring, privatization, and the transformation process in general have also been frequently noted in the transition literature (Fischer and Gelb, 1991; Portes, 1993; Frydman *et al.*, 1993; Estrin, 1994). Yet, there has been little detailed information about the nature and scope of enterprise-level provision of social benefits, let alone any attempts to analyse either their diversity or their determinants. Finally, although there are frequent assertions about how enterprise-level social provision is changing with transition, privatization, and the emergence of the new private sector, there is no hard evidence on the matter. It is these inadequacies in our knowledge that we seek to redress in this paper, which draws on the evidence from a three-year panel of approximately 200 Polish firms. A companion paper to this (Belka *et al.*, 1995) discusses adjustment by the surveyed enterprises more generally.

Non-wage social provision is an interesting issue because it is a factor influencing both labour supply and product market structure in the transition process. Although analysts know that social provision to employees was often extensive, there has been little empirical indication of its scale, its diversity, and the factors encouraging its use by some firms but not others. These factors are important because overextensive social provision could raise the costs of enterprise restructuring, and might alienate potential foreign investors if they are forced to take these assets on along with the more productive ones. Aghion *et al.* (1994) have suggested that the degree of social provision may also influence the structure of coalitions emerging in support of unbundling, typically in

25

the direction of hindering restructuring. On the labour side, social provision restricts labour mobility, so its sectoral and structural pattern may be an important explanatory factor in regional unemployment differences. By raising the effective wage paid in the state sector, social provision also places pressure on private firms that wish to recruit – either to match in terms of social provision or to substitute through higher pay. Finally, the pre-existence of social benefits provides the state sector with a simple route to raise total remuneration even in the presence of tax-based incomes policies. We will test hypotheses based on these ideas in the later sections of the paper.

The main findings of the paper are that social benefits are concentrated in state-owned firms. To a considerable extent, they are also present in privatized companies, but are found considerably less frequently in the *de novo* (i.e. newly established) private sector. The extent of provision within the state sector is primarily determined by enterprise size and is correlated with the level of wages. However, it is interesting to find that provision is also positively related to indicators of employee power. Social provision has been declining in state-owned and privatized firms, but increasing (modestly) in new private firms. On average the decline in the state-owned and formerly state-owned sectors is surprisingly small. The key determinants of the pace of change are the size of the firm and its profitability; in the case of the state-owned sector, provision also declines more slowly when the tax-based incomes policy (the '*popiwek*') binds.

In the next section, we briefly outline the methodology of the survey and provide summary statistics about enterprise behaviour in Poland over the sample period, 1991–3. The nature and scope of social benefits are outlined in the third section, and simple hypotheses about the determinants of provision are tested. In the fourth section, we summarize and attempt to explain the recent changes in social provision, including changes in investments in social assets. Conclusions are drawn in the final section.

Sample size, selection, and characteristics

The survey was sponsored by the World Bank Research Project on Enterprise Behaviour and Economic Reform, and was undertaken between November 1993 and March 1994 by a team of Polish economists headed by Professor Marek Belka. A survey questionnaire in two parts was administered to 200 enterprises in the manufacturing sector. Eight of the original 200 firms withdrew from the survey after they had supplied most of the requested information and were replaced with eight additional firms, giving a total sample size of 208. The first part of the questionnaire was undertaken primarily by interview with senior managers, and involved qualitative questions about a variety of subjects including marketing, technology, employment, finance, and corporate governance. A few of these questions covered social benefits and social issues. The second part of the questionnaire was quantitative and drew on various elements of the firm's profit and loss accounts, balance sheets, and other economic data for the three years 1991–3.

The minimum firm size covered in the survey was 10 employees. The sample was stratified by ownership form as follows: 41 enterprises were emerging (*de novo*) private firms (DNs); 45 were privatized firms (PRIs); 41 were state-owned firms that had been converted into joint stock companies ('commercialized', 'corporatized') and were awaiting privatization (SAs), and 81 were traditional (not yet commercialized) state-owned firms (SOEs). Within these categories the selection of firms was random. All major manufacturing subsectors are well-represented. In our analysis we do not weight by size, and there are only minor differences in the sectoral distribution of the firms in our sample compared with the weight of sectors in aggregate manufacturing employment.

Tables 2.1–2.4 provide a picture of the firms in our sample and of the key differences in situation and enterprise economic performance by ownership type in Poland at the end of 1993. This picture is of considerable interest in its own right because of the shortcomings of the available data on the Polish private sector published by the Polish Central Statistical Office (CSO). Though the quality of these data is probably the best among transition countries, they suffer from two important drawbacks. First, the CSO data make no distinction between the *de novo* private sector and the privatized sector. Second, the CSO definition of the 'private sector' in use since 1991 includes cooperatives. Poland began the transition with a substantial number of manufacturing cooperatives, accounting for 12 per cent of industrial employment in 1989 compared with 15 per cent for the emerging private sector proper.[1] During the communist period, Polish cooperatives had little real autonomy, but the situation in the transition is quite different and in this sense cooperatives are correctly classified as part of the private sector. Cooperative performance has, however, been quite poor during the transition, and over the period 1989–93 the output and employment of industrial cooperatives roughly halved, though even now their weight in manufacturing is still substantial relative to the emerging private sector. At the same time, the emerging private sector, by all accounts, has enjoyed explosive growth and now accounts for perhaps one-third or more of total industrial output. The Polish CSO statistics on the private

Table 2.1. Poland: employment size in 1993 vs. ownership

Employment in 1993	% of firms in given ownership class				
	DN	PRI	SA	SOE	All
< 50	31	2	0	3	7
51–250	62	36	8	29	33
251–1,000	8	45	53	41	38
> 1,000	0	16	40	28	22
Total	100	100	100	100	100
Median	68	350	838	375	352

DN = emerging private sector (*de novo*) firm
PRI = privatized firm
SA   = state-owned and commercialized
SOE = state-owned, traditional (unincorporated)
Note: Figures may not sum to 100 due to rounding.

sector thus unfortunately combine what are several quite distinct ownership groups: *de novo* private firms, formerly state-owned firms that have
been privatized, and cooperatives.[2]

We note first from table 2.1 that, as expected, most *de novo* private firms
are small, and most state firms (SAs and SOEs) are large. However it is
encouraging that there are already a few *de novo* private firms employing
more than 250 persons, and that more than one-third of privatized firms
are small or medium sized (250 employees or fewer). It is also noteworthy
that virtually all commercialized firms are large. The reason for this is
that the bulk of these firms are to be included in the Polish Mass
Privatization Programme (MPP) and so had to be converted into joint
stock companies.

The Polish industrial sector began to grow again in 1992 after a deep
recession, and total manufacturing output grew by 12 per cent in 1993.
Tables 2.2 and 2.3 provide a picture of how the growth was distributed
between the ownership types. Commencing with sales growth in table
2.2, we find rapid real growth concentrated in the private sector and
especially in *de novo* private firms; median real sales growth in 1993 was
16 per cent in privatized firms and 30 per cent in *de novo* firms. Only a
minority of SOEs and merely a quarter of commercialized firms displayed
sales growth in excess of 10 per cent in 1993. On the other hand, the
macroeconomic expansion is leaving few firms out completely; only 5 per
cent of private firms and 20 per cent or less of state-owned firms were still
shrinking in 1993.

The picture is rather different for employment growth, reflecting the

Table 2.2. Sales growth in 1993 vs. ownership

Sales growth in 1993 (%)	% of firms in given ownership class				
	DN	PRI	SA	SOE	All
< −10	5	12	20	16	14
−10 to 10	21	31	53	43	38
10 to 25	13	29	18	23	21
> 25	61	29	10	18	27
Total	100	100	100	100	100
Median	30	16	0	6	10

DN = emerging private sector (*de novo*) firm
PRI = privatized firm
SA   = state-owned and commercialized
SOE = state-owned, traditional (unincorporated)
Note: Figures may not sum to 100 due to rounding.

Table 2.3. Employment growth in 1993 vs. ownership

Employment growth in 1993 (%)	% of firms in given ownership class				
	DN	PRI	SA	SOE	All
< −10	16	27	28	35	28
−10 to 10	31	66	73	59	58
> 10	54	7	0	5	14
Total	100	100	100	100	100
Median	13	−3	−4	−6	−4

DN = emerging private sector (*de novo*) firm
PRI = privatized firm
SA   = state-owned and commercialized
SOE = state-owned, traditional (unincorporated)
Note: Figures may not sum to 100 due to rounding.

fact that current and former state-owned firms often still had significant amounts of hoarded labour, and that private firms need to employ extra workers in order to grow. Thus a third or more of PRIs, SAs, and SOEs recorded rapid employment reductions; in each case, higher proportions than displayed rapid declines in sales. Almost none of the state-owned and formerly state-owned firms recorded rapid increases in employment, as against 54 per cent of *de novo* private firms. Thus sales growth was fairly widely dispersed, though more marked in the private sector, whereas employment growth was concentrated in *de novo* private firms.

Table 2.4. Profit margin in 1993 vs. ownership

Profit margin in 1993 (%)	% of firms in given ownership class				
	DN	PRI	SA	SOE	All
< −5	8	30	37	45	33
−5 to 5	60	39	24	44	42
>5	33	32	39	12	26
Total	100	100	100	100	100
Median	2.6	2.9	0.5	−1.8	1.2

DN = emerging private sector (*de novo*) firm
PRI = privatized firm
SA = state-owned and commercialized
SOE = state-owned, traditional (unincorporated)
Note: Figures may not sum to 100 due to rounding.

Finally, the pre-tax profit margin by ownership type is reported in table 2.4. Although there is considerable dispersion of profitability within ownership groups, the patterns are more or less as predicted. The bulk of emerging private sector firms had near positive (margins of −5 per cent to 5 per cent) or high (margins above 5 per cent) profitability; the privatized and commercialized categories had substantial numbers of firms with large losses (margins below −5 per cent) as well as firms with large profits; and most traditional state-owned firms were either roughly breaking even or making large losses. It is also interesting that a slightly higher proportion of commercialized firms had profits in excess of 5 per cent of sales than did privatized firms.

In summary, most *de novo* private firms are small, whereas most state-owned firms and especially the commercialized ones are large. Privatized firms can be both medium sized or large. Growth in 1993 was widely diffused through the economy, but rather more concentrated in privatized and especially in newly established private firms, while financial distress as revealed by low profit margins was concentrated in the state-owned sector.

The scope and determinants of enterprise social provision

The survey instrument contained questions about the nature of social provision within each firm, as well as information about factors that might in principle explain the extent of enterprise-level social benefits. In this section, we briefly survey the scope of social provision, before testing some simple hypotheses about its determinants.

Table 2.5. The scope of social provision in late 1993

(a) By benefit type

Benefit	% of firms
1. Child care	34
2. Health care	63
3. Food subsidy/cafeteria	29
4. Housing/housing subsidy	52
5. Holiday subsidy/resort	74
6. Other responses (volunteered by the interviewee),[1] e.g.	22
– Travel assistance	3
– Compassionate leave	11
– Payment in kind	3
– Children's recreational camps, etc.	7
– Cultural events	2

(b) By number of benefits

Number of benefits	% of firms
0	11
1	10
2	25
3	24
> 3	31

[1] Since the responses in (6) were volunteered by the interviewee, the frequencies are not directly comparable with those for (1)–(5).

We report information about the nature and scale of provision in the 200-odd firms sampled in table 2.5. The data reveal that social provision in late 1993 remained quite extensive in both range and extent four years into the transition process. A majority of firms sampled offered holiday subsidies, health care provision, and a housing subsidy. More than one-third of firms offered childcare facilities and almost one-third provided some form of food subsidy. Textual questions allowed the interviewers to discover more about the extraordinary variety of social provision in Poland. Almost a quarter of sampled firms offered social benefits in addition to the major five categories in table 2.5a; these included arrangements for compassionate leave, payments in kind, and other gifts such as sending children to recreational camps. It is clear from table 2.5b that social benefits are not regarded by management as substitutes for one another; most firms offer three benefits or more and only 11 per cent of sampled firms offer no social benefits at all.

A number of common assertions about social provision can be tested on this sample. The first concerns the relationship between social benefits, enterprise size, and ownership form. Enterprise provision of social benefits was an important feature of the large socialist enterprise, and as such seems likely to be concentrated in state-owned firms, or former state-owned firms. In contrast, one might expect very little social provision in the *de novo* private firms, which would have to build social assets or use valuable revenue to match state-owned sector provision. Privatized firms would probably take an intermediate position, with management gradually seeking to reduce social provision but perhaps having made little progress in the short term. An alternative approach to the issue is to note that a variety of what we call 'social benefits' are frequently provided by employers in developed countries as part of the remuneration package offered to their employees, and that in many socialist countries the scale of social benefits offered, measured in cost terms, was not actually particularly high. In Poland, for example, the expenditures of the social and housing funds (including financial transfers and loans to workers) of industrial enterprises in the late 1980s amounted to about 5 per cent of gross wage costs.[3] This view would suggest that emerging private sector firms may need to start offering social benefits in order to attract more labour and that they may not find it prohibitively costly to do so.

An important distinction between commercialized and unincorporated state-owned firms rests in their sector and financial situation; the former have been deemed eligible for the MPP and are likely on average to be in a somewhat better position. In so far as the run-down of social provision is related to financial distress, one might expect lower levels of provision in the SOEs. Given economies of scale in certain forms of social provision – notably health, crèches, and perhaps holiday homes – one might expect a clear correlation between provision and size. This would operate independently of the ownership–size relationship noted in table 2.1, which established that private firms, and especially *de novo* private firms, are smaller than their state-owned counterparts.

We examine these ideas through a number of cross-tabulations before testing them more formally in a regression framework. The relationship between social provision and ownership is reported in table 2.6. As expected, the frequency of provision of most benefits is very high in the state sector and rather lower in the private sector. This is true for each type of benefit and for the number of benefits. Thus, the majority of SAs and SOEs offer more than three benefits, but no DNs offer more than two. However, there are some surprises in table 2.6. First, there is a higher degree of provision of social benefits in the *de novo* private sector

Table 2.6. Social benefits and ownership

(a) By benefit type

| | % of firms in ownership class providing benefit | | | |
Benefit type	DN	PRI	SA	SOE
1. Child care	8	47	46	35
2. Health care	29	64	83	70
3. Food subsidy/cafeteria	10	31	41	31
4. Housing/housing subsidy	2	49	78	65
5. Holiday subsidy/resort	15	80	95	89

(b) By number of benefits

| | % of firms in ownership class | | | |
Number of benefits	DN	PRI	SA	SOE
0	46	4	0	1
1	27	2	5	7
2	27	33	12	25
3	0	27	32	31
> 3	0	33	51	36

DN = emerging private sector (*de novo*) firm
PRI = privatized firm
SA   = state-owned and commercialized
SOE = state-owned, traditional (unincorporated)

than one might have expected; more than half of the sample firms in this ownership category do make some social provision despite the fact that, as we saw in table 2.1, these firms are typically small or medium sized. This suggests that private firms may need to offer social benefits to compete in the labour market with the state sector. We return to this possibility below.

Even more striking is the very high degree of social provision in the privatized firms – a level by benefit type and by number of benefits not greatly different from that observed in the state sector. Thus only 4 per cent of privatized firms offer no social benefits, and the pattern of provision matches that of the state-owned firms. This suggests that privatization in Poland has not entailed to a significant degree the unbundling – especially of social assets, and the reduction of non-wage employee provision – that had been hoped for by some outside observers. One reason may be that the majority of privatizations in this period were to insiders – coalitions of managers and workers – who had only limited interests in unbundling or in adjusting the balance of money wage to non-wage payments. An alternative (though not necessarily a competing)

Table 2.7. Social benefits by size class

(a) By benefit type

	% of firms in size class providing benefit			
Benefit type	≤ 50	51–250	251–1,000	$> 1,000$
1. Child care	13	21	37	58
2. Health care	27	45	74	84
3. Food subsidy/cafeteria	7	9	33	60
4. Housing/housing subsidy	13	32	58	84
5. Holiday subsidy/resort	7	59	86	96

(b) By number of benefits

	% of firms in size class providing benefits			
Number of benefits	≤ 50	51–250	251–1,000	$> 1,000$
0	53	21	0	0
1	27	12	7	2
2	13	35	25	11
3	7	21	33	18
>3	0	11	34	69

DN = emerging private sector (*de novo*) firm
PRI = privatized firm
SA   = state-owned and commercialized
SOE = state-owned, traditional (unincorporated)

explanation is that the returns to unbundling (cost savings, revenues from sales of social assets) are often low compared with the returns to keeping these assets in their current uses.

The relationship between social provision, enterprise size, and union-ization is reported in tables 2.7 and 2.8. Table 2.7 confirms that provision is extensive in large firms and modest in small ones, though the picture is not as simple as one might have expected: some larger firms provide few benefits, while more than one-third of small firms provide more than two benefits.

Poland is unusual amongst the economies in transition for the magnitude and importance – political as well as economic – of its trade union movement. The Solidarity union played the leading role in bringing down the communist government, and studies confirm the continued importance of trade unions in enterprise decision-making (see Estrin *et al.*, 1995). In the West, one would expect some degree of association between the degree of unionization (as a proxy for employee bargaining power) and the level of remuneration, both in money wages

Table 2.8. Unionization, ownership structure, and social provision

(a) Unionization by ownership type

% of labour force unionized	% of firms in ownership class			
	DN	PRI	SA	SOE
< 10	100	24	5	10
11–30	0	18	5	19
31–60	0	47	59	51
61–100	0	11	32	20

(b) Unionization and size

% of labour force unionized	% of firms in size class			
	≤ 50	51–250	251–1,000	> 1,000
< 10	93	56	9	2
11–30	7	11	16	9
31–60	0	24	57	61
61–100	0	9	18	27

(c) Unionization and social benefits

% of firms in unionization class providing:	% of labour force unionized			
	< 10	11–30	31–60	61–100
1. Child care	17	24	44	47
2. Health care	34	68	74	88
3. Food subsidy/cafeteria	11	36	37	32
4. Housing/housing subsidy	18	56	69	68
5. Holiday subsidy/resort	32	84	91	97

and via social benefits. Given the availability of detailed data on this subject in the questionnaire, the relationship could be investigated in this survey.

The relevant cross-tabulations are contained in table 2.8. The *de novo* private sector is totally non-unionized, regardless of size and sector. The proportion of the labour force unionized is typically more than 30% in all other ownership forms, with almost one-third of firms reporting unionization ratios in excess of 60 per cent. The largest proportion of firms is found in the category 31–60 per cent unionized in all three state and formerly state-owned firm categories. Unionization is, however, noticeably lower in privatized firms, almost one-quarter of which have extremely low unionization rates. The causality, however, almost certainly runs from unionization to ownership form rather than the other way round. This is because Polish unions wield significant influence over the privatization process in firms where they are powerful (see Estrin *et al.*, 1995), often to hinder or prevent the ownership change. Hence privatization was probably more easily effected in enterprises where unionization levels were low.

Table 2.8b indicates that the conventional positive relationship between unionization and size holds in the Polish economy. Given the findings in table 2.1, table 2.8b in part merely reconfirms the relationship between unionization and ownership type. Table 2.8c reveals a clear correlation between the extent of social provision and the level of unionization. Note, however, that a reasonable proportion of firms with virtually zero or very low unionization rates still offer social benefits, and that the proportion of firms offering each type of benefit differs little between the 31–60 per cent unionization and the 61–100 per cent unionization categories.

The descriptive statistics indicate that the nature and scope of social provision are positively related to ownership form, size of firm, and unionization rate. To test this view more rigorously, we used regression analysis, with the number of benefits being the dependent variable. The dependent variable is assumed to convey ordinal information only[4] and so we use an ordered logit estimating equation. In an ordered logit procedure, the probability of observing outcome n – here, the number of benefits – is estimated as a linear function of independent variables and a set of cut-off points k_n corresponding to the set of outcomes:

$$\text{Probability(number of benefits} = n)$$
$$= \text{Probability}(k_{n-1} < \mathbf{x}_i \boldsymbol{\beta} + u_i \leq k_n),$$

where $\mathbf{x}_i$ is the vector of independent variables for firm i, $\boldsymbol{\beta}$ is the vector of coefficients on the independent variables, and u is an error term, assumed to be logistically distributed.[5] By assumption, k_{-1} is taken as $-\infty$, and k_N, where in this case N is the maximum number of benefits observed in the sample, is taken as $+\infty$.

Ownership type was controlled for via ownership dummy variables (with state-owned firms as the basis for comparison) and size (after some experimentation, by the natural logarithm of employment).[6] Employee bargaining power is proxied by the percentage of the labour force that is unionized and by the response to a qualitative question about the objectives of the firm.[7] The equation reported in table 2.9 also tests two other hypotheses that have emerged in our discussion. The first is the idea that firms in a less favourable financial situation either will be unable to offer social benefits – this might apply to *de novo* private firms

– or, if already providing them in the state sector, will be under pressure to reduce provision. We noted above that this might explain the observed differences between SAs and SOEs in the extent of provision. We test this view by including as independent variables two indicators of current enterprise performance: the growth of sales in 1993 as against 1992 and the profit margin over sales in 1993.[8]

The second issue raised by the cross-tabulations concerns the nature of the remuneration package offered in the private and state sectors, respectively, and the impact of tax-based incomes policies. *A priori*, one might expect that firms that pay higher money wages would offer fewer social benefits, *ceteris paribus*. However, in enterprises where tax-based incomes policies might potentially apply (e.g. the state sector) one would expect social provision to be more extensive as a mechanism of raising total remuneration without breaching tax norms. We test these ideas by including the average wage in 1993 and a dummy variable for firms in which the '*popiwek*' was binding in either 1992 or 1993.

The results are reported in table 2.9, and for the main variables confirm many of our prior views. There is no significant difference between SOEs and SAs in the number of benefits provided, but *de novo* firms provide significantly fewer (the coefficient on DN is negative and significantly different from the benchmark ownership class, which we have taken to be SOEs[9]). However, the regression also confirms that privatized firms are not statistically significantly different from state-owned ones in the scale of social provision. In short, the ownership form division that is statistically significant in determining social provision is between *de novo* private and current and formerly state-owned firms, rather than between state and private firms *per se*.

The size effect on social provision is positive and statistically significant, even where we control for ownership, and the distribution of the impact is lognormal. Once we control for size and ownership form, unionization is not quite significant.[10] However, the general impact of employee power on non-wage social benefits is supported by the nearly significant (at the 5 per cent level) positive coefficient on the dummy variable indicating the importance of employee preferences in decision-making.

The finding that state-owned and privatized firms do not differ significantly in the number of benefits offered even after controlling for differences in employee power is consistent with the proposition that state-owned and formerly state-owned firms inherit historically accepted norms for the provision of social benefits as part of their compensation packages. Employees expect these services, and firms do not readily drop them even as ownership changes occur. *De novo* private firms, by contrast, have greater leeway and do not have the burden of this

Table 2.9. Number of social benefits, ordered logit estimates

Ordered logit estimates

Log likelihood = −240.65376

Number of obs. = 189
$chi^2(10)$ = 180.51
Prob > chi^2 = 0.0000
Pseudo R^2 = .2727

core_ben	Coeff.	Std. Err.	z	$P > |z|$	[95% conf. interval]	
log_sg93	−1.501477	.5735828	−2.618	.009	−2.625679	−.3772755
w93	.0600763	.012897	4.658	.000	.0347986	.085354
log_l	1.01859	.1793243	5.680	.000	.6671208	1.370059
log_pm93	−.908585	.8161238	−1.113	.266	−2.508158	.6909882
lpower	.5294094	.2861096	1.850	.064	−.0313551	1.090174
unionper	.0094951	.0075539	1.257	.209	−.0053104	.0243005
tipbind	.2551516	.3517094	0.725	.468	−.4341861	.9444892
sa	−.2217492	.3859986	−0.574	.566	−.9782926	.5347942
pri	−.6358484	.4398842	−1.445	.148	−1.498006	.2263088
dn	−2.282608	.6731489	−3.391	.001	−3.601956	−.9632606
			(ancillary parameters)			
_cut0	4.497226	1.20463				
_cut1	6.779219	1.204053				
_cut2	8.703618	1.241445				
_cut3	10.26566	1.304947				
_cut4	11.95994	1.385563				

core_bens	number of core social benefits offered: child care, health care, food subsidy/cafeteria, housing/housing subsidy, holiday subsidy/resort
log_sg93	sales growth in 1993 (log form)
wg93	average wage in 1993
log_l	log employment
log_pm93	log profit margin = log[sales/(sales − profit)]; see note 8
lpower	dummy variable: = 1 if wage or employment growth are among the main objectives of the firm, 0 otherwise
unionper	percentage unionization
tipbind	dummy variable: = 1 if the tax-based incomes policy (*popiwek*) was binding in 1992 or 1993, 0 otherwise
sa	dummy variable: = 1 if firm is state-owned and commercialized, 0 otherwise
pri	dummy variable: = 1 if firm is privatized, 0 otherwise
dn	dummy variable: = 1 if firm is *de novo* private, 0 otherwise
_cut0	upper cut-off k_0 corresponding to break between zero benefits and one benefits offered (see text)
_cut1	upper cut-off k_1 corresponding to break between one benefit and two benefits offered
_cut2	upper cut-off k_2 corresponding to break between two and three benefits offered
_cut3	upper cut-off k_3 corresponding to break between three and four benefits offered
_cut4	upper cut-off k_4 corresponding to break between four and five benefits offered

Bottom cut-off $k_{-1} = -\infty$ and top cut-off $k_5 = +\infty$ by assumption.

Table 2.10. Social assets by ownership form

	% of firms in ownership class owning asset			
Asset type	DN	PRI	SA	SOE
1. Crèche	0	0	5	5
2. Health clinic	0	22	63	58
3. Buffet/cafeteria	3	22	37	27
4. Apartments	0	33	71	53
5. Hostel for workers	0	18	27	15
6. Holiday resort/facilities	5	29	76	63

DN = emerging private sector (*de novo*) firm
PRI = privatized firm
SA   = state-owned and commercialized
SOE = state-owned, traditional (unincorporated)

historical legacy. They are freer to arrive at total compensation packages that may or may not include such non-wage benefits.

There is only mixed evidence for the effect of the firm's financial situation on social provision. Surprisingly, firms that grew fast in 1993 offered fewer social benefits, even when we control for size and ownership. This might suggest that widespread social provision exercises a constraining influence on the growth of the firm, perhaps because managers are more concerned with employee welfare issues than with taking advantage of the new growth opportunities. There is, however, no significant effect from profit margins, perhaps because social provision is probably more closely related to previous than to current returns on capital.

Finally, the results concerning wage trends appear to refute the view of wages and social benefits as substitutes – the two are in fact significantly associated in this equation. This is consistent with the view of social benefits as part of a typical total remuneration package offered to employees, as well as with an efficiency wage type-of-view in which some firms offer high pay in both money and non-money terms. In the Polish context, the latter may arise from managers and workers agreeing to extract most or all available surplus to employee remuneration, whether in wages or non-wage benefits. Both wages and social provision are therefore lower in enterprises with smaller firm-specific costs to distribute. Such a view fits with the surprising finding that social provision is not greater in firms where the tax-based incomes policy is binding.

The questionnaire also yielded information about the social assets owned by the firms, which offers a slightly different picture of the nature and scope of social provision. The distribution of social assets by type and ownership form is reported in table 2.10. The most common social

Table 2.11. Provision of social benefits vs. ownership of social assets

Benefit type	% of firms in ownership class							
	DN		PRI		SA		SOE	
	BP	NA	BP	NA	BP	NA	BP	NA
Child care	8	7	47	47	46	41	34	30
Health care	29	29	64	42	83	20	70	12
Cafeteria	10	7	31	9	42	5	31	4
Housing	2	2	49	9	78	5	65	9
Holiday-related	15	10	80	51	95	20	89	26
No. of firms	41		45		41		81	

BP: Benefit provided
NA: Benefit provided *without* ownership of corresponding social asset

DN = emerging private sector (*de novo*) firm
PRI = privatized firm
SA = state-owned and commercialized
SOE = state-owned, traditional (unincorporated)

asset is holiday homes and housing, followed closely by health clinics. In fact crèches and cultural assets were very rare in our sample, and even company dining facilities were relatively infrequent. The pattern by ownership is more striking than for the provision of benefits, presumably because, even if they provide benefits, *de novo* firms have neither the available resources nor the motivation to purchase social assets. Thus virtually no *de novo* private firms own any social assets at all, and ownership is concentrated in the state-owned sector. Privatized firms own fewer assets than state-owned ones, though it is unclear whether this is because the assets have been disposed of, or because privatization was easier in firms with fewer social assets, or because privatization was easier in small firms and small firms tend to have few social assets.

The relationship between the provision of social benefits and the ownership of social assets is clarified with reference to table 2.11. Very few firms offer housing or food assistance without owning the asset. Moreover, most firms that provide childcare assistance do not own a crèche. However, the limited ownership of social assets in health and holiday areas does not prevent widespread offering of social benefits.

Table 2.11 also highlights the differences in the nature of provision between state and private sectors. The lack of social assets does not prevent relatively widespread provision of social benefits in the private sector, especially in the area of health care. However, private firms have

Table 2.12. Change in level of social provision 1991–3 vs. ownership

Change in level of benefits	% of firms in given ownership class				
	DN	PRI	SA	SOE	All
Increase	12	7	5	5	7
Constant	83	51	41	31	48
Small fall	2	27	29	21	20
Big fall	2	16	24	43	25
Total	100	100	100	100	100

DN = emerging private sector (*de novo*) firm
PRI = privatized firm
SA   = state-owned and commercialized
SOE = state-owned, traditional (unincorporated)
Note: Figures may not sum to 100 due to rounding.

steered away from social benefits that might entail large sunk costs in social assets – housing and childcare facilities. In state-owned firms there is a closer correlation between ownership of assets and social provision.

Finally, we note that only 13 of the firms in our sample had made recent major investments in social assets. Although *de novo* private firms were the most likely to do so, the percentage of investing DN firms was still only 10 per cent.

The determinants of changes in social provision

Analysts of transitional economies tend to believe that the provision of social benefits will decline across the board, because of privatization, tightening budget constraints, and increasing market pressures. The questionnaire contains information about changes in the scale of social benefits over the preceding two years that allows for the testing of some simple hypotheses.

The changes in social provision by ownership type are reported in table 2.12, as the answer to a question about adjustments in social provision coded in four categories between an increase and a big fall.[11] Social provision declined in around 45 per cent of firms, but increased in 7 per cent. Perhaps more significantly, a majority of firms in the sample registered either an increase or no change in social provision. It is clear from these figures that, although Polish firms may be restructuring in various ways pre or post privatization (see Belka *et al.*, 1995; and Pinto *et al.*, 1994), relatively few of them are adjusting their provision of social benefits downwards in a significant way. This is especially apparent in the figures for disposals of social assets: only 32 firms disposed of social assets between 1991 and 1993, only three of these being privatized firms. The main reason given for asset disposal was to allow the firm to concentrate on its core business (59 per cent of cases) or to repay debts (19 per cent). The relatively low number of asset disposals, and the fairly high frequency of disposals via gifts (nearly one-third) compared with sales or leasings, provide support for our earlier suggestion that the return to disposals may be relatively low.

The findings by ownership type are also revealing. The largest falls in social provision are recorded in the state-owned sector, and especially in SOEs, where a majority of enterprises display some sort of fall. The decline is more *modest* in privatized firms, an absolute majority of which have kept social provision constant! It is also interesting that *de novo* private firms are more likely to be increasing than decreasing provision, though of course the majority keep their level of provision constant (at or near zero).

In attempting to explain the change in provision of social benefits, we included in our estimating equation all the factors predicted to be relevant in our understanding of the level of provision, as well as variables to control for changing enterprise circumstances, especially financial situation. Hence, as before, we include ownership dummies, a proxy for size (the natural logarithm of employment), and indicators of employee power (the unionization rate and our indicator for labour power). The equation also contains as independent variables the profit to sales ratio in 1993, the growth in sales in 1993, and a dummy variable for the imposition of the tax-based incomes policy (TIP). Since the non-wage benefit is now specified in rate of change form, the wage variable is also entered as a percentage change. Finally, the questionnaire also contains information about whether employee power is increasing or declining, which is extended to include the proxies for workers' influence over changes in social provision. As before, the dependent variable is assumed to contain ordinal information only and is coded such that a larger value implies a larger decline in benefits offered.

The results of the ordered logit regression are reported in table 2.13. The decline in social benefits is most marked in state-owned and commercialized firms; there is no significant difference between them (SOEs are the benchmark and the coefficient on the SA dummy variable is insignificantly different from this benchmark). However, the decline is significantly *less* in privatized firms and the negative coefficient is even larger (though not significantly so) for *de novo* private firms. The results suggest that, far from encouraging the reduction in social provision, privatization appears to hinder it! The size effect, however, follows

Table 2.13. Changes in level of social provision, ordered logit estimates

Ordered logit estimates

Log likelihood = −192.98805

Number of obs. = 186
chi²(12) = 59.97
Prob > chi² = 0.0000
Pseudo R^2 = .1345

dec_bens	Coeff.	Std. Err.	z	P > |z|	[95% conf. interval]	
log_sg93	.3872371	.5755846	0.673	.501	−.7408881	1.515362
log_wg93	−.2440438	.2293651	−1.064	.287	−.6935912	.2055036
log_1	.4565321	.1775231	2.572	.010	.1085933	.8044709
log_pm93	−2.55687	.8415811	−3.038	.002	−4.206339	−.9074016
lpower	.1553798	.3034023	0.512	.609	−.4392777	.7500374
lpow_con	−.88111	.4585097	−0.192	.848	−.9867735	.8105515
lpow_dwn	.3078642	.5568883	0.553	.580	−.7836169	1.399345
unionper	.0009049	.0087041	0.104	.917	−.0161547	.0179646
tipbind	−.664386	.3630424	−1.830	.067	−1.375936	.0471639
sa	−.7647363	.4228121	−1.809	.070	−1.593433	.0639602
pri	−1.154766	.4461527	−2.588	.010	−2.029209	−.2803224
dn	−1.939957	.6842845	−2.835	.005	−3.28113	−.5987844
			(ancillary parameters)			
_cut0	−1.407995	1.163268				
_cut1	2.119904	1.146466				
_cut2	3.239967	1.161623				

dec_bens   decline in scale of social benefits in the preceding two years (1 = increase, 2 = constant, 3 = small decline, 4 = big decline)

log_sg93   sales growth in 1993 (log form)

log_wg93   real wage growth in 1993 (log form)

log_l   log employment

log_pm93   log profit margin = log[sales/(sales − profit)]; see note 8

lpower   dummy variable: = 1 if wage or employment growth are among the main objectives of the firm, 0 otherwise

lpow_up   dummy variable: = 1 if firm said labour power had been increasing over the preceding two years, 0 otherwise [DROPPED]

lpow_con   dummy variable: = 1 if firm said labour power had been constant over the preceding two years, 0 otherwise

lpow_dwn   dummy variable: = 1 if firm said labour power had been falling over the preceding two years, 0 otherwise

unionper   percentage unionization

tipbind   dummy variable: = 1 if the tax-based incomes policy ('popiwek') was binding in 1992 or 1993, 0 otherwise

sa   dummy variable: = 1 if firm is state-owned and commercialized, 0 otherwise

pri   dummy variable: = 1 if firm is privatized, 0 otherwise

dn   dummy variable: = 1 if firm is *de novo* private, 0 otherwise

_cut0   upper cut-off k_0 corresponding to break between an increase and no change in social benefits offered (see text)

_cut1   upper cut-off k_1 corresponding to break between no change and a small fall in social benefits offered

_cut2   upper cut-off k_2 corresponding to break between a small fall and a large fall in social benefits offered

Bottom cut-off $k_{-1} = -\infty$ and top cut-off $k_3 = +\infty$ by assumption.

expectations, with greater declines in larger firms (the coefficient on log employment is positive), *ceteris paribus*. Since we know that more benefits are provided in larger firms, there is presumably a scale effect, with social benefits tending to be reduced in proportion to initial provision. Employee power, whether indicated by objectives, changing authority in the firm, or unionization rate, appears to be unrelated to the decline in benefits, suggesting that observed changes are influenced more by 'push' factors (external circumstances) than by internal structures.

This view is broadly confirmed by looking at the coefficients and *t*-statistics on the indicators of the enterprises' economic situation. Firms with larger profit margins display significantly smaller declines in social provision, suggesting a pivotal role of financial circumstances in the decision to reduce provision. However, since the recent growth of sales (which may be a better indicator of likely future profitability) is not significant, changes in social provision may be driven primarily by short-term financial pressures. Finally, though we found a positive relationship between the level of social provision and the level of wages in table 2.9, the relationship breaks down in rate of change form; there is no significant relationship between the change in benefits and the change in wages in table 2.13. However, we do find evidence that social provision is being used strategically by firms; the coefficient on the TIP variable is nearly significant at the 5 per cent level and negative, indicating that benefits are reduced less in enterprises in which the tax-based incomes policy is biting.

Conclusions

In this paper, we provide one of the first quantitative evaluations of the scale of non-wage social provision in transitional economies, as well as a preliminary effort to explain both the level and the change in provision. Our main findings are that social provision remains surprisingly wide-spread, and has not been greatly reduced in either the state-owned or the privatized sectors. Moreover, even *de novo* private firms offer a surprising range of social benefits to workers and, if anything, they are tending to increase rather than reduce the scale of their provision.

The main determinants of the scale of social provision are ownership structure, size of firm, and employee power, the last not explicitly via the union structure. Money wages and the provision of social benefits appear to be complementary rather than substitutes. Social assets are concentrated in state-owned firms, but there is relatively little social asset disposal; the *de novo* private sector is expanding the range of social benefits offered but is not investing significantly in social assets. Changes in the provision of social benefits have been modest, and are explained by ownership form, size, and profitability. There is also some evidence of substitution between money wages and social benefits in firms subject to the tax-based incomes policy.

NOTES

This is a revised version of a paper prepared for the March 1994 CEPR/IHS Conference on Social Protection and the Enterprise in Transitional Economies. The authors would like to thank seminar audiences at the IHS and the World Bank for comments and suggestions, and Donata Hoesch for excellent research assistance. The statistical package used was Stata 3.0. The paper is a product of the World Bank Research Project on Enterprise Behaviour and Economic Reform in Central and Eastern Europe. The views expressed in the paper are those of the authors and not those of the World Bank or other institutions.

1 See *Rocznik Statystyczny 1991*, p. xvi.
2 Our sample of 208 firms included 5 cooperatives founded during the communist period. Given that the transition has meant that control of these cooperatives was devolved to their members, we classify the 5 cooperatives in our sample as 'privatized' firms (PRIs).
3 See *Rocznik Statystyczny Przemysłu, 1990*.
4 That is, we are assuming that the scale of social services implied by 'two benefits' is greater than that implied by 'one benefit', and that 'three benefits' means more services than 'two benefits', but we make no assumptions about how the jump in the scale of social provision from 'one benefit' to 'two benefits' compares with the jump from 'two benefits' to 'three benefits'.
5 Assuming a normal distribution for the error term corresponds to the ordered probit estimating procedure. As it happens, ordered probit estimations gave virtually identical results.
6 Employment is the relevant indicator because it is workers who receive the non-wage social benefits, and employment has typically adjusted less than sales or output to the new market conditions. Goodness-of-fit tests indicate the dominance of the logarithmic specification.
7 The variable LPOWER is equal to unity if the firm responds that increasing wages or employment (rather than profits, sales growth, or some other goal) is its main objective; zero otherwise.
8 The profit margin is used in log form, log[sales/(sale−profits)], i.e. roughly the log sales/costs ratio. The log specification is less sensitive to outliers and (hence) dominated the levels specification (profit/sales) in goodness-of-fit tests, though the results were quite similar.
9 An example of how to interpret the estimated coefficients is as follows. Consider an SOE firm whose score (the fitted number of benefits obtained by applying the estimated coefficients to the observed values of the firm's independent variables) is 9.0. The cut-off k between three and four benefits offered is 10.27 (_cut3 in table 2.9). The probability that the firm offers four or more benefits is $1 - [1/(1 + e^{(9.0 - 10.27)}] = 22\%$. Now consider a firm with identical values for all independent variables except that it is a *de novo* private

firm. The coefficient on the dummy variable DN is -2.28, and so this firm's score is $9.0 - 2.28 = 6.72$. The probability that this firm offers four or more benefits is $1 - [1/(1 + e^{(6.72 - 10.27)})] = 3\%$.

10 Though the extent of social provision is correlated with unionization rates, we cannot discern an effect independent from enterprise size and ownership.

11 A small number of firms that answered 'not applicable' to this question had their answer recoded as 'no change' ('constant level of social provision'). Most of these were *de novo* firms that responded 'not applicable' because they provided no social benefits.

REFERENCES

Aghion, P., O. Blanchard, and R. Burgess (1994), 'The behaviour of state firms in Eastern Europe, pre-privatisation', *European Economic Review* 38(6), June.

Belka, M., S. Estrin, M. E. Schaffer, and I. J. Singh (1995), 'Enterprise adjustment in Poland: evidence from a survey of 200 private, privatized, and state-owned firms', Centre for Economic Performance Discussion Paper No. 233.

Estrin, S. (ed.) (1994), *Privatization in Central and Eastern Europe*, London: Longman.

Estrin, S., A. Gelb, and I. J. Singh (1995), 'Shocks and adjustment by firms in transition: a comparative study', *Journal of Comparative Economics* 21(2), October.

Fischer, S. and A. Gelb (1991), 'The process of socialist economic transformation', *Journal of Economic Perspectives* 5(4), Fall.

Frydman, R., A. Rapaczynski, and J. S. Earle *et al.* (1993), *The Privatization Process in Central Europe*, London: Central European University Press.

Gregory, P. R. and R. C. Stuart (1989), *Comparative Economic Systems*, 3rd edn, Boston: Houghton Mifflin.

Pinto, B., M. Belka, and S. Krajewski (1994), 'Transforming state enterprises in Poland: evidence on adjustment by manufacturing firms', *Brookings Papers on Economic Activity*, No. 1.

Portes, R. (ed.) (1993), *Economic Transformation in Central and Eastern Europe: A Progress Report*, London and Brussels: CEPR and European Commission.

Wiles, P. J. D. (1977), *Economic Institutions Compared*, Oxford: Blackwell.

3 Do East European enterprises provide social protection?

Employee benefits and labour market behaviour in the East European transition

JOHN S. EARLE

Introduction

It has often been observed that various forms of in-kind benefits made up a large proportion of the compensation paid to the employees of state-owned enterprises in socialist Eastern Europe. Kornai (1992: 222), for instance, explained this as a function of the firm as follows:

> [A firm plays] the role of a local branch of paternalistic provision. Many firms provide institutionally owned apartments and have their own doctor's office, holiday center, kindergarten, and day nursery. The bosses decide how these services are allocated. In many countries and periods, firms also deal with distribution of rationed foodstuffs and perhaps other scarce goods (such as color televisions or cars).[1]

There seem to have been several motivations for state-owned firms to provide non-wage compensation. By contrast with many other parts of their accounts, the cash wages paid by enterprises were strictly controlled by central planners. As has so often been the case with incomes policies throughout the world, the attempt to restrict the growth in cash wage payments in socialist economies led to various forms of evasion. Chief among them may have been the substitution of forms of compensation that were less tightly controlled. In an environment of continual labour shortage, it was very important that non-wage benefits allowed enterprises to increase the level of total compensation they could offer. Moreover, in an economy dominated by shortages of many commodities, enterprises may have had superior access (for instance through political connections) to valuable goods that had a greater value to employees than their nominal equivalents in cash. Managers could also use fringe benefits to create larger payment differentials within the firm than were permitted by the centrally planned wage system. Thus, benefits could in principle have functioned to recruit, retain, and motivate workers, as well as to achieve any political or personal goals of the managers and industrial nomenklatura, while the more easily observed and measured cash wage differentials remained within rather narrow limits.

The continued existence of non-wage compensation, particularly if it represents a large item in either the costs of the firm or the benefits to the workers, poses a number of interesting social and economic problems in the transition to a market economy. From one point of view, which may for instance be inferred from the above quote from Kornai, these activities epitomize the remaining paternalistic atavisms of the command economy from which firms should now unburden themselves. Fundamental to the restructuring process, as firms are privatized and as they 'rationalize' their activities, is the 'unbundling' of the different activities that constituted the state-owned firms (SOEs). For instance, Aghion *et al.* (1993: 4) argue that '[n]on production activities, schools, housing, hospitals and the like should be operated independently'. This view has also been prominently associated with such international financial institutions (IFIs) as the World Bank, despite their large-scale provision of such services to their own employees.

An alternative point of view stresses the desirability that East European firms continue these activities until either the state or the market achieves sufficient competence to be able to provide them. There may be significant social costs if such necessities as housing, medicine, and child care are even temporarily unavailable, and the supply responsiveness of these goods and services may be quite inelastic in the short run. It also may not make sense to maintain the hypothesis of robust secondary markets for the assets associated with these benefits, as though it were easy enough for an East European firm to sell an asset to an entrepreneur likely to continue its operation. Under these conditions, peculiar to the transition economies but not always clearly acknowledged by the IFIs, there may be a discrepancy between the private and social benefits for firms to continue performing these functions: the market is perhaps not the best judge of the optimal boundaries of the firm.

Of course, the other side of the debate may reverse this argument with the easy riposte that there is no clearly superior alternative to the market, and that the East European countries should by now have had enough bad experiences with those claiming that they know better 'the needs of the people'. A third, more conciliatory party might try to calm the disputants by pointing out that, because such a wide variety of goods and services may be included under the general rubric of employee benefits, it would be better first to define carefully all the relevant categories, while holding out the hope that each side might be correct in their arguments when applied to different types of benefits.

This paper takes a less normative tack by and large, exploring the positive role of employee benefits, including social protection expenditure and other types of non-wage compensation, in several aspects of labour market behaviour in the transition countries of Eastern Europe. The paper begins by pointing out that the employment package contains many types of working conditions in addition to compensation, narrowly construed; these affect both the attractiveness of the firm's jobs to workers – the labour supply to the firm – and the firm's costs. One critical but neglected dimension of social protection that firms can provide their workers, for example, is job security. Work-sharing arrangements of various types have been quite widespread in most East European countries, and, indeed, the obverse of the oft-noted drop in productivity, measured as output per worker, is the preservation of jobs. The paper substantiates the empirical importance of these observations through an analysis of layoffs, hiring, and hours of work in several East European economies, with a particular emphasis on this behaviour in Romania, the only country for which consistent time-series information seems to exist.

On the other hand, an important theoretical determinant of a firm's choice of labour market adjustment, and thus the extent to which it preserves jobs in the short run, is the degree to which labour represents one-time ('quasi-fixed'), per worker-year, or per hour costs to the firm. Thus, there is a certain interdependence between the 'social protection' arising from job preservation and that coming from conventional social expenditures made by firms. The cost to the firm of some fringe benefits, including some categories of social expenditures, seems to be invariant to the number of hours of work, thus increasing the incentives of the firm to use layoffs rather than hours reductions to reduce labour costs. The paper therefore examines the importance of some standard categories of fringe benefits for the choice between employment and hours adjustments, using disaggregated data for sub-branches of industry in Romania. In the event, there seems to be only weak and inconsistent evidence that non-wage labour costs are significant determinants of the choice of method of adjustment.

A possible explanation for the lack of clear findings on these effects is that non-wage compensation is less significant than commonly believed. Although incompleteness and comparability problems preclude strong statements, existing evidence for the Czech Republic in 1993 and Romania in 1992 seems to imply that these categories of expenditures are no greater than in the United States, and significantly less than in some West European countries. This may be a result of much shedding of 'non-productive' activities that has occurred or, possibly, because they were never particularly large.

However, the small measured size of non-wage labour costs may also be accounted for by another factor, one that brings us full circle to the normative debate portrayed at the beginning of this paper. It may be that firms incur relatively low current costs for the provision of social services to their employees, since they have already made fixed investments some time ago in the assets (clinics, recreation facilities) from which the services (health care, vacations) are generated. In this case, the apparent low level of benefits would be simply an artefact of accounting conventions that fail to amortize the cost of sunk investments over the full life of the asset. By the same token, it is possible that workers would then value the service much more highly than is represented by the firm's cost accounts.

In principle, the appropriate tool for determining the value placed by the market on fringe benefits and other working conditions is the hedonic wage function, and the paper estimates such a function for various categories of social and other fringe benefits. No evidence is found for the contention that workers value benefits more than their cost to the firm or more than the equivalent of the firm's cost in cash wages. Of course, the application of this method makes strong assumptions about the extent of labour mobility and about the ability of the researcher to control for other influences on wages, neither of which is likely to be satisfied in the transition countries of Eastern Europe. Indeed, empirical investigations of equalizing differences in the West have also generally failed to confirm the theory. The paper thus concludes somewhat agnostically about the role these benefits play in total compensation, and about the appropriate role for public policy either in mandating them or in substituting public provision.

Layoffs and alternatives

Firms and workers have a variety of methods by which to adjust the use and cost of labour in response to exogenous shocks (see, for instance, Earle, 1988). Most important for present purposes is the possibility of short-time working during hard times as an alternative to laying workers off. The reduction of working hours may take a variety of forms – fewer hours per day, an occasional full day off, or short-term leaves for a week or more – but they generally share an important feature: they spread the burden of adjustment over all or most employees rather than concentrating it entirely on a few workers, generally the least skilled and lowest paid, who would be subject to layoffs. On the other hand, work sharing may be an inferior method of adjustment to certain kinds of shocks, especially those that require a permanent reallocation of labour across firms.

Given the importance of these issues in the transition context, it is surprising that so little attention has been paid to labour market adjustments other than those of employment. For instance, the frequent observation that 'productivity' declined in all East European countries in the early 1990s refers, practically without exception, to the fall in output per employee, while overlooking the possibility that hours of work may also have declined significantly. No doubt there is also some measurement error in output in such a direction as to magnify the true output decline, owing to 'index number relativity' and the difficulties of adaptation by national statistical offices and in monitoring hundreds of thousands of new legal entities (see Earle, 1995, for further discussion). These problems are enormously exacerbated when one attempts measurement for the whole economy; I therefore focus on the industrial sector in the subsequent analysis.

A further choice of alternatives, within the general category of employment adjustments, is that between a policy of active layoffs and a policy of workforce reduction through attrition, by encouraging voluntary retirement and slowing or halting the rate of hiring. Once again, the latter method tends to cushion currently employed workers from shocks. But this does not mean it is always superior from a social viewpoint, both because the bulk of adjustment falls on new entrants to the labour force and because the rate of labour reallocation may be slowed.

Table 3.1 illustrates the empirical importance of these observations with data from Romania, perhaps the only country for which consistent time-series are available.[2] From 1989 to 1992, real GNP fell by 32 per cent and real industrial production by 54 per cent, which, leaving measurement problems aside, represent shocks of enormous magnitude. Employment of production workers in state-owned industrial firms first rose in 1990 through a large increase in the hiring rate from 17 to 21 per cent, perhaps as the planners' restrictions eased, permitting enterprises to respond with an instinctive lunge for more labour before realizing that the environment had changed. Voluntary quits exactly doubled, from 9 to 18 per cent, with the increase accounted for by a commensurate increase in both the job-to-job quit rate and the rate of retirement from the labour force. A temporary reduction in the retirement age, adopted in most East European countries in 1990, goes some way to explaining the latter phenomenon, while the opportunities in the new private sector must play some role in the former. The involuntary dismissal rate was little changed from 1989.[3]

Table 3.1. Romania: labour market adjustments, 1989–92

Indicator	1989	1990	1991	1992
Real GNP index	100.0	92.6	79.9	67.9
Industrial production index	100.0	76.3	58.9	46.0
Average number of workers ('000)	3,339.3	3,387.4	3,161.3	2,763.1
Dismissal rate (%)	4.2	4.6	6.7	7.8
Quit rate (%)	8.9	18.0	9.5	6.9
Other separations rate (%)	1.5	1.8	1.4	3.7
Hiring rate (%)	17.0	21.0	9.0	5.4
Total hours worked (million)	6,970.2	5,891.2	5,048.1	4,176.0
Average annual hours of work	2,087.3	1,739.2	1,596.8	1,511.4

Source: National Commission for Statistics and author's calculations.
Note: Employment, turnover, and hours data refer only to workers in the state and cooperative sectors, because consistent estimates for private sector employment are unavailable. The real GNP and industrial production indexes, however, are estimates of total output, including production originating in the private sector. It is unlikely, however, that the private sector contributed substantially to industrial output over this period.

After 1990, however, employment began to fall, only gradually in 1991 but more rapidly in 1992. In 1991, the hiring rate collapsed to 9 per cent, and it fell further to 5 per cent in 1992. Separations, meanwhile, showed quite divergent patterns: layoffs (which may also include some of the separations classified as 'other') began to increase gradually, while quits fell dramatically, so that by 1992 both the overall quit rate and the job-to-job quit rate were much lower than in any of the previous five years.

The pattern of adjustments indicates, therefore, that firms initially attempted to maintain employment, then tried to adjust employment downwards through voluntary attrition, and have only recently undertaken active layoffs. Firms were interested in preserving both their overall size of employment and the jobs of their workers.

This interpretation is further corroborated by the data on hours of work. The Romanian National Commission for Statistics provides data on the total number of hours worked by production workers in state-owned industrial firms for each of these years. Dividing by the number employed yields a plausible estimate of average hours of work per production worker over the course of the year. In 1989, workers had an average of 2,087 hours of work for the year, or, assuming a 50-week year, nearly 42 hours per week. Hours fell drastically in 1990, with the abolition of Saturday working in state-owned industrial enterprises, and continued to fall to a level of 1,511 hours per year on average, or just over 30 hours per week, in 1992. Average hours of work, therefore, decreased much more than did employment, 27.6 compared with 17.3 per cent over this period.[4]

Evidence from other countries of the region, although less complete, suggests that some of the Romanian patterns may not be wholly unique. According to Beleva *et al.* (1993), writing on the state sector in Bulgaria, quits dominated layoffs as a source of separations in the years 1990–1992, although it appears from their figures that the proportion accounted for by layoffs increased from 6 to over 25 per cent over this period. The hiring rate fell significantly from 1990 to 1991, but is unreported in 1992. One might infer from these data that Bulgaria may be lagging Romania slightly in the evolution of its adjustments. Unfortunately, no hours-of-work data are supplied.

With respect to Poland, Coricelli *et al.* (1993) show data only for total separations, so it is not possible to assess the prevalence of active layoff versus passive attrition policies of firms. Hiring behaviour shows the interesting pattern of declining from 1988 to 1990 and rising thereafter. However, their data pertain to the state sector until 1991 and include the private as well as the state sector in 1991 and 1992, rendering it impossible to conclude anything about the job preservation behaviour of the large state enterprises in the more recent period. Average annual hours of work are provided for the years 1988–92, but it is not clear from the text whether they refer to the state sector or both state and private. Assuming they are state, they show much less adjustment compared with Romania: in industry, average annual hours of work fell by only about 9 per cent from 1989 to 1991, and in the 'total' they fell by only 9.4 per cent to 1992 (for which hours in industry are 'not available').

Russia, of course, is the country where firms seem to have adopted employment preservation on a massive scale, the chief evidence being the very low unemployment rate: 1.5 per cent registered with local labour offices and about 5.5 per cent according to the Labour Force Survey.[5] And an astoundingly low proportion of the registered unemployed – 21 per cent in December 1993 – had been laid off, whereas nearly half had quit their former job. Moreover, total employment had fallen only slightly – by about only 4 per cent in 1993, in the Goskomstat. And, according to Yemtsov (1994), only a trivial proportion of separations, certainly under 10 per cent, are layoffs, while Roxburgh and Shapiro point out, on a more disaggregated basis, that no sector had layoffs accounting for more than 12 per cent of separations.[6]

Although these data might be interpreted as proof that the insiders of Russian firms are taking care of their own, it is notable that gross flows of labour in and out of employment remain quite high, with hiring and separation rates both above 20 per cent in most sectors. Thus, jobs have been preserved, but they are in many cases occupied by different individuals.

On the other hand, there is substantial evidence of various kinds of work-sharing arrangements in Russia. According to Yemtsov (1994), Goskomstat data for March 1994 show that 20–33 per cent of enterprises had 'significant shares of their workforces' working shorter hours or taking involuntary leaves.[7] It is interesting that the average duration of involuntary leaves was only about 19 days, implying that there may have been a fair amount of churning of workers in and out of unpaid leave in some firms. As emphasized by Meacher (1994), these adjustments are encouraged by a kind of short-time compensation from the Employment Fund to workers on unpaid leave or working short hours.

To some extent, real wage adjustments may also be considered a measure of social protection by enterprises, insofar as they also represent an alternative to layoffs, which distribute the burden of adjustment more widely. Throughout Eastern Europe and the former Soviet Union, real wages have fallen. The measures usually reported, however, have several failings: they neglect the greater availability of goods and the end of time wasted in queuing (as argued by Lipton and Sachs, 1990) and they ignore changes in hours of work, usually being based on monthly earnings. When real hourly earnings are computed for Romania, for instance, the results look quite different from the reported figures for real monthly earnings: comparing the end of 1992 with 1989, the monthly figures fell 30 per cent while the hourly figures actually rose by 15 per cent!

Fringe benefits and the choice of adjustment

This section investigates the interaction between two different kinds of 'social protection' activities of firms in transition economies: the preservation of jobs and the provision of social benefits. Standard labour demand theory suggests that firms respond to different types of labour costs with different choices of the level and adjustment of employment and hours of work. Thus, the decision to share the work and avoid layoffs during a downturn will be influenced by the marginal cost saving from reducing hours compared with that from reducing employment. If benefits vary at the margin with hours worked, then firms paying higher

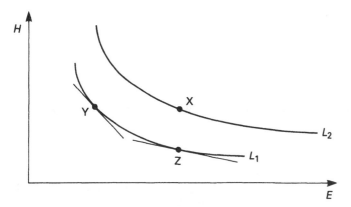

Figure 3.1 Employment and hours adjustments

benefits are more likely also to engage in work sharing compared with the situation when benefits are invariant to hours of work. Thus, the degree to which the two types of social protection activities are complementary depends on the nature of the costs to firms of providing benefits.

The firm's total labour input can be expressed as

$$L = L(E, H),$$

where E=number of employees and H=average hours of work per employee. Implicitly, employment and hours are treated as two separate factors of production, with the usual assumptions about positive but decreasing marginal products.[8] Isoquants plotted in E–H space with the usual convex shape trace out the level surfaces of labour input or, if labour is the only factor of production, of output, as shown in figure 3.1. Ignoring overtime premia and one-time costs of hiring and training, labour costs are

$$C = WHE + BE,$$

where W=average hourly wage, including the firm's costs for benefits that vary with H, and B=employer costs for employee benefits that vary with E but are unrelated to the level of H. The equation for an isocost curve in E–H space is

$$E = C/(WH + B),$$

with slope given by

$$dE/dH = -CW/(WH + B)^2 < 0,$$

$$\partial(dE/dH)/\partial W = \frac{E^3}{C^2}(WH - B), \quad \text{and}$$

$$\partial(dE/dH)/\partial B = 2WE^3/C^2 > 0.$$

Thus, the isocost curve is non-linear, with a negative slope varying positively with B and ambiguously with W.

The problem for East European firms, as described in the previous section, is how to cope with a negative demand shock as well as to adjust to a different set of objectives. Cost minimization in the combination of inputs was not an objective of state-owned enterprises subject to central planning and 'guidelines'.[9] The starting point is point X, where a total labour input of L_2 is used; no tangency with an isocost curve reflecting relative prices of H and E is assumed.

With the demand shocks, hardening of budget constraints, and changes in objectives, the firm seeks to reduce labour input from L_2 to L_1 on the graph. We may therefore expect non-positive changes in both dimensions of labour input, but the relative importance of hours and employment declines should be influenced by the relative cost-saving from each. Faced with a decline in demand and the need to reduce labour input, cost-minimizing firms with relatively high B tend to reduce E relatively more than H, by moving to a point such as Y; those with relatively high W should have the reverse behaviour, moving to a point such as Z.[10]

I test this model by examining the dependence of hours and employment adjustments on the structure of labour compensation. Indeed, we can observe wide variation in the extent of adjustment of employment and hours in Eastern Europe. The previous section documented international differences in these adjustments. But they also display significant variation within countries, as shown in figure 3.2 for Romanian industries. Because of data limitations, the employment changes are computed from 1990 to the end of 1992, while those for average hours worked are from 1989 to 1992 (average over year). Although the graph shows that branches with large hours changes also tend to have large employment changes (the raw correlation coefficient is .49), this is probably because a third factor – demand shocks – affects both. Our test must therefore take this third factor into account.

The simple test adopted here is that the responsiveness of average work hours and of employment to changes in output is dependent on the structure of compensation. The framework is a 'random coefficients model' where the coefficient on output is a function of the proportion of

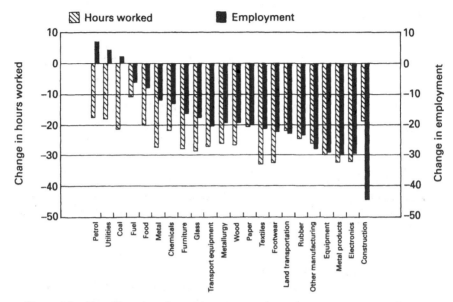

Figure 3.2   Layoff vs. work sharing: employment and hours adjustments in Romania

Source: National Commission for Statistics.

Note: Change in employment covers the period 1990 to end 1992 and change in hours worked the period 1989–92

compensation varying with hours and employment. The starting point is the general equation

$$\Delta Y_i = \alpha + \beta \Delta X_i + u_i,\tag{1}$$

where $Y = E$ and H in different equations, $X =$ industrial output of sub-branch i, and u is a random disturbance. β is then postulated to be a function of the division of compensation among three categories: W_1, compensation dependent on hours of work; W_2, compensation dependent on the number of workers; and W_3, quasi-fixed (hiring and training) costs:

$$\beta = f(w_2, w_3),$$

where lowercase letters indicate the proportion of the category in total compensation (with w_1 omitted to avoid perfect collinearity).[11] Assuming a linear functional form for f and substituting in the equation (1),

$$\Delta Y_i = \alpha + \beta_1 \Delta X_i + \beta_2 \Delta X_i w_2 + \beta_3 \Delta X_i w_3 + \mu_i,$$

whereas μ is a composite error term, suggesting the possibility of heteroskedasticity.

Table 3.2. Labour costs and employment and hours adjustments

ΔY	α	β_1	β_2	β_3	R^2
ΔH	−19.3	0.29	−2.87*	1.82*	.33
	(10.3)	(0.21)	(0.02)	(0.07)	
ΔL	18.2	0.99*	−4.95*	3.50*	.55
	(10.9)	(0.21)	(0.01)	(0.07)	
$\Delta H/\Delta L$	4.8		−0.52	0.05	.14
	(2.3)		(0.30)	(1.26)	

Note: Results for ΔH and ΔL from OLS estimation of equation (1) in the text. Results for $\Delta H/\Delta L$ are based on the equation in the text. Number of observations = 22. Standard errors are shown in parentheses. For ease of reading, an asterisk is attached to those estimates for which the point estimate is at least twice the corresponding standard error.

The results, shown in table 3.2, are rather inconclusive. The effect of an increased proportion of compensation tied to employment, β_2, is to lower the responsiveness of average hours of work to output changes, as hypothesized. It is also consistent with the model that higher quasi-fixed costs (training) are associated with more adjustments of hours. However, the responsiveness of employment adjustments to these same factors is the same as that for hours, contradicting the theory. The final equation shown tries to get at the question of relative adjustment, as follows:

$$\Delta H_i/\Delta L_i = \alpha + \beta_2 w_2 + \beta_3 w_3 + \mu_i.$$

β_2 is not very precisely measured, but the point estimate implies that higher per worker costs tend to lower the adjustment of hours relative to the adjustment of employment, consistent with the model, while training costs have no effect.

These results are difficult to interpret, but in any case should not be construed as providing unambiguously strong support for the hypothesis that the composition of labour costs may be an important factor in the choice of method of labour adjustment. One possible explanation could be that fringe benefits, at least those that vary with numbers employed rather than with average hours worked, are a relatively unimportant part of total compensation.[12] The next section turns to the problem of quantifying the size of benefits.

International comparisons of compensation structure

Table 3.3 shows a disaggregation of labour costs in the Czech Republic and Romania, and figures 3.3 and 3.4 depict the breakdown into major

Table 3.3. Employment costs in the Czech Republic and Romania

Category	Czech Rep. (1993) (%)	Romania (1992) (%)
Wages and salaries	**58.3**	**66.5**
For hours worked	55.5	64.7
● base wage	NA	49.2
● bonuses	NA	11.9
● premia (seasonal & annual)	NA	2.4
● profit sharing	NA	1.2
Overtime	2.6	1.8
Call-out bonuses	0.1	NA
Payments for time not worked	**10.0**	**9.2**
Vacation payment	7	7.8
Vacation allowance	NA	0.3
Public holiday payment	2.2	NA
Other paid leave	0.5	0.2
Slack work	0.3	0.4
Sick leave paid by employer	0	0.7
Accident allowances paid by employer	0	0.1
Benefits in kind	**3.4**	**1.9**
Company products	0	NA
Company car	0	NA
Staff housing & boarding contribution	1.8	0.3
Anniversary rewards	0.3	NA
Other benefits	1.2	1.6
● equipment for protection & sanitation	NA	0.5
● food	NA	0.4
● business trips	NA	0.7
● holiday & spa tickets	NA	0.1
Statutory social security contributions	**24.8**	**22.1**
Pension contribution	16.4	NA
Sickness insurance contribution	6.1	0.9
Unemployment insurance contribution	2.0	3.5
Accident insurance contribution	0.3	0.0
Penalty taxes on excess wages	NA	1.2
Contribution for maternity	0[1]	0.9
Contribution to social security in addition to direct payments to employees	0	15.4
Non-statutory social security contributions	**0**	**NA**
Supplementary pension schemes	0	NA
Other supplementary insurance	0	NA
Social benefits	**0**	**NA**
Hiring and training costs	**3.5**	**0.3**
Severance payments	1.2	NA[2]
Recruitment costs	0.1	NA
Training costs	2.2	0.3

NA = not available
Source: Romania: National Commission for Statistics; Czech Republic: Statistical Office.
1 These are paid by a state fund.
2 These are included in the category 'other paid leave'.

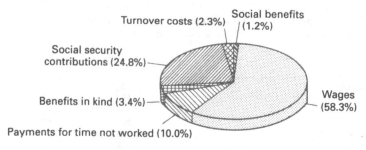

Figure 3.3   Employment costs in the Czech Republic
Source: Statistical Office.

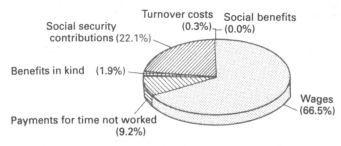

Figure 3.4   Employment costs in Romania
Source: National Commission for Statistics.

categories. The Czech data are taken from the pilot survey done in late 1993 of the European Employment Cost Index (EECI). The data refer to the third quarter of 1993 and were taken from 70 largely manufacturing companies of greater than 99 employees each, and with total employment of 109,000. The Romanian data are the result of a survey, based approximately on the EECI and on ILO recommendations, and conducted at the end of 1992 in nearly the entire state enterprise sector. Thus, the two sets of data differ in both timing and coverage.

Nonetheless, the aggregate behaviour implied by these data is not entirely dissimilar in the two countries; nor seems it to be very different from that in the USA in 1991 or in countries of the European Community in 1988.[13] Payments for time worked were 58.3 per cent of total compensation in the Czech Republic, 66.5 per cent in Romania, and 71.8 per cent in the USA.[14] In the European Community, these payments varied from 57.6 per cent (France) to 83.9 per cent (Denmark).

Cash payments for time not worked accounted for 10 per cent of employment costs in the Czech Republic, 9.2 per cent in Romania, and

9.1 per cent in the USA. These occupied the middle of the range of EC countries – from 6 per cent (Portugal) to 12.3 per cent (Denmark). Since the beginning of 1993, sick leave is financed by the enterprise for the first 10 days in Romania, although these payments may be deducted from the social insurance contribution liability. The latter statement also holds for accidents on-the-job ('worker's compensation' in the US terminology), but without the 10-day limit. Sick leave is financed completely by the state in the Czech Republic.[15]

Benefits in kind were 3.4 per cent, 1.9 per cent, and 0.6 per cent for the three countries, respectively, and under 1 per cent in Western Europe. Most of the difference is accounted for by the slightly greater role that continues for Czech firms in providing subsidized housing. 'Other benefits in kind' include health care, but this seems to be a negligible component in both the Czech Republic and Romania.

Statutorily required social security contributions represent the biggest difference between the two East European countries (25 and 22 per cent, respectively) and the USA (6.4 per cent). West European countries show enormous differences here: from 1.9 (Denmark) to 7.3 (the UK) to 25.6 (Belgium) to 30.6 per cent (Italy), to give a few examples. Non-required payments, for instance for pensions and insurance, are essentially non-existent in Eastern Europe, while accounting for 12.1 per cent of compensation in the USA and 1.1 (Denmark) to 9.4 per cent (France) in Europe.

From these data it therefore seems difficult to assert that East European enterprises are a more important 'pillar' of social protection than are capitalist firms in the West. Why then do so many observers, including Kornai (1992), hold to this belief? There may be several reasons for the discrepancy.

First, perhaps these social functions of firms were important in the past, but have already been eliminated. If a primary motivation for firms in providing them was to compensate workers for shortage commodities, then price liberalization should have largely obviated the need for this behaviour. Benefits may also have been shed as part of initial restructuring in response to hard budget constraints: unbundling of costly activities that produce no revenue. But if the benefits are valued by workers, then firms should have found some way to structure compensation to keep them.

Second, these functions may have been and still remain important in some countries or in some regions, so that the conclusions from the aggregate data in the Czech Republic and Romania may not be generalized. For instance, some limited survey evidence from Russia (Commander and Jackman, 1993) indicates much higher proportions of the 'social fund' in total labour costs – over 25 per cent in large firms – and total benefits of about 35 per cent. But the sample size is quite small and limited to firms in the Moscow area, so it is difficult to draw strong conclusions. And Rose (1994) finds that benefits from employment contribute little to household well-being in a survey of 1,975 Russians in mid-1993. It is possible that, throughout the region, social protection arrangements in isolated 'one-company towns' are organized by firms. Perhaps in some areas, even of Romania and the Czech Republic, there are remote pockets where social benefits from firms are critical.

But the most important explanation for the apparently low proportion of benefits in total labour costs could be related to the discrepancy between costs, as accounted for by the enterprise, and benefits, as valued by workers. Benefits such as health care, vacations, and meals are provided based on facilities likely to have been constructed and fully amortized some time ago. Only the operating cost would show up in the firms' balance sheets, and opportunity costs and current depreciation are likely to be omitted. As a result, it may be that the true economic cost to the firm and the value placed upon the benefits by workers are much higher than the account books reveal. The next section examines this hypothesis.

What is the value of employee benefits?

We have seen that the cost of providing benefits to workers, as reported by firms in the Czech Republic and Romania, is not particularly large compared with reported costs in Western Europe. As argued in the previous section, however, it is possible that the (marginal) value of benefits to workers far exceeds the (average) cost to firms. This section investigates this hypothesis by estimating a hedonic wage function.

The starting point is a standard human capital earnings function:

$$\log(C_i) = \alpha + X_i' \beta + u_i, \tag{2}$$

where C_i is total hourly compensation for individual i, X is a vector of factors affecting productivity and earnings, and u is an error term. Because (suppressing individual subscripts) $C = W + \Sigma_j B_j$, where W is wages and B_j are various types of benefits indexed by j, we can write

$$C = W(1 + \tau_j b_j), \tag{3}$$

where the b_j are the proportions of the various benefits in total compensation and the τ_j measure the value placed on B_j by individuals. If benefits are valued more than the equivalent amount of cash wages, the

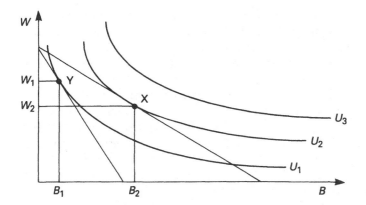

Figure 3.5   Substitution of wages and fringe benefits

$\tau_j > 1$; if workers would prefer to have cash, $\tau_j < 1$; if workers are indifferent, $\tau_j = 1$.

The outcome depends, in general, upon the distribution of the preferences of individuals and the cost functions of firms. Factors affecting costs of benefits from the firm's point of view include standard considerations such as tax policy and the desire to screen job applicants and reduce turnover (see, for example, Rosen, 1986). In the transition context, one should also add that it may not be easy to unbundle the asset; so sunk investments in social facilities may continue to be operated rather than being sold off, because the price they would fetch on the underdeveloped asset markets would be lower than the value of the stream of services they provide.

These considerations are illustrated in figure 3.5 by the isoprofit functions in W–B space, where the tradeoff between wages and a single benefit is assumed for graphability. Note that the isoprofit curves may be non-linear, for instance if there are economies of scale or set-up costs of providing certain benefits, and that the slope indicates the marginal cost of benefit provision. The flatter isoprofit function in the diagram (with slope greater than -1) presumes some greater economies realized by the firm in providing benefits, resulting in a benefit–wage combination of (B_2, W_2). If the firms lose their cost advantages, the isoprofit curve will become steeper, rotating from the same point on the W axis. In the diagram, the substitution effect dominates the income effect, and the new optimal combination is at point Y, with higher W and lower B.

Workers' preferences between wages and benefits include tax considerations, loss of discretion (especially if substitution effects towards greater consumption of the commodity are induced), and convenience (for instance, of having the cafeteria at the work site, or even lunch provided to employees at their desks, as in some Wall Street operations). A further factor likely to be important in socialist and transition economies is the presence of shortages prior to price liberalization and of underdeveloped markets for some goods and services thereafter. Even if the money cost to the firm of providing housing is no less than the official price for the apartment, if no apartments are available for that price then their shadow value is higher than the equivalent of the cost received in wages. These considerations are illustrated by the indifference curves drawn in W–B space in figure 3.5, the slope measuring the marginal rate of substitution between wages and benefits.

Assuming perfect information and costless mobility, individuals are matched with firms so that preferences are satisfied in the least-cost way. The set of tangencies in which the marginal cost of benefits is set equal, for each individual, to his/her marginal rate of substitution produces an equilibrium market locus, the average slope of which can be estimated as the τ_j above. The estimating equation is derived by substitution of equation (3) into equation (2) above. If benefits represent a small proportion of total compensation and the τ_j are also not too large,[16] then $\log(1 + \Sigma_j \tau_j b_j) = \Sigma_j \tau_j b_j$. Under these conditions,

$$\text{Log}(W) = \alpha + \mathbf{X}'\beta + \Sigma_j \tau_j b_j + u. \tag{4}$$

Unfortunately, information on these variables for individual employees was unavailable, so I have utilized existing data on industries in Romania to provide some preliminary results. X includes standard human capital and wage determination variables: average age (AGE) of employees in the industry, average number of years of schooling (EDC), and percentage female (FEM). In some specifications, it also includes the proportion of employees in the industry working for firms that are *regii autonome*, state-owned enterprises not included in the large privatization programme (RA), and the proportion of unskilled workers whose wage exceeded the norms established in the wage policy in 1991 (EXW). The purpose of including the last two variables is to control for the possibility that the determination of employee compensation in Romania is not based solely on productivity; in particular, some industrial branches seem to have obtained much larger wage increases than merited on productivity grounds, the explanation for which may be strong unions or strong ties to the government.[17] RA and EXW are only imperfect instruments for this behaviour, but both are highly correlated with the average wage and EXW is also highly correlated with the proportion of

Table 3.4. Summary statistics for regression variables

Variable	Mean	Std	Range	Min	Max	N
Avg wage[1]	279.88	97.10	506.06	95.57	601.63	50
BTC	0.33	0.04	0.17	0.26	0.42	50
EDC	11.10	1.28	8.43	8.57	17.00	47
AGE	35.08	2.02	10.00	33.20	43.20	47
FEM	39.86	20.47	78.60	6.40	85.00	50
RA	38.25	42.79	100.00	0.00	100.00	20
EXW	50.54	23.18	98.98	0.00	98.98	50
TNWRKTC	0.11	0.03	0.13	0.04	0.17	50
INKINDTC	0.02	0.02	0.14	0.00	0.14	50
SIUETC	0.18	0.02	0.12	0.14	0.26	50

Sources: For EDC, the Survey of Registered Unemployed. For all others, the National Commission for Statistics.
1 The average wage is expressed in '000 lei 1992.

total compensation paid as benefits.[18] This suggests they must be included in the equation to avoid omitted variable bias.

Table 3.4 contains summary statistics for the variables; 'Std' refers to the standard deviation, and 'N' the number of industries for which information is available. The average annual wage in 1992 varied from 96,000 to 602,000 lei, and the proportion of benefits in total compensation (BTC) varied between 0.26 and 0.42. The three final variables are disaggregations of BTC: TNWRKTC is the proportion of compensation for time not worked (vacation and sick leave, etc.), INKINDTC is the proportion of compensation in kind, and SIUETC is social security contributions, both legally required and voluntary.

The results of OLS estimation of four different specifications of equation (4) appear in table 3.5. In the first specification, τ is large and positive, implying, if naively interpreted, that benefits are negatively valued, because the compensating differential is positive. As noted above, however, this specification likely suffers from an omitted variable bias: excluded factors tend to raise both wages and benefits, leading to a spurious positive correlation. RA and EXW are therefore added to the equation, reducing estimated τ to insignificance. Specifications 3 and 4 repeat this exercise for disaggregated measures of benefits. Again, the estimates of τ_j are positive in the third specification, but this time they are too imprecisely measured to permit any judgements. The fourth specification again adds RA and EXW, affecting all the τ_j estimates. The point estimates for the coefficients on payment for time not worked and for in-kind benefits actually increase, while that on social insurance contributions falls below -1. But, again, the coefficients are so imprecisely

Table 3.5. Hedonic wage function: estimations

	Eq 1	Eq 2	Eq 3	Eq 4
Constant	4.93*	8.63*	5.60*	5.87*
	(1.05)	(2.13)	(1.13)	(2.54)
BTC	2.73*	−0.36	−	−
	(1.05)	(1.35)		
EDC	0.6	0.017	0.06	0.06
	(0.45)	(0.09)	(0.04)	(0.09)
AGE	−0.02	−0.101	−0.04	−0.03
	(0.02)	(0.05)	(0.02)	(0.06)
FEM	−0.006*	−0.005	−0.004*	−0.005
	(0.002)	(0.003)	(0.002)	(0.003)
RA	−	0.003*	−	0.002*
		(0.001)		(0.001)
EXW	−	0.008*	−	0.007*
		(0.003)		(0.003)
TNWRKTC	−	−	0.33	1.38
			(1.78)	(1.82)
INKINDTC	−	−	3.16	4.03
			(2.14)	(3.46)
SIUETC	−	−	3.95	−1.30
			(2.21)	(2.32)
R^2	.39	.78	.37	.82
N	45	21	45	21

Note: Estimates result from application of OLS to equation (4) in the text. For ease of reading, an asterisk is attached to those estimates for which the coefficient point estimate is at least twice its standard error.

measured that the null hypothesis of $\tau_j = 0$ cannot be rejected in any of the cases.

Thus, these results provide no support for the view that the value of social benefits provided by firms in Eastern Europe exceeds their reported costs. For the most part, point estimates were positive, implying that employees must actually be compensated for benefits. The data set is far from ideal for this purpose, and perhaps more sophisticated methods would yield different results. At this point, however, all we can say is that this approach has failed to find evidence of $\tau_j < -1$.

Policy conclusions

This paper has investigated several aspects of the social protection activities and labour market behaviour of firms in Eastern Europe. It began by pointing out that firms may function as part of the 'welfare mix' through a variety of means. One critical, but often overlooked, way that firms may provide protection or insurance to their employees is by choosing methods of adjustment to exogenous shocks that avoid large-scale layoffs, for instance through work sharing. Job security is particularly important in economies where many social services are provided by firms rather than the state, so that social insurance for the unemployed is unavailable or inadequate. However, such employment-stabilizing arrangements may also have the drawback of discouraging the reallocation of labour, which is part of the essence of the transition in Eastern Europe. And they also protect insiders, those already in good jobs, and place greater hardships on outsiders, such as new entrants to the labour force. Public policy would ideally take this tradeoff into account, encouraging labour-shedding in such places and at such a rate that the growing sectors may absorb the displaced workers and that provision from markets and government may replace lost benefits, while elsewhere encouraging job preservation, work sharing, and generally more gradual adjustment. The difficult aspect in the East European context, of course, is for the state, given its poor record, to make and implement such decisions.

The paper then analysed the possibility that the provision of social services by firms may itself carry implications for the adjustment strategy the firm chooses. Because many services represent per worker rather than per hour costs, a firm that is attempting to reduce costs will have increased incentives to lay workers off rather than reducing their work hours, the greater the proportion of such benefits in total compensation. This argument is strengthened if the firm faces difficulties in unbundling its social assets, either for political reasons or because of the lack of development of markets. Policy-makers must be aware of the potential tradeoff between the two types of social protection activities of firms, because a policy to encourage firms to retain benefits may be more likely to lead to job losses. In an analysis of the employment and hours behaviour of Romanian industries, however, only weak empirical support for these effects was found.

The paper then documented recently released information on the structure of labour compensation in the Czech Republic and Romania, and compared this structure with those in the United States and several West European countries. The surprising (to the author) result was that, as a proportion of compensation, every type of measured benefit in the Czech Republic and Romania falls within the Western range. The aggregate data, therefore, suggest no more important role for firms as a 'social protection pillar' than would be the case in the West.

However, it is also possible that standard cost accounting practices, insofar as they are based on current cash flows rather than capital budgeting, fail to measure the true value of social services provided by firms. The importance of social protection expenditures by firms could far exceed their nominal cost, carrying large implications for policies. The paper examined the hypothesis that the value of benefits exceeds their accounting cost by estimating a hedonic wage function. Although the limitations of both data and method preclude strong statements, no evidence for the hypothesis was found.

Who then – firms, families, or the state – should provide social protection in Eastern Europe? Is it appropriate for the state to mandate that firms provide insurance and services to their employees? In favour, one may argue that, if the organizational and physical capital to support the services already exists in firms, then it may be costly to change. Governments may be less efficient providers, and markets may exhibit small supply elasticities, particularly in the short run. But this presumes that employees of East European firms value the services more than they would the cash equivalent, a contention for which the paper could find no empirical support.

To this may be added standard Western arguments about avoiding the 'public provision trap' and the smaller distortion of mandated provision as compared with taxation plus state provision (these arguments are summarized in Summers, 1992). Both are significantly weakened in the East European context. The former claims that the variety and quality of services will be lower under state provision than if they are organized in a decentralized fashion, but in Eastern Europe the critical issue currently is whether they are provided at all. The latter presumes that the internal functioning of firms is already efficient, and the state can exploit this through requirements consistent with social objectives. In Eastern Europe, however, firms have huge internal distortions and inefficiencies; not allowing them to adjust by imposing restraints on their behaviour hardly seems the way to promote a smooth transition to a market economy.

Thus, in addition to the problems of inadequacy of coverage of 'outside' groups – the unemployed, the retired, etc. – a policy of mandating benefit provision in Eastern Europe faces quandaries peculiar to the transition. The state may be incompetent as a provider of social services, but it may be no better at monitoring firms, and firms may be no better than the state at providing. If some firms have cost advantages, for instance owing to sunk investments, they will provide benefits; others will not. The continued provision of benefits by firms may also have the effect of decreasing the mobility of labour, certainly undesirable given the massive reallocation of labour that the transition demands.

The most fundamental objection, however, to mandating benefits in

Eastern Europe is that it represents continued involvement by the state in the behaviour of firms. Policies in the transition should be designed with careful attention to their effect on the clarity of the boundary between the state and private sectors. The problems of monitoring firms imply that enforcement will be uneven, and therefore at least somewhat arbitrary. Tempting as it may be to 'save state resources', scarce as they admittedly may be, by requiring firms to provide social services, this carries the danger of perpetuating the murkiness of the permitted spheres of public and private action and thus of slowing the growth of the autonomous private sector.

NOTES

I thank Simona Spiridon for assistance with statistical calculations, Tanya Nemeth, Doina Rachita, and Nicusor Ruiu for data collection, Becky Schumann and Hunter Bost for help with the figures, and Douglass Lippoldt for comments. The Centre for Economic Policy Research (London), the Institute for Advanced Studies (Vienna), and the CEU Privatization Project provided financial support. The National Council for Soviet and East European Research supported data collection early in the project.

1 Many others have made similar claims. For instance, according to Pestoff *et al.*, '[i]n Eastern Europe the social responsibilities of firms were very extensive prior to the collapse of their planned economies. Many social benefits and services were provided directly to employees by the public enterprises or authorities where they were employed. Such benefits and services included housing, day-care for children, medical services, access to vacations sites, etc. Full employment guaranteed that such services were available to everyone, although at various levels and of different quality' (1993: 6).
2 Unfortunately, the Romanian National Commission for Statistics discontinued the use of the questionnaires on labour turnover and hours of work after 1992, so it is impossible to follow this behaviour thereafter.
3 At least in terms of labour market turnover, 1989 was fairly typical compared with previous years. See Earle and Oprescu (1995) for longer time-series, more disaggregation, and more analysis of these data.
4 Calculations of productivity are therefore sensitive to the definition of labour input: when the denominator of productivity is the number of workers, productivity fell by 44.4 per cent; but when the denominator is the total number of hours of work, productivity fell by 23.2 per cent. The extent to which this fall in productivity reflects measurement errors in output is beyond the scope of this paper.
5 These and the following figures in this and the next paragraph are taken from Layard and Richter (1994), except as noted.
6 Yemtsov (1994) also cites survey evidence that 'less than 25 percent' of separations are involuntary, but even this number is quite low compared with East European countries in 1991–2.
7 The figures in Layard and Richter (1994) are quite different: according to

them, the Goskomstat statistics show that 2.1 per cent of employees were on involuntary leave and 4.4 per cent were working shorter hours in March 1994. It is also unclear whether Yemtsov's figures refer to the percentage of firms or that of workers.

8 Chapman (1909) was probably the first to conceive of hours of work as a separate factor of production. Also see Rosen (1968), who is to some extent concerned with similar issues, but focuses on one-time costs of hiring and training, the theoretical analysis of which is due to Oi (1962).

9 This leaves aside the question of production efficiency, but it is surely debatable whether SOEs were on the boundary of their production sets.

10 Another intervening factor, although one not possible to measure in the current context, could be differences in the substitutability of fixed factors, such as capital, for numbers employed and hours worked. To take an extreme example, it may be relatively easy to reduce the length of the shift in a factory from 8 to 6 hours, but not to reduce the number of workers by 25 per cent, because of a relatively unadjustable worker-to-machine ratio. In this case, we would expect to see hours rather than employment adjustments. The same holds for a workforce that is heterogeneous in skill composition: the reduction in labour input may be so large that essential skills would be lost through layoffs.

11 Included in W_2 are cash payments such as seasonal and annual bonuses, profit sharing, vacation allowances (above regular pay), and time off for studies and special events. Also included are in-kind benefits such as subsidies for rent and utilities in company housing, food, and holiday and spa tickets. W_3 includes training costs and payments upon retirement, decease, layoff, and job transfer. For more detail, and aggregate numbers corresponding to these categories, see the following section.

12 It is also probable that the explicit one-time costs for recruitment, training, and separation measure the quasi-fixed costs only very imperfectly. Opportunity costs of forgone worktime by managers, experienced co-workers, and trainees are probably more important. See Barron *et al.* (1989).

13 The US data are taken from US Chamber of Commerce (1992), cited in Ehrenberg and Smith (1994). The European data come from Eurostat (1991).

14 'NA' stands for 'not available' in the table. Note, however, that, in most cases, this is the result of not being able to disaggregate the figures comparably across the two countries; except for some minor exceptions, it does not imply that the categories are completely uncounted.

15 Regarding the USA, where sick leave is financed wholly by the employer up to a limit stipulated by contract, the Bureau of Labor Statistics survey on employer costs for employee compensation in March 1992 found a somewhat lower figure for 'paid leave', at 6.8 per cent in private industry and 7.7 per cent in state and local government. See Braden and Hyland (1993).

16 As argued in the case of pensions in Montgomery *et al.* (1992).

17 The excessive wage increases in those sectors seem to be paid through a variety of direct and indirect state subsidies. See Earle and Oprescu (1995).

18 The raw correlation between Log(Wage) (for time worked) and BTC (the proportion of benefits in total compensation) is .46, that between Log(Wage) and RA is .68, that between Log(Wage) and EXW is .69, that between BTC and EXW is .66, and that between BTC and RA is .21.

REFERENCES

Aghion, P., O. Blanchard, and R. Burgess (1993), 'The behavior of state firms in Eastern Europe: pre-privatization', European Bank for Reconstruction and Development, Working Paper No. 12.

Barron, J., D. Black, and M. Lowenstein (1989), 'Job-matching and on-the-job training', *Journal of Labor Economics* 7(1), January.

Beleva, I., R. Jackman, and M. Nenova-Amar (1993), 'The labor market in Bulgaria'. Paper presented to the World Bank Conference on 'Unemployment, Restructuring, and the Labor Market in East Europe and Russia', Washington, October.

Braden, B. and S. Hyland (1993), 'Cost of employee compensation in public and private sectors', *Monthly Labor Review*, May.

Chapman, S. (1909), 'Hours of labour', *Economic Journal* XIX, September.

Commander, S. and R. Jackman (1993), 'Providing social benefits in Russia: redefining the roles of firms and government', Policy Research Working Paper of the Economic Development Institute, World Bank, September.

Coricelli, F., K. Hagemejer, and K. Rybinski (1993), 'Poland'. Paper presented to the World Bank Conference on 'Unemployment, Restructuring, and the Labor Market in East Europe and Russia', Washington, October.

Earle, J. (1988), 'Empirical studies of cyclical labor market adjustments in the post-war United States'. Unpublished PhD dissertation, Stanford University.

(1995), 'Interpreting the decline of "output" and the prospects for "recovery" ', in J. Gacs, R. Holzmann, and G. Winckler (eds.), *Output Decline in Eastern Europe – Prospects for Recovery?*, Dordrecht: Kluwer Academic.

Earle, J. and G. Oprescu (1995), 'Aggregate labor market behavior in the restructuring of the Romanian economy', in O. Blanchard *et al.* (eds.), *Unemployment, Restructuring, and the Labor Market*, Washington DC: Economic Development Institute of the World Bank.

Ehrenberg, R. and R. Smith (1994), *Modern Labor Economics: Theory and Public Policy*, 5th edn, New York: HarperCollins.

Eurostat (1991), *Labour Costs: Survey 1988 – Initial Results*, Theme 3, Series C.

Kornai, J. (1992), *The Socialist System: The Political Economy of Communism*, Princeton NJ: Princeton University Press.

Layard, R. and A. Richter (1994), 'Labor market adjustment – The Russian way', photocopy, 8 June.

Lipton, D. and J. Sachs (1990), 'The creation of a market economy in Eastern Europe: The case of Poland', *Brookings Papers on Economic Activity*.

Meacher, M. (1994), 'Options for employment policy in Russia'. Paper presented to the Conference on Employment and Unemployment in Russia from a Microeconomic Perspective at IIASA, June.

Montgomery, E., K. Shaw, and M. E. Benedict (1992), 'Pensions and wages: An hedonic price theory approach', *International Economic Review* 33(1).

Oi, W. (1962), 'Labor as a quasi-fixed factor of production', *Journal of Political Economy* 70, December.

Pestoff, V., J. Hoos, and V. Roxin (1993), 'Institutional changes in basic social services in Central and East Europe during the transition to market economies', Cracow Academy of Economics.

Rose, R. (1994), 'What is the value of fringe benefits in Russia today?' in *Studies in Public Policy* No. 225, Centre for the Study of Public Policy, University of Strathclyde.

Rosen, S. (1968), 'Short-run employment variation on class-I railroads in the U.S., 1947–1963', *Econometrica* 36(3–4).

(1986), 'The theory of equalizing differences', in *Handbook of Labor Economics*, vol. 1, Amsterdam: North-Holland.

Summers, L. (1992), 'The simple economics of mandated benefits', *American Economic Review, Papers and Proceedings*, May.

US Chamber of Commerce (1992), *Employee Benefits 1991*, Washington DC.

Woodbury, S. (1983), 'Substitution between wage and non-wage benefits', *American Economic Review* 73(1), March.

Yemtsov, R. (1994), 'Ingoing and outgoing flows in employment'. Paper presented to the Conference on Restructuring and Recovery of Output in Russia, IIASA, June.

4 Wage and non-wage labour costs in the Czech Republic – the impact of fringe benefits

RANDALL K. FILER, ONDREJ SCHNEIDER, and JAN SVEJNAR

Introduction

This paper discusses the development of non-wage benefits in the Czech economy during the transition from a planned to a market economy. This development is perhaps best understood as a two-step process. In the first stage many fundamental welfare activities, such as health insurance and pensions, were shifted from the state budget to parallel, quasi-private insurance funds. This stage was, in large part, completed in 1994. In the second stage, which is much less far along, there is an ongoing shift away from uniform, mandated benefits towards individualized packages designed by and for each firm.

After an initial discussion of the benefit system in the pre-transition Czechoslovak economy, we discuss the evolution of the national insurance scheme following the transition. We then present a detailed breakdown of the total labour cost, which consists of wages and non-wage benefits. Finally, we offer some evidence regarding the extent of non-mandatory fringe benefits provided by individual employers and discuss why we believe such benefits are likely to become increasingly important in coming years.

Employee benefits in Czechoslovakia before 1989

Social policy in 'socialist' Czechoslovakia was characterized by a striking gap between proclaimed successes and rather mixed actual results. There was full employment, but at the price of an inefficient allocation of resources. Another result of central planning was an extremely equalized wage distribution. This system left firms with limited scope to choose. Benefits were overwhelmingly supplied on the basis of legal requirements, with only a small part varying according to the profitability of a firm. Many areas that are commonly treated as firm benefits in the West (such as pensions and medical insurance) were part of the state budget and financed out of general government revenues. Trade unions were obligatory in all firms and were subordinated to the Communist Party. Trade union leaders were nevertheless granted the power by the Communist Party to decide on the allocation of some employee benefits, predominantly heavily subsidized recreation facilities. This power provided a major reason for joining a trade union for the majority of workers.

In the former Czechoslovakia[1] the social sphere was under the direct control of the state. All benefits were financed through the state budget and were therefore often treated according to the interests of the government rather than those of firms or their workers. For example, taxes were adjusted every year in order to achieve a formally balanced government budget. There were no independent funds that provided medical or pensions insurance. The level and accessibility of benefits were therefore totally dependent on the discretion of state authorities.

State policy concentrated mainly on family welfare. A number of measures were taken to support family incomes (the Family Act, No. 94/1963 and its amendment in 1992). For instance, family allowances were increased several times in the 1980s, as were maternity allowances. The conditions for claiming an old-age pension while remaining employed were very liberal. Due to this, and to the low real level of pensions, almost 25 per cent of pensioners were also employed. State intervention was common in the housing market, too, with the costs of constructing and maintaining housing being covered mostly by the state budget and by funds provided by industrial firms. A certain proportion of dwellings were specifically designed to serve social purposes, for instance housing for the elderly or specially adapted apartments for disabled persons (the Social Security Act, 100/1988 and its amendments 1990–3).

Although the structure of benefits in the former Czechoslovakia resembled that in Western countries, it is difficult to assess these benefits because of the vagueness of their definition and the lack of transparency in accounting practices in the state budget. The main disadvantage for people depending on these benefits was their infrequent updating and the bureaucratic system of provision. As a result, benefits often did not keep pace with hidden inflation and their real value decreased over the 1980s.

Enterprises had only a negligible influence over the state's decisions regarding social policy. They were obliged, however, to secure possibly inconsistent goals such as full employment and the 'reproduction of physical and mental abilities'.[2] Crucial for the purposes of this paper is the fact that enterprises were *forced to provide these benefits by law*. In 1973, the Czechoslovak government adopted regulations and principles

concerning workers' welfare in enterprises. According to these regulations, enterprises had to make provision for employing all sections of the population. This included creating special working conditions for young workers, mothers of young children, and handicapped persons. Enterprises were also responsible for satisfying 'vital needs'. As the vague term suggests, this included not only provision of health care and catering, but also such imprecise items as the reproduction of physical and mental abilities mentioned above. A final class of enterprises' responsibilities was labelled 'conditions for personal development'. This included educational and cultural activities, sporting and hobby facilities, holiday camps for children, etc. Very popular among workers were enterprise-owned vacation facilities that offered subsidized accommodation and services for employees. In 1986 these facilities had sufficient capacity to provide a five-day stay per worker per year. Enterprises were also obliged to improve the education of workers by establishing enterprise schools. The wording of all these laws was, however, very vague ('the enterprise helps workers to find or build appropriate accommodation', etc.) and therefore the reality was often quite bleak.

Another peculiarity of the non-wage benefit system before 1989 arose from the difficulties of the centrally planned economy. There were shortages of many commodities at official prices. Since market forces were absent, the state shifted responsibility for allocating these scarce items to enterprises. Enterprises therefore provided commodities that were simply consumption goods and had only limited social protection merit. Although this allocative mechanism was common to all centrally planned economies, it appears not to have been as extensive in the former Czechoslovakia as in some other countries.

Formally, the programmes provided by enterprises were divided into four groups. Catering was in the first of these. The law specified at length the conditions under which enterprises could, or had to, provide catering. Nevertheless, no specific amount of subsidy was set. Trade unions had the legal power to 'control the quality of meals and the efficiency of production'.

A second group of benefits consisted of pre-school facilities for children. Facilities were built at the expense of enterprises but stayed under state control, and the state could order them to accept non-employees' children.

Recreation supervised by trade unions was the third main part of employees' benefits. Programmes included both special camps for children and recreational facilities for whole families. Prices were subsidized by trade unions, usually by around 50 per cent (or even more for children's camps).

The last programme addressed the housing problems of workers.

Profitable firms were allowed to contribute to building and maintenance costs. However, this programme never achieved significant results and most new housing was constructed through consumer cooperatives rather than by employers.

An indication of the extent of these firm-based benefits can be obtained by examining the amounts transferred to 'funds for social and cultural needs', the category in the official Czech system of accounts that came closest to traditional fringe benefits and included most of the expenditures discussed above. Firms paid employee benefits from this fund, including subsidies to catering and recreation and 'presents to loyal employees'. This fund also provided interest-free loans to workers, which were often used to assist housing acquisition. According to official statistics, non-capital expenses paid by these funds grew from around Kcs 4 billion in 1980 to about Kcs 6.5 billion by the end of the decade. Such expenditures were reported to be between 2 and 3 per cent of total payrolls. This level seems unbelievably low in comparison with levels typical in developed countries (even allowing for the fact that many insurance needs were met from general budget revenues) or in comparison with the obligations assumed by firms in the areas supposedly funded from these accounts. It is likely that such a low level of reported benefit expenditures is best explained by inaccurate accounting practices rather than as accurately expressing the level of employees' benefits in pre-transition Czechoslovakia.

It is plain from this discussion that the system of employee benefits provided by firms in Czechoslovakia before 1989 was developed in a typical 'socialist' way: broad definitions with little concrete meaning and with no possible control. It is not, therefore, surprising that accurate measures of the extent of these benefits are hard to come by. Whether this lack of reliable information is due to bureaucratic incompetence, lack of interest, or a deliberate attempt to mask the deterioration in workers' status is an open question.

Developments after 1989

Following the fall of the Communist government in late 1989, the years 1990 and 1991 were devoted to preparing reforms and introducing basic macroeconomic changes. Firms spent this period preparing their new business plans. Many larger firms were divided into several smaller units in an attempt to reduce the monopolistic structure of the previous system. The social sphere was initially left almost unchanged. The only significant changes were that firms frequently shed their extensive recreational and sports facilities by selling them to the private sector and

many firms that previously provided housing began the process of turning these units into cooperatives.

At the end of 1991 the situation was as follows (Salkova, 1991):

(1) Enterprises provided a system of health care that covered almost 70 per cent of their employees as well as many of their family members.
(2) Enterprises still owned many flats, for which they provided an annual subsidy of some Kcs 2.2 billion in 1990. Approximately 40 per cent of tenants in these flats, however, had no connection with the owning enterprise.
(3) Subsidies to catering in 1991 were around Kcs 2,000 per employee, equivalent to slightly less than 10 per cent of payroll costs.
(4) Pre-school facilities were subsidized by Kcs 7,000–21,000 per child.
(5) Firms continued to support recreational facilities and heavily subsidized children's summer camps, with parents paying only around 20 per cent of actual costs.

The legal system reacted to the social changes by omitting most of the vague requirements previously imposed on state enterprises. The private sector has been exempted from these duties from the outset and has also not been obliged to subsidize trade unions through funds derived from payrolls.

There was a major shift in the provision of social protection at the beginning of 1993. A National Insurance Company consisting of four independent funds was established. These funds assumed the responsibility from both the state budget and individual enterprises for providing pensions, health insurance, disability insurance, and unemployment benefits. (The last of these, of course, was a new addition to the social protection scheme since unemployment was not recognized in the pre-1989 economy.) All four funds are financed by payroll taxes. Nominally, these taxes are imposed on employers and employees in a ratio of slightly less than three-to-one, although their true incidence obviously depends on elasticities of supply and demand for labour and has not yet, to our knowledge, been studied. The 1993 tax rates for these four funds are shown in table 4.1.

The high tax rates shown in table 4.1, plus the fact that these taxes are imposed on the entire wage bill, rather than on wages up to a maximum level as in the United States, result in an unusually high level of mandatory indirect labour costs in the Czech Republic when compared with the typical Western market economy. Mandatory insurance payments comprise almost 25 per cent of labour costs in the Czech Republic as opposed to 6.4 per cent of labour costs in the USA, 7.6 per cent in the UK and 16.4 per cent in Germany (US Chamber of

4.1. Czech Republic: social insurance tax rates in 1993 (%)

Type of insurance	Employer	Employee	Total
Health insurance	9.0	4.5	13.5
Pension fund	20.4	6.8	27.2
Disability insurance	3.6	1.2	4.8
Unemployment insurance	2.25	0.75	3.0
Total	35.25	13.25	48.5

Commerce, 1992; Mitchell and Rojot, 1993). Obviously, such a high tax burden serves to reduce the labour cost advantage that Czech manufacturers would otherwise have in competing in global markets.

Administration of the individual social insurance funds varies somewhat. Basic pensions are still handled through the state budget, in a manner similar to Social Security in the USA. The government argues that this is necessary because current revenues are needed to pay pension obligations incurred by the state for current retirees. Recently, however, there has been pressure from trade unions and other labour organizations to transfer the obligation for current retirees to the general state budget and to use current social insurance taxes to support a fully funded and vested pension system for current workers. In addition, tax-advantaged supplemental private pension plans to which employers and/or employees can contribute began to develop in 1994 and 1995.

The situation with respect to health insurance is somewhat more complicated. In January 1992, a government-owned corporation (the General Health Insurance Office, or GHIO) was established to assume health insurance activities. From January 1993, however, other companies have been allowed to compete in the health insurance market. These companies are free to sign a contract with an employer to represent that employer's workers, with revenues being transferred to the insurance company from the general insurance fund according to the number of workers covered.[3] As of January 1994, there were 18 private health insurance companies insuring approximately 16 per cent of Czech citizens. Interestingly, whereas workers and the self-employed made up only 43 per cent of the clients of the GHIO, they comprised 61 per cent of the clients of the private insurance companies (Ministry of Health, 1994).

Wages and benefits

This section contains 1993 data on average wages and other benefits from a sample of about 3,500 Czech firms. The data are cross-tabulated

at varying levels of detail with respect to the sector of the economy, the ownership type of firms, and firm size. Access has been provided to the tabulated data reported below, but not to the underlying firm-level data.

Table 4.2 presents a relatively detailed breakdown of the total hourly labour cost in the sampled firms. The hourly labour cost is decomposed into several sub-categories within each of the following major categories: earnings (wages and bonuses), employer-paid wage-related benefits, non-insurance benefits, social security (insurance) benefits, and hiring and training costs. The first two categories are referred to as direct costs, while the last three are termed indirect costs. The data are presented for nine aggregate sectors of the economy: mining, manufacturing, utilities (electricity, gas, and water), construction, trade in and repair of motor vehicles, restaurants and hotels, travel agencies, financial and insurance institutions, and real estate, research, etc.

As can be seen from table 4.2, there are major differences in average hourly wages, earnings, and the total costs across the nine sectors. In terms of average hourly earnings, for instance, the hotel and restaurant sector paid Kcs 32.99, whereas firms in financial services and insurance paid almost twice as much – Kcs 64.43. Within the earnings category, base wages represented the most important item, averaging Kcs 27.08 (71 per cent of average earnings) across all sectors. As far as other components of earnings are concerned, firms in most sectors paid regular periodic bonuses (wage premia) that amounted to about 15 per cent of hourly earnings. Financial and insurance companies and travel agencies were an exception in that they paid little in the way of periodic bonuses. In contrast, however, financial and insurance firms paid by far the largest share of total hourly earnings (31 per cent) in the form of 'sharing in economic results', profit-sharing, extra (usually year-end) monthly salaries, and 'other salaries'. Travel agencies in turn paid 9 per cent of earnings in the form of sharing in the economic results of the firm.

Employer-paid wage-related benefits amounted on average to a significant 11.5 per cent of earnings. Major expenses in this category were primarily paid vacations (equal to 8.9 per cent of earnings) and, to a lesser extent, paid holidays (1.3 per cent of earnings). All sectors except for travel agencies provided significant paid vacations, with mining (where paid vacations amounted to more than 10 per cent of total hourly earnings) being the leading sector in this area. In contrast, travel agencies spent very little on paid vacations but devoted significant amounts of money to payments for 'obstacles to work' when employees were available for work but could not through no fault of their own.

It should be noted that a significant share of these wage-related expenditures were mandatory under the terms of the Labour Code.

4.2. Components of the average cost of labour in 1993 (Kcs per hour)

	Average of all sectors	Mining	Manufacturing	Electricity, gas, and water	Average of (2)–(4)	Construction	Trade and repair of motor vehicles	Hotels and restaurants	Travel agencies	Financial and insurance companies	Real estate, research, etc.
	(1)	(2)	(3)	(4)	(5)	(6)	(7)	(8)	(9)	(10)	(11)
1 Earnings	38.09	47.81	35.27	41.79	36.97	39.27	34.81	32.99	46.92	64.43	42.28
Composed of:											
2 Base wages	27.08	30.20	24.92	25.62	25.48	29.35	25.89	23.81	39.14	42.52	32.50
3 Regular (periodic) bonuses	5.61	7.58	5.35	7.18	5.70	6.87	5.18	5.88	1.80	0.56	5.59
4 Bonuses based on economic results	0.85	0.18	0.88	0.78	0.81	1.02	0.99	0.23	4.09	1.44	1.78
5 Profit-sharing bonus	0.42	0.18	0.30	0.43	0.30	0.21	0.50	0.33	0.58	3.76	0.35
6 Extraordinary (13th & 14th) salaries	1.43	3.16	1.07	3.48	1.45	0.73	0.80	0.75	0.06	8.48	0.83
7 Overtime pay	0.29	0.47	0.32	0.22	0.33	0.31	0.19	0.23	0.16	0.12	0.23
8 Other bonuses	1.26	4.56	1.41	1.77	1.74	0.28	0.42	0.72	0.91	0.98	0.40
9 In-kind wages	0.02	0.22	0.01	0.01	0.03	0	0.01	0	0.03	0.02	0.02
10 Bonuses for emergency work readiness	0.06	0.19	0.03	0.45	0.08	0.02	0.03	0.01	0	0.02	0.07
11 Other wages	1.07	1.07	0.99	1.85	1.06	0.48	0.79	1.03	0.15	6.53	0.50
12 Employer-paid wage-related benefits	4.38	6.73	4.47	4.83	4.73	4.16	3.15	2.90	4.02	5.37	3.87
Composed of:											
13 Work stoppages	0.20	0.16	0.29	0.06	0.26	0.19	0.03	0.02	0	0.06	0.07
14 Paid vacation	3.40	5.00	3.36	4.07	3.57	3.18	2.61	2.60	0.86	4.91	3.31
15 Paid holidays	0.48	0.84	0.53	0.34	0.55	0.58	0.27	0.18	0.16	0.07	0.35
16 Obstacles to work	0.31	0.73	0.30	0.36	0.35	0.21	0.23	0.11	3.00	0.33	0.14
17 1–16 Direct costs	42.47	54.54	39.74	46.62	41.70	43.43	37.96	35.89	50.94	69.80	46.15
18 Non-insurance benefits	1.74	4.92	1.57	3.18	2.01	0.81	1.21	0.87	0.34	3.64	1.32

Composed of:

19 Discounted products of the firm	0.08	0.14	0.09	0.03	0.09	0.05	0.15	0.05	0	0	0.02
20 Contributions to housing	0.34	2.58	0.29	0.56	0.53	−0.04	−0.01	0	0	0.28	0
21 Use of company cars for private purposes	0.07	0.02	0.04	0.02	0.03	0.09	0.18	0.05	0.06	0.11	0.18
22 Contributions to food	0.68	1.41	0.66	0.82	0.74	0.41	0.51	0.43	0.26	1.20	0.68
23 Contributions in the form of savings, sale of shares	0.02	0	0.01	0	0.01	0	0.01	0	0	0.38	0.01
24 Contribution to the recreational and social fund	0.45	0.57	0.37	1.54	0.48	0.24	0.26	0.29	0.02	1.57	0.36
25 Contributions to trade unions	0.11	0.20	0.11	0.20	0.12	0.05	0.11	0.04	0	0.09	0.09
26 Insurance benefits	16.59	23.98	15.24	18.14	16.30	16.44	14.59	13.49	19.40	29.70	17.64
Composed of:											
27 Compulsory contributions to social security	15.90	21.18	14.67	17.42	15.50	16.16	14.13	13.24	18.94	28.08	17.11
28 Additional programmes of social security	0.06	0.61	0.02	0.03	0.08	0.01	0.03	0.01	0	0.22	0.02
29 Employer-paid sickness benefits	0.10	0.34	0.11	0.25	0.14	0.03	0.02	0.02	0	0.02	0.01
30 Severance pay	0.48	1.61	0.41	0.42	0.52	0.17	0.39	0.21	0.45	1.37	0.47
31 Other social contributions	0.04	0.24	0.03	0.02	0.05	0.06	0.01	0.01	0	0.02	0.03
32 Hiring and training costs	1.24	1.81	1.25	1.22	1.30	1.05	0.99	1.82	0.13	1.94	1.11
Composed of:											
33 Hiring costs	0.05	0.03	0.05	0.02	0.04	0.03	0.09	0.13	0.02	0.08	0.09
34 Apprenticeship costs	0.30	0.28	0.41	0.20	0.38	0.28	0.17	0.40	0	0	0.04
35 Professional training costs	0.34	0.15	0.29	0.44	0.28	0.15	0.44	0.26	0.06	1.47	0.56
36 Other personnel costs	0.54	1.35	0.51	0.56	0.59	0.59	0.29	0.73	0.04	0.39	0.42
37 Taxes and subsidies	0.16	0.30	0.11	0.24	0.14	0.55	−0.51	0.30	0.36	0.60	0.24
Composed of:											
38 Taxes linked to employment	0.28	0.37	0.15	0.25	0.18	0.56	0.24	0.31	0.36	0.60	0.29
39 Subsidies linked to employment	−0.12	−0.07	−0.04	−0.01	−0.04	−0.01	−0.75	−0.01	0	0	−0.05
40 Indirect costs	19.73	31.01	18.17	22.78	19.75	18.85	16.28	16.48	20.23	35.88	20.31
41 Total labour cost	62.20	85.55	57.91	69.40	61.45	62.28	54.24	52.37	71.17	105.68	66.46

Thus, for example, firms were required to provide four weeks of paid vacation for employees who had worked for more than 15 years since their 18th birthday. In addition, partial pay for days off sick was required under the Labour Code. Since, however, firms often offered more generous vacations than are required or paid full compensation for days off sick, it is impossible to divide amounts spent under this general heading into mandatory and voluntary components. Differences across firms or industries may represent differences in the generosity of the voluntary component or differences in age, experience, and illness history of the workforce. For example, it is likely that the relatively low expenditures for vacations in the travel industry represents the relative newness of firms in that industry and the related relative youth of their workforces.

As we mentioned earlier, indirect benefits can be divided into non-insurance benefits (equivalent on average to 4.6 per cent of earnings), social security contributions (initially equal to 48.5 per cent of earnings but later decreasing to 43.5 per cent, with further reductions proposed), and hiring and training costs (3.3 per cent of earnings). Within the category of non-insurance benefits, mining companies contributed significantly to employee housing, mining companies and financial–insurance institutions provided sizeable food subsidies, and utilities as well as financial–insurance companies contributed meaningfully toward a social fund. Benefits in terms of access to a firm's products or using company cars were quantitatively small across the board. As with wage-related benefits, the bulk of social security contributions were legally mandated, although mining and financial–insurance firms also paid out significant severance benefits. In the category of hiring and training costs, there were significant training expenditures in the finance–insurance sector and on 'other personnel costs' in mining.

Overall, it can be seen from table 4.2 that mining and finance–insurance were the sectors with the highest indirect labour costs. These were also the two highest-paying sectors, followed by travel agencies, utilities, and real estate–research.

Tables 4.3–4.5 present information on wages and benefits according to a finer division of industries, type of ownership, and size of firm, respectively. The information in these tables is based on monthly rather than hourly labour costs and, therefore, differences in some categories of the pay package may be associated with differences in hours worked in an average month in addition to the structure of employee compensation.

Table 4.3 provides a breakdown of the labour cost data by two-digit industrial classification. As can be seen from the table, coal mining

dominated other types of mining by paying higher employer-paid wage-related benefits, social benefits, voluntary social security, and hiring and training costs.

Within manufacturing, there was a relatively uniform pattern with the following outliers. Coke production and oil refining had the highest overall labour cost, brought about to a significant extent by the high social benefits and training expenditures observed in this industry. The production of transport equipment provided the second-largest social benefits and training expenditures, followed by the chemical industry. Interestingly, the textile industry dominated other industries in the extent of its voluntary insurance contributions.

Among utilities, the electric and gas industry had higher benefits than water systems in all categories. Within the finance–insurance sector, financial institutions paid much higher wages than insurance companies, but they provided lower voluntary fringes as a percentage of direct labour costs. In addition, there are differences in the composition of fringe benefits, with financial institutions placing a greater emphasis on voluntary insurance contributions and training, whereas insurance companies paid more in non-insurance benefits.

Table 4.4 provides a breakdown of the main categories of total monthly labour costs by firm ownership type. Since by the end of 1993 many new (small and medium-size) private firms had emerged, almost one-half of firms existing prior to 1989 had been privatized, and substantial Western investment had taken place, all types of ownership are relatively well represented in the sample. As can be seen in the table, foreign-owned firms provided the highest wages and voluntary fringe benefits, both in absolute value and as a percentage of the base wage. Their total labour cost was 59 per cent above the all-firm average, with the largest differential between them and other firms being in the category of recruitment and training. The fact that foreign firms paid more and engaged in more (costly) recruitment and training is consistent with a greater concern on the part of these firms with the quality of their workforce. State organizations, international organizations, and joint ventures ranked next in wages and non-wage benefits, while local governments and cooperatives paid their workers the least. State organizations in fact furnished the highest non-insurance benefits and voluntary insurance contributions.

Table 4.5 shows how labour cost components varied with firm size. Small firms (11–24 workers) paid 22 per cent higher base wages than did larger firms but they provided much smaller non-wage benefits. The wages of small firms were so much greater, however, that total monthly labour cost per worker in small firms was still 13 per cent higher than in

Table 4.3. Components of the monthly labour cost by two-digit industrial classification

	Total labour cost (1)	Earnings (2)	Employer-paid wage-related benefits (3)	Direct costs (2)+(3) (4)	Non-insurance benefits (5)	Compulsory insurance benefits (6)	Voluntary insurance benefits (7)	Hiring and training costs (8)	Taxes and subsidies (9)
1 Coal mining	12,379	6,883	950	7,833	732	3,055	443	266	50
2 Gas extraction	10,675	6,700	716	7,416	205	2,761	75	220	−3
3 Other mining	9,894	5,688	965	6,653	457	2,509	97	185	−7
4 Total mining	12,048	6,734	948	7,683	690	2,984	395	255	43
5 Food and beverages	8,320	5,140	546	5,686	201	2,118	61	260	−6
6 Textile industry	6,732	3,901	601	4,503	207	1,668	225	94	36
7 Apparel industry	6,361	3,879	480	4,359	173	1,617	36	171	5
8 Leather industry	6,902	4,289	535	4,824	159	1,769	62	84	4
9 Wood industry	7,392	4,668	501	5,169	164	1,917	54	91	−2
10 Paper industry	8,171	5,050	613	5,663	243	2,072	41	143	10
11 Printing industry	9,684	6,148	584	6,733	211	2,527	65	141	8
12 Coking & oil refining	11,400	6,387	754	7,141	1,079	2,716	12	450	2
13 Chemical industry	9,835	5,851	687	6,538	353	2,581	81	243	39
14 Rubber and plastics	9,007	5,549	697	6,246	219	2,311	36	167	28
15 Other mineral products	8,661	5,258	657	5,915	239	2,237	69	182	19
16 Metal production	10,131	6,173	804	6,978	336	2,504	95	209	9
17 Production of metal constructions	8,406	5,238	615	5,853	172	2,131	60	168	22
18 Machinery industry	8,193	4,955	693	5,647	209	2,079	75	170	12
19 Office machines and computers	6,916	4,473	542	5,015	154	1,523	75	120	30
20 Electrical machines	8,944	5,457	737	6,194	192	2,279	105	151	23
21 Production of radios and TVs	7,177	4,378	654	5,032	139	1,862	72	88	−16
22 Medical equipment and watches	7,977	4,882	626	5,508	153	2,030	122	136	29
23 Motor vehicles	9,062	5,469	681	6,150	226	2,253	92	316	25
24 Other transport equipment	9,174	5,420	723	6,142	414	2,238	74	266	40
25 Furniture and other industries	7,217	4,483	591	5,074	89	1,877	57	93	26

26 Manufacturing of semifinished materials	9,861	6,148	708	6,856	149	2,526	59	158	113
27 Manufacturing industries	8,376	5,101	647	5,748	227	2,121	83	180	16
28 Production and distribution of electricity and gas	11,585	6,881	759	7,640	636	2,886	165	223	34
29 Production and distribution of water	8,605	5,326	652	5,978	245	2,194	25	124	39
30 Production and distribution of energy	10,354	6,239	715	6,954	475	2,600	107	182	36
31 Industry total	8,883	5,346	681	2,027	291	2,242	115	188	20
32 Construction	9,651	6,085	645	6,730	126	2,503	43	163	86
33 Sale and repair of motor vehicles	7,886	4,979	538	5,517	117	1,996	97	144	15
34 Wholesale trade	10,515	6,872	584	7,456	270	2,704	82	231	−228
35 Retail trade	6,961	4,444	400	4,844	134	1,810	59	95	18
36 Trade and repair of vehicles	8,355	5,362	485	5,847	185	2,176	71	153	−78
37 Hotels and restaurants	7,954	5,040	443	5,483	133	2,023	38	232	46
38 Travel agencies	11,184	7,372	631	8,004	54	2,977	72	20	57
39 Financial institutions	16,800	10,273	828	11,101	523	4,463	278	328	108
40 Insurance companies	12,934	7,702	805	8,508	768	3,449	87	124	−1
41 Financial and insurance companies	16,229	9,894	825	10,718	559	4,313	249	298	92
42 Real estate	7,483	4,647	501	5,149	172	1,887	162	65	48
43 Rental of machinery & equipment	8,612	5,492	439	5,931	233	2,277	6	149	16
44 Data processing	10,267	6,630	559	7,189	240	2,638	76	133	−9
45 Research and development	9,833	6,282	630	6,912	255	2,520	81	73	−7
46 Other commercial services	11,235	7,159	624	7,782	192	2,904	57	238	61
47 Real estate, research and development	10,170	6,470	592	7,062	202	2,618	81	170	36
48 All-industry average	9,236	5,663	648	6,311	257	2,362	102	183	21

Table 4.4. Components of the monthly labour cost by ownership of firm

	Total labour cost (1)	Earnings (2)	Employer-paid wage-related benefits (3)	Direct costs (2) + (3) (4)	Non-insurance benefits (5)	Compulsory insurance benefits (6)	Voluntary insurance benefits (7)	Hiring and training costs (8)	Taxes and subsidies (9)
1 Private firms	8,794	5,522	596	6,118	182	2,262	68	158	6
2 Cooperative firms	6,850	4,271	486	4,757	134	1,778	75	79	27
3 State organizations	9,175	5,476	701	6,177	348	2,303	143	172	32
4 Municipal and local organizations	6,510	4,265	285	4,550	113	1,766	2	38	41
5 Social organizations	8,992	5,334	448	5,782	238	2,454	77	57	385
6 Foreign firms	14,678	9,092	724	9,816	300	3,626	64	846	25
7 International organizations	10,907	6,856	656	7,512	219	2,739	58	350	29
8 Joint ventures	10,678	6,474	727	7,201	296	2,810	123	219	29
9 All-firm average	9,236	5,663	648	6,311	257	2,362	102	183	21

Table 4.5. Components of the monthly labour cost by size of firm

	Total labour cost (1)	Earnings (2)	Employer-paid wage-related benefits (3)	Direct costs (2)+(3) (4)	Non-insurance benefits (5)	Compulsory insurance benefits (6)	Voluntary insurance benefits (7)	Hiring and training costs (8)	Taxes and subsidies (9)
1 All-firm average	9,236	5,663	648	6,311	257	2,362	102	183	21
2 11–24 employees	10,357	6,847	479	7,326	129	2,713	26	154	9
3 25+ employees	9,160	5,596	656	6,252	263	2,335	105	184	21
4 Within 25+: 25–49	9,523	6,333	497	6,830	145	2,520	38	194	−204
5 50–99	9,348	6,005	535	6,540	154	2,427	49	141	37
6 100–199	8,957	5,620	569	6,189	192	2,325	55	140	56
7 200–499	7,809	4,834	582	5,416	151	1,993	76	127	45
8 500–999	8,683	5,287	661	5,948	239	2,186	99	190	21
9 1,000+	9,852	5,853	744	6,598	366	2,490	149	223	26

larger firms. An interesting implication of the data in tables 4.4 and 4.5 is either that small firms were not dominantly private or that small private firms paid considerably higher wages than large private firms. This follows from the finding in table 4.4 that workers in domestic private firms earned below-average wages and total compensation and the result in table 4.5 that small firms had the highest wages and labour cost.

Among firms with 25 and more employees, table 4.5 shows that monthly earnings and hiring and training costs per employee fell with firm size up to firms containing 200–499 employees and increased with size afterwards. Non-insurance benefits increased with size until firms reached 100–199 employees, fell for the 200–499 group, and grew with size thereafter. Finally, insurance benefits increased monotonically with size.

Overall, wages and benefits increased with firm size except for the smallest firms. Small firms in turn provided a more generous overall package and placed more emphasis on wages than on non-wage benefits.

The determinants of non-wage benefits

Some simple regression analyses provide insight into the development of fringe benefits in the Czech Republic. Table 4.6 reports the results of regressing various measures of fringe benefits as a proportion of base wages on firms' characteristics. The units of observation for these analyses are industry averages by two-digit industry. Observations are restricted to mining, manufacturing, and utilities (rows 1–29 of table 4.3, excluding rows 4 and 27) since it was only for these industries that average firm characteristics were available.[4]

The results indicate that fringe benefits were more important relative to wages in industries with higher labour force productivity (calculated as sales per worker rather than value-added per worker owing to data limitations). On the other hand, private firms offered a lower share of compensation as fringe benefits than other firms. The reference group for this comparison is dominated by state-owned firms and does not reflect the result of voucher privatization distributions that occurred during 1993. There was no difference between state-owned firms and foreign firms or joint ventures with respect to the division of compensation between wages and benefits.

Finally, there was a negative relationship between changes in the size of firms' labour forces and the share of compensation that consisted of non-regular cash payments (bonuses, profit sharing, etc.) plus benefits, but not the share that consisted solely of benefits. This implies that firms that were shrinking in size made greater than average use of bonuses and

Table 4.6. Regression results: benefits as a share of base wages (*t*-statistics in parentheses)

	Bonuses, profit sharing, non-insurance benefits and voluntary insurance	Non-insurance benefits and voluntary insurance
Productivity (sales per worker), 10,000 Kc	.22 (1.62)	.23 (2.14)
Percentage change in labour force (1992–1993)	−.0035 (1.72)	−.0015 (0.93)
Percentage change in sales (1992–1993)	.00029 (0.30)	.00020 (0.26)
Percentage of firms privately owned	−.387 (2.55)	−.292 (2.37)
Constant	.164	.054
R^2	.34	.38

profit sharing. Such a pattern is consistent with these firms being further along in a restructuring process that involves both labour shedding and greater use of incentive compensation schemes.

The incidence of specific fringe benefits

Additional evidence regarding the incidence of fringe benefits in the Czech labour market during the transition can be obtained from the results of annual compensation surveys conducted by the consulting firm Coopers & Lybrand. Primarily conducted in order to aid international clients in setting compensation policies, these surveys are not designed to be representative of the labour market as a whole. Rather, they focus on larger firms with some foreign participation. The firms included, however, may fall into several of the categories in table 4.4, since the foreign participation may be a minority stake in a private or still majority state-owned domestic firm. As large firms with some connection to the international market, it might be appropriate to regard these firms as leaders in the labour market. Although it would appear that they offered greater current levels of many benefits, one

Table 4.7. Proportion of firms with international connection offering various benefits (%)

	1993	1994		
	Offering	Offering	Planning to offer	Total
Pension plan[1]	15	10	40	50
Profit-sharing plan	10	20	7	27
Medical insurance[1]	25	30	25	55
Life insurance	15	25	40	65
Disability insurance[1]	15	32	20	52
Housing assistance	5	23	5	28
Loans to employees (inc. mortgage)	15	30	20	50
Reduced-price meals	60	75	5	80
Public transit subsidies	35	30	10	40
Discounts on products	20	40	7	47

[1] Figures for pension plans, medical insurance, and disability insurance refer to benefits offered *in excess* of the required participation in the social insurance scheme.

would expect competitive pressures in the currently tight Czech labour market to cause other firms to match these firms' compensation packages in the near future.

In the survey conducted in the first quarter of 1994, 58 firms provided information on the compensation of over 3,500 employees in selected occupations ranging from senior management to drivers and receptionists (Coopers & Lybrand, 1994). Line production workers were not among the types of workers covered. Table 4.7 shows the proportion of firms that provided each of several common types of fringe benefits in 1993 and 1994. In addition, firms surveyed in 1994 that did not offer a specific benefit were asked if they planned on offering that benefit in the near future and these results are also reported.[5]

It is clear from the table that, although most benefits were not offered by a majority of firms, there is a continual pattern of increasing penetration. By 1994 over half of all firms either offered or expected soon to offer at least some of their workers pension plans and medical insurance in excess of the mandatory social security coverage, as well as life insurance and loan programmes or housing assistance. If these trends continue, the incidence of common types of fringe benefits in the Czech Republic should soon approach that of Western Europe and North America.

Conclusions

Taken as a whole, the evidence cited in this paper indicates that voluntary insurance payments in excess of what is mandated to the social insurance funds play a small but increasing role in labour compensation in the Czech Republic. There is reason to believe that their importance will continue to increase in the future. The Czech government has recently approved the registration of the first domestic private pension funds and there are applications pending that would dramatically increase the number of such funds. The plan is to authorize private medical insurance companies to offer policies that are more generous in their payment schedule than those offered by the national insurance funds. Several private clinics have opened in Prague to take advantage of these expected higher insurance payments by offering improved facilities and services. In private conversations, operators of these clinics have claimed that their intended market is private firms' employee benefit programmes. Indeed, clinics currently in operation typically accept direct payments from firms for their employees' care while awaiting reform of the insurance industry.

There are several reasons why it would be economically rational to expect the provision of voluntary fringe benefits to become more prevalent in the Czech Republic. Among these are:

(1) The extremely high social insurance and income tax rates (maximum of almost 50 per cent) make it attractive for firms to offer compensation in the form of fringe benefits that are not subject to these taxes.

(2) The very tight labour market, with unemployment rates of around 3 per cent for the country as a whole and less than 0.5 per cent in Prague, makes it important for firms to reduce turnover and retain valuable employees who might be subject to recruitment by other employers. As is well established, fringe benefit programmes (especially pensions) can be used to bind employees to firms and reduce turnover in ways that simple wage payments cannot.

(3) Prior to August 1995, the existence of wage controls made it attractive to increase compensation in the form of benefits that were not subject to these restrictions.

Thus, we would anticipate that the role of non-mandatory fringe benefits in the Czech Republic will increase substantially in the next few years as firms continue the process of evolving normal market relationships with their employees.

NOTES

1 The main source for this section was The Labour Act, No. 65/1965, and its later amendments from 1968 to 1994.
2 Quotations in this section are from The Labour Act, No. 65/1965.
3 There is also a complex equalization formula based on the age and sex of covered participants designed to reduce the disparities that would be created by private insurance companies 'creaming off' the best insurance risks.
4 These were calculated from data for all industrial firms provided by the Ministry of Industry. Thus, they are for the entire population of firms rather than for the sample used to generate the wage and benefit data. This should not pose a problem as long as the wage sample is representative.
5 It must be emphasized that the figures given are for the proportion of *firms* offering a benefit. As such, they probably overstate the proportion of *workers* receiving that benefit because some firms will offer a given benefit to only a fraction of their workers.

REFERENCES

Coopers & Lybrand (1994), *1994 Czech Republic Wage Survey*, Prague, Summer.
Ministry of Health (1994), *Analysis of the Contemporary Situation of Transformation of Czech Health Care*, Report for the Committee for Social Policy and Health Care of Parliament, 28 February.
Mitchell, D. and J. Rojot (1993), 'Employee benefits in the Single Market', in L. Ulman, B. Eichengreen, and W.T. Dickens, *Labor and an Integrated Europe*, Washington DC: The Brookings Institution.
Salkova, H. (1991), 'Socialni politika v prubehu transformace', *Socialni politika*, vol. 2.
US Chamber of Commerce (1992), *Employee Benefits, 1991*, Washington DC.

5   Firms and government in the provision of benefits in Russia

SIMON COMMANDER and
RICHARD JACKMAN

Introduction

Russian firms commonly provide a substantial range of non-monetary benefits to workers, including a number of important social services such as housing and some aspects of education and health care. Some also supply services not simply to their workers but to the local community as a whole, for example sewerage, hospital buildings, or other public infrastructure. Taken together, non-monetary benefits and services may amount to something of the order of 35 per cent of total firm labour costs, which is large in comparison with firms in most OECD settings. Although the types of benefits and services range widely across firms, it is a reasonable generalization that most in a market economy would normally be the responsibility of local government rather than of a commercial firm.

There is a common presumption that Russian firms should transfer the social services and benefits they currently provide to local government or some other agency. Indeed, firms have been induced to transfer the bulk of their housing stocks to municipalities. The arguments behind this emphasis on divestiture are that Russian firms will not be able to compete effectively in the market if they are at the same time burdened with having to run various social services, and that, at least in some contexts, enterprise closure could lead to a collapse in the provision of essential services if these had previously been provided by the enterprise. In practice, the situation is rather more complex, and the prospects for achieving benefits from divestiture in the absence of parallel reforms of the housing and local government finance systems are much less clear-cut than these simple claims suggest. Most obviously, it will not help an enterprise to be divested of its services if it then has to pay as much in taxation to the local government as it previously paid in direct costs. Nor will it help people in a company town to have entrusted services to a local government when the closure of the company would precipitate a corresponding collapse of local tax revenues.

Thus it may be helpful to examine explicitly the question of the appropriate assignment of functions between public agencies, such as local government, and the firm sector. There are a number of potential inefficiencies associated with firm provision of social benefits:

(1) To the extent that the services constitute a net burden rather than a benefit of employment to the workers (see below), this net burden may fall differentially on different firms, hence distorting competition between them. It would be the objective of a well-designed tax system that the costs of supporting local public services would be borne by non-distorting taxes (Wallich, 1994).

(2) If firms pay the costs of social services for their workers, they may become reluctant to hire or to employ workers in 'high-risk' groups, e.g. women with young children.

(3) If changing jobs means the loss of access to social benefits, or the disruption of access, firm-linked benefits will hinder labour mobility.

(4) There are arguments for managerial specialization. Firms, it is argued, should have a set of objectives dominated by considerations of productive efficiency and profit maximization. There may also be arguments for having provision of a service such as education, health, or housing under a single management rather than these activities being scattered around among many providers.

(5) In a company town, or a town dominated by a single industry, the closure of the company or industry will have the additional consequence of disrupting the provision of local social services.

Prior to discussing in more detail the arguments for specific benefits programmes and their methods of implementation, we attempt to give a short overview of the type of benefits currently provided by firms before attaching costs and/or income flows to those benefits. We use two data sources. The first comes from two rounds of a World Bank firm survey carried out in the Moscow region in November 1992 and April 1993.[1] The information covers the period from pre-transition in 1991 through the first quarter of 1993. This sample is both small – 41 firms – and localized. The second source is a far larger and more representative World Bank survey covering 439 industrial firms throughout Russia that was implemented in July 1994 with data points going back to 1990/91.

Firm benefits: a description

A listing of the types of benefits provided by firms is given in tables 5.1 and 5.2. It can be seen that a significant proportion of the total labour force continues to have entitlements to child care, paid vacations,

Table 5.1. Benefits: type and availability by firm size, Moscow survey, November 1992

	Firm size				
Type of benefit	80–350	351–700	701–900	901–1,500	1,501 +
Housing (permanent)	2	5	8	5	0
Housing (temporary)	1	3	4	3	0
Kindergarten	1	5	8	6	2
Land for dachas	3	7	7	6	3
Canteen (subsidized)	4	6	8	7	2
Policlinic access	2	2	5	5	2
Community House	0	1	3	3	0
Fitness facilities	0	0	1	2	0
Sanatorium	0	6	4	4	1
Food store with subsidized prices	8	9	7	6	2
Sick pay	0	0	3	2	1
Housing rent assistance	0	0	0	1	0
Other forms of housing help	0	6	4	4	0
Transport allowance	3	3	1	3	2
Maternity allowance	10	11	10	7	2
Childcare allowance	10	11	9	7	3
Paid vacation	4	8	7	3	0
Pre-dismissal allowance	8	10	8	4	3
Sanatorium vouchers	8	10	9	6	3

$N = 41$.
Source: World Bank Moscow survey.

housing, and holiday homes, whether in the small Moscow sample or in the larger survey with information on mid-1994. Benefits are both varied and pervasive across all firm size classes. By 1994, although we find some increase in the number of firms providing no benefits, the overall picture is of considerable inertia.[2] Throughout there is a positive association between firm size, as measured by employment, and range of benefits. Larger firms generally provide more benefits and these are likely to include not only housing but also access to healthcare facilities (commonly in-firm) and other social functions, such as pre-school education. This is clearly true for firms that act as locally dominant employers and in 'company-town' settings (see Standing, 1992). The 1994 survey found that concentration in employment was unambiguously associated with higher shares of benefit provision across all categories. Here, the functions normally assigned to local authorities in OECD contexts have been almost completely absorbed within firms.

Table 5.2. Benefits: large World Bank survey, mid-1994 and 1990/91

Type of benefit	% of firms mid-1994	% of firms 1990/91
Child care/childcare subsidy	66	79
Healthcare facility	70	71
Food subsidy/cafeteria	78	83
Food and/or consumer goods sold	60	52
Construction of new housing	50	73
Housing/housing subsidy	55	59
Holiday resort/holiday subsidy	45	57
Transportation/transportation subsidy	57	57

Source: World Bank survey, 1994.

But although the motivation for providing a wide scale of benefits in larger firms had economic content, particularly in the desire to attach workers and reduce turnover, it is important to appreciate the non-economic factors behind the phenomenon. Indeed, concepts such as prestige and benevolence have been and remain important considerations and, in some sense, enter directly into the utility function of managers of state firms. This may explain in part the current reluctance or inability of those managers to shed such benefits. Indeed, without appreciating the underlying idea that the firm has an explicit social function and set of responsibilities, we are unlikely to understand the current responses.

Among smaller firms with less local labour market dominance, the evidence suggests that firm-provided benefits may not exceed those covered by local authorities. Indeed, in the small Moscow sample, for housing, child care, and health facilities firm expenditure at the local level was comparable to or in excess of local authority or non-firm expenditures in only 10–30 per cent of cases, depending on the function (table 5.3). As these items constitute the major expenditure charges on the benefits side, this cautions against a simplistic view of the scale of firm-level functions.

From both surveys we are also able to get some handle on the response of firms to the current and future provision of benefits. Several results stand out. First, although larger firms offering wider benefits have begun to scale back these obligations, in general large firms were those that have adjusted benefits provision the least. This appears to be related to continuing receipt of subsidies and/or tax breaks, often from local government sources, that at least in part compensate for the cost of provision. Declining provision was more likely among small and medium-sized firms. In particular, provision of kindergartens and some healthcare facilities was significantly reduced. Roughly one-third of enterprises providing child care in mid-1994 expected to cut provision in

Table 5.3. Enterprise benefits programmes

Programme share at local level relative to local government expenditures	Moscow	Moscow *oblast*	Other	Total
Housing				
None	14	3	0	17
Smaller	6	7	3	16
Comparable	2	3	0	5
Higher	0	3	0	3
Child care				
None	14	7	1	22
Smaller	3	3	1	7
Comparable	4	3	1	8
Higher	1	3	0	4
Health				
None	13	8	3	24
Smaller	8	5	0	13
Comparable	1	3	0	4
Higher	0	0	0	0

Source: World Bank Moscow survey.

1995. In a significant number of cases in both surveys, firms had begun to increase cost recovery by raising user fees, generally by applying differential tariffs for non-employee access to services. Thus, despite a clear preference for all firm size classes to dispense with, or curtail, the range of benefits, more striking is the generally sluggish adjustment on benefits by firms, though, of course, we have no way to correct for quality of services or rationing. Part of the likely reason behind this inertia in the Moscow survey was the reasonably buoyant financial position of most sample firms in 1992,[3] but this is not strictly true if we look at the larger sample. Although there is a loose correlation between current profitability and benefits provision, many firms have continued to receive financial supports (see Alfandari *et al.*, 1996).

In summary, evidence from both surveys suggests that firms have widely tried to economize on providing benefits, but the extent of divestiture to date is less than might have been expected.

The costs of benefits

Little hard evidence exists that allows computation of the share of benefits costs in firms' labour payments. The Moscow survey allows us to get a reasonably detailed picture on this score. First, wages as reflected in the firms' wage bills (inclusive of the wage tax) account for roughly 50 per cent of total labour costs. Including bonuses raises this share to just over 60 per cent for the entire sample. The remaining costs are distributed over pensions, social insurance taxes, Employment Fund payments and, in terms of benefits, Social Fund allocations.[4] The latter amount to over 20 per cent of total labour costs. These orders of magnitude are confirmed by the 1994 data. Gross costs of benefits at that time were around 18 per cent of the wage bill. Aggregate data for the first quarter of 1994 similarly indicate that expenditure on social benefits and services by Russian industrial enterprises was about 21 per cent of the wage bill. This suggests a fairly stable cost share since the start of the transition.

Taken from the income side, we find that wages accounted for roughly 50 per cent of total labour income, rising to around 65 per cent when factoring in bonus payments. In summary, it seems that benefits, dissociated from more conventional cash wage or effort-related incentives, comprised approximately 35 per cent of labour income in 1992/93. Over time, a clear pattern has emerged in which workers have commonly accepted low cash wages for employment security. This will have reduced the monetary share of total compensation. The 1994 data clearly indicate that the non-monetary share in total compensation has increased over the course of the transition. This has been one important factor in continuing to attach workers to firms. In addition, it explains why workers have widely picked attachment and low effort in the employment offering them social benefits, while gaining monetary compensation by participation in the informal sector.[5]

The divestiture problem

It is clear that Russian firms do indeed provide a wide range of non-monetary benefits. To make the analysis more tractable, it may be helpful to characterize the activities at issue under three broad titles.

(1) *Services provided for current workers at the firm during the course of their work and as a benefit of employment* (e.g. subsidized meals in the works canteen, paid vacations, holiday accommodation in dachas or sanatoria, sports facilities). Such services constitute part of the workers' wage package; they can be balanced by a lower cash wage and therefore do (or need) not add to firms' costs. Whether or not workers wish to be remunerated in this way may be open to question, though we may note that, under current tax laws, benefits in kind are not liable for payroll or personal income tax, and hence may be an attractive option for

employers. Tax considerations aside, the form of the wage package would appear to be a matter for the workers and the firm concerned and not for public policy and hence, in principle, might be primarily a function of firm-level performance and priorities. There is no obvious reason for government to take responsibility for the provision of such benefits for unemployed workers or for those whose employers do not provide them.

(2) *Services provided for current workers and their families* (for example, pre-school education or health clinics). This category differs from the first because the cost of these services can differ enormously across different workers. In principle, it is important to distinguish between cost differences that arise as a result of insurable risks, where the differences in costs incurred in relation to different workers though large *ex post* is unpredictable *ex ante*, as against differences due to identifiable worker characteristics.

Examples of insurable risks that a firm may take on could include pensions, provided that these are computed on an actuarially fair basis, or medical facilities to treat accidents and other unpredictable health problems. If these services would not otherwise be available for the workers, then in principle, as in case (1), the benefit of provision of the services can be balanced by a lower cash wage. The firm is in a sense acting as a private insurance company for its workers and can reduce wages by an amount representing the insurance premium. As in case (1), this activity need not add to the firm's costs. Pensions lie outside the scope of this paper, but as far as health services are concerned the picture is further complicated:

- in many localities it appears that a substantial part of the costs of health clinics, in particular the wages and salaries of medical staff, medical supplies and equipment, and in some cases also the maintenance and upkeep of buildings, is paid by local authorities even in respect of enterprise-based clinics;
- in general there are other health clinics in the locality that workers from the firm would be able to use if their own employer did not provide one. Hence there is no benefit to the worker, save that of greater convenience, from employer provision.

Essentially, the firm can pay lower wages to recover the costs of provision only in circumstances either where the service would not be available at all, or where the worker would otherwise have to pay for it.

Identifiable risks arise with services such as pre-school education, where, even if the firm cannot tell in advance how much taking on a particular worker will cost it, it can very reasonably expect that women with young children are likely to cost it much more than, say, prime-age men. Retention of these services in the enterprise leads to a number of potential difficulties, most obviously that, to hold down costs, enterprises are likely to become reluctant to hire workers from 'high-risk' groups. In principle, with competitive markets, the market wage of different groups would adjust to equate the expected total cost of employing different types of workers to their marginal products, so that, even if equally productive, 'high-risk' workers would get paid less. If firms were not allowed, or not prepared, to discriminate in wages in this way, the outcome would be unemployment of high-risk groups. If public policy is to shield individuals from the costs of pre-school education or health care, these services cannot be left to the enterprise but would have to be supported from public funds. Even though, amongst large firms, the incidence of such costs per worker may be approximately equal *ex post* by virtue of the law of large numbers, firms will still have an incentive to hire only low-risk workers in order to save on such expenses.

In principle, user fees could achieve much the same result as wage flexibility and hence mitigate some of the adverse incentive problems that differential risk categories might impose. However, the current practice in Russia whereby generally 20 per cent of the cost of pre-school education is borne directly by the parents and the remaining 80 per cent by the parents' employer or employers, though alleviating the financial imbalance between enterprises that provide pre-schools and those that do not, continues to impose a potential financial burden on the employers of workers with young children.

(3) *Services provided for the local community, whether or not employees of the enterprise* (for example, public infrastructure, hospitals, or transport subsidies). If access to these services is open to all citizens of a locality, they cannot form part of the wage package and hence, unlike in cases (1) and (2), their cost will be incident on the enterprise itself and cannot implicitly be shifted to workers in the form of a lower cash wage. Whether the costs of these services be transferred to consumers, to the local government, or to central government depends ultimately on whether they are private goods, local public goods, or have an income redistribution objective. For example, in current conditions in Russia there is probably not much justification in terms of either economic efficiency or income distribution for public transport subsidies, while hospitals might reasonably be made a responsibility of local government.

It is evident that many of the benefits offered by enterprises would in most market economies be provided by local rather than by central government. But this raises the problem of the adequacy of local government finance, and whether divestiture to local authorities simply recreates the problem at the community rather than the enterprise level. Most obviously it will not help an enterprise to be divested of its non-remunerative services if it then has to pay in taxation to the local government as much as it previously had to pay in direct costs. A general view is that the system of local government finance would need to compensate for two dimensions of differences between localities, namely differences in spending needs and differences in resources. Irrespective of the tax base, the amount of revenue a local government can expect to raise from local taxation is likely to depend crucially on the strength of local industry. A local government supported by resource equalization grants can continue to provide social services that local enterprises can no longer afford to finance, but in this context the local authority grants need to be in place before the divestiture of services.

There is the associated question of the relationship between management and finance. Clearly the burden on enterprises could be alleviated as effectively by a system of subsidies from public funds in support of non-remunerative activities. What are the advantages of transferring the management of such services, as opposed to just the cost, to government? And does the transfer of managerial responsibility necessarily entail the physical relocation of the facilities themselves in the case, say, of clinics or kindergartens? Again, in the case of one-company towns, it would be wasteful to build new facilities and close down what already exists, but in a town with a number of small enterprises each providing health or pre-school education services on a small scale, there may be considerable efficiency gains from rationalization of the service by a single authority. It may be that the shortage of funds rules out building new facilities, so that by default divestiture would entail local authorities running services using the same facilities. But if so, it might be as logical for central government to pay compensation direct to enterprises, based on numbers of pre-school-age children, etc., as to pay grants to local authorities on the same criteria.

The immediate implications appear to be that, apart from a small range of services that might reasonably be regarded as part of the wage package, enterprise provision of social services is likely to lead to inefficiency, most obviously in affecting the job prospects of high-risk groups, such as women with young children or the elderly. A second problem is that the burden of supporting social benefits may not fall on enterprises in proportion to their number of workers, since they may

Table 5.4. Housing programmes by firm size, November 1992

	Firm size class				
Type of programme	80–350	351-700	701-900	901–1,500	1,500 +
Permanent	2	5	8	5	0
Temporary	1	3	4	3	1
Housing loans	0	6	4	4	0
No programme	7	3	1	1	2
% of workforce housed	0	13.3	26.7	75.4	2.0
% of non-firm tenants	0	37.7	36.9	39.4	45.4
% of tenants that have privatized	0	3.3	1.3	1.1	6.1

$N = 41$.
Source: World Bank Moscow survey.

support activities used by the local community as a whole rather than just their employees.

Housing

Housing programmes provide the single largest component of benefits. Although by no means universally provided, a significant proportion of firms – over 50 per cent of both samples – had some form of direct housing programme. There seems to be a clear positive association with firm size but, save among the smallest firms, housing programmes were offered by a majority of enterprises. In all, over 28 per cent of the total labour force covered by the Moscow sample was housed in firm property and this share rose to over 75 per cent in the case of the second-largest firm size class (see table 5.4). Although these programmes were commonly built up in the Soviet period to reduce labour mobility, this objective has been made largely irrelevant; between 40 and 60 per cent of tenants in the housing stock in both surveys were not current firm employees.

By end 1995, a significant proportion of firms had been induced to transfer their housing stock to municipal governments as a result of explicit policy. Although removing most of the direct financing burden from firms, this transfer has left untouched major issues concerning ownership and cost recovery. Rents still remain regulated and yield derisory current incomes. Further, maintenance charges, including the cost of energy, to tenants have remained heavily subsidized by local governments. Consequently, energy subsidies to households exceeded 5 per cent of GDP in 1995 on a rising trend.

From the Moscow data we can estimate the impact of reducing such price controls. For simplicity, we assume that the objective of the firm is simply to close the financing gap generated by maintenance expenditures. Bearing in mind that such outlays were 50 per cent lower in 1992(3) than in 1991(3), we can calculate that it would require an additional rental payment by each current tenant of around 320 roubles per month in order to cover maintenance costs for 1992(3). The figure doubles if we assume that 1991(3) expenditures were a more appropriate target level. This implies that 15–30 per cent of average monetary wages would need to be directed at housing rents simply to cover maintenance.

The absence of adequate offsetting revenue from the extant housing stock and low cost recovery on services, in many cases, have led to a reduction or suspension of maintenance, reducing the quality of the housing stock. Recent decrees and other measures aimed at facilitating the privatization of housing and creating a framework for forming condominiums have had limited effect, partly because of continuing confusion over their status and legal validity. And privatization has been held back by the perception that large-order price adjustments may be unequally distributed over tenanted and privatized units. This suggests that privatization of the housing stock will proceed rapidly only if uncertainties over rights and prices are resolved. To do this will require several types of action. In the first place, there remains much uncertainty regarding the institutional-cum-legal framework. Tax and other incentives for the formation of condominiums and other agencies for the management of common property remain key. Second, a rapid, and hence large, adjustment to administered prices, particularly for maintenance charges, accompanied by a system of transitional income support would reduce the dynamic incentive problems associated with a gradual relaxation of price controls. At the same time, by tapering the transitional income support, there would be clear room for fiscal savings relative to the current system of subsidies.[6]

Types of firms and their settings

Any discussion of benefits has to distinguish not only the type of benefit but also the type of firm as given by its place in the labour market. This is important given the immense diversity of firms in addition to the problem of concentration in employment.

At first approximation, we can characterize the Russian economy in terms of numbers of semi-closed economies in which labour is largely immobile. In addition, we can try and characterize in terms of degree of concentration over regions and within regions. Russian industrial structure has generally been characterized by high concentration. Brown *et al.* (1993), using a large firm data set for 1989, qualify these

Table 5.5. Employment concentration by region, 1989

Region	Shares of employment in industries with:	
	1 firm	1–4 firms
Central	1.7	16.7
Chernozem	15.5	49.0
E. Siberia	10.7	36.6
Far East	12.4	24.3
Kaliningrad	26.3	70.6
N. Caucasus	8.8	24.9
North	19.4	36.8
North West	17.2	51.8
Urals	8.2	29.6
Volga	7.1	41.4
V-Vyatka	14.8	51.7
W. Siberia	6.5	29.5

Source: Brown *et al.* (1993).

assumptions in several significant ways.[7] First, they argue that, at national level, there is little robust evidence of concentration; further, Russian industry is not generally characterized by very large firms and those very large firms that do exist are not generally in heavily concentrated industries. In addition, most very large firms are not in company towns, but are located in areas with reasonably diversified industrial bases.

Nevertheless, employment concentration is quite significant. Further, given labour immobility across regions – exacerbated by the housing constraint – local concentration in employment is the more appropriate indicator for our purposes. Excluding the Central Region, which incorporates Moscow, 25–70 per cent of industrial employment in each region was concentrated in industries that had four or fewer firms in that region in 1989, as indicated in table 5.5.

Further, even where a number of firms exist in a locality, in some cases they may all operate within the same industrial sector, so that the local economy is wholly dependent on the fortunes of one particular industry. Local government in Russia, at both *oblast* and *raion* levels, is financed wholly from taxes levied on local enterprises; a collapse in local industry therefore translates directly into a collapse in local authority revenues. There is at present no indication that the Russian government is prepared to contemplate the introduction of equalization grants for local authorities, along West European lines and as recommended by the World

Bank (see Wallich *et al.*, 1993), so that there is at present no revenue provision for social benefits in the event of widespread enterprise bankruptcy in a locality.

Concentration in employment is likely to be closely correlated with concentration in the provision by enterprises of services and benefits. This implies that shocks to employment likely translate into shocks to services. In the most extreme case, when services are provided entirely within the firm, this means cessation of benefits. This is less likely to be a problem in multi-firm settings with services provided largely outside the firm. This has both practical and analytical aspects and motivates making a distinction over such settings.

As a consequence, we modify our assumptions regarding the labour market setting. So far we have implicitly worked with a setting assuming multi-firm and multi-industries. It has been assumed that there is some local labour market mobility, outside opportunities for workers, and diversity in the provision of services; loss of employment may have marginal implications with respect to access to basic services. With reasonable local labour market mobility firms face an exogenously determined supply price of labour; the package of wage and non-monetary benefits they offer has to be at least equivalent to what the worker could earn elsewhere. In such settings, one would normally presume greater municipal provision of services, because it is unlikely to be sensible for each firm to provide its own. Further, with a diversified industrial base sustaining local authority revenues, the bankruptcy of an individual enterprise can take place within a context where local government can take over the services that the enterprise previously provided.

At the other extreme are settings where one industry, or even a single company, dominates employment in the locality; we refer to this as a 'company town'. Access to services and employment are strongly correlated. Value-added in (or credits to) the enterprise or industry provides the only resource base for the finance of local social services. If there is no alternative source of employment, it is feasible for enterprises to tax workers in the form of a lower cash wage in order to pay for the services. Using this crude distinction over settings, we try and think through the implications of such differences.

Concentration in employment

We now examine the issues that arise when a single firm or a small number of firms dominate in the labour market and where the economic base is limited. There is, in the extreme case, an identity of interest between the enterprise and the local community and this has continued after the breakdown of monolithic authority through an equivalence of interest between an enterprise concerned with the well-being of the workforce and a democratic local government, because the population and the workforce are essentially the same constituency. It follows (for a proof, see the Appendix) that the level of provision of social benefits will be the same whether they are provided directly by the enterprise (financed by reduced wages) or by local government (financed by taxation).

However, this equivalence no longer holds if the enterprise cuts back employment, as is likely with restructuring. For this creates a divergence of interests between the 'insiders' employed in the firm and the 'outsiders' who are not. Typically this may mean that, if social benefits are left in the hands of the enterprise, it will cut back, insofar as the insiders prefer higher wages for themselves to better services for the community as a whole (see Appendix). The conflicting interests of different groups in the society are most appropriately resolved through the political process rather than by relying on the benevolence of the enterprise workers.

Although interesting, the case of the company town is, as noted above, something of a rarity. More common is the single-industry town. In a single-industry town there may be many enterprises and factories, with none particularly dominant in terms of employment, and a mix of social benefit provision between the local authorities and the larger enterprises. However, everyone depends on the same source of finance – the earnings of (or credits obtained by) enterprises all of which are concentrated in the same industry. If the industry fails there is no way that a rejuggling of services between sectors can help.

The dependence of local public services on the profitability of local industry may appear to be a serious structural defect in the Russian system of local government finance, though it is to some extent mitigated by the fact that almost all taxes are initially collected at the local level, with a share, in principle, predetermined but, in practice, subject to bargaining passed up to the federal government. As long as enterprises can still borrow to pay their taxes, the system can function. But, with the present system of local government finance, the imposition of hard budget constraints would have devastating effects on social service provision in industrially depressed localities.

Conclusion

Russian firms continue to provide workers with significant non-monetary components of compensation. Indeed, as the transition has progressed the non-monetary share in total worker compensation appears to have increased. One result has been to maintain attachment of workers to firms and to encourage the development of an informal private sector alongside. The principal benefit of the Soviet period – housing – has now seen some acceleration in the rate of privatization. By 1995 possibly as much as one-third of the housing stock had been privatized. But significant parts of the housing stock remain on the books of enterprises and, given government policy, increasingly on the books of municipalities. Cost recovery rates remain low, particularly for maintenance and energy provided to tenants. As such, the subsidy bill for housing had dramatically expanded to over 5 per cent of GDP by 1995. Transfer of housing to municipalities may have shifted the financing burden but it has done little to address the fundamental questions of cost recovery and ownership. We suggest that a more rapid programme of price decontrol, linked to transitional income supports, would have definite advantages both in financing terms and in terms of the viability of privatization. A more inclusive programme of divestiture is essential, explicitly associated with a new institutional arrangement addressing the management problem and a shift away from controlled prices. Implementing a transitional income support to offset part of this increase in charges to the population would also be critical.

The paper further discussed the divestiture problem and associated financing questions in a number of settings, focusing in particular on company towns or contexts where lack of diversity in production results in serially correlated shocks that are likely to amplify the size of any fiscal or financial shock. Given such shocks, the resulting separation of workers from the firm(s) generates a potential problem of coverage of benefits over retained and separated workers. This likely requires that decisions over benefits be divorced from the decisions of the firm and suggests a greater role for local government. In addition, it raises quite explicitly the difficult financing problem. Negative financial shocks to a company town or single-industry town imply a need for compensating financial supports, which under the existing budgetary arrangements are either absent or difficult to pinpoint. These issues stray directly into the overall question of fiscal relations between the centre and the regions. Although these questions are obviously important, we do not deal with them in greater detail in this chapter.

Appendix: benefits provision where employment is concentrated

Let there be two goods, a private consumption good (c) and a collective consumption good, which takes the form of a good that is supplied (or available) in the same quantity to all households (either by policy or because it is non-excludable) and is measured in units of consumption per household (g). The representative worker/household (ignoring differences between households) has a utility function:

$$U = U(c, g),$$

with all the usual properties.

The firm produces value added per worker q, and the price of its output (value-added), relative to the price of the consumption good, is p. Normalizing prices on the consumption good, and measuring the collective consumption good in units such that the price per unit is 1, the per worker budget constraint for the town is:

$$pq = c + g.$$

If each worker/household inelastically supplies one unit of labour and production technology is linear, the maximum the firm can produce per worker/household is set by choice of units at $q(s) = 1$. If the revenue-maximizing level of production per worker is denoted $q(d)$, production is given by:

$$q = \min[q(s), q(d)].$$

The enterprise will not produce beyond its revenue-maximizing output. We can then distinguish 'surplus labour' regimes $(q(s) > q(d))$ from labour shortage regimes $(q(s) < q(d))$. In this instance, we are interested in the surplus labour regime. Here, revenue per worker/household is maximized at R with $h = q(d)/q(s)$ equal to the proportion of labour input used (the rest being on-the-job leisure, short-time work, or unpaid leave). We refer to $h(< 1)$ as 'hours worked'.

'Full employment' outcome

First, assume all the workers remain in employment. The solution in this case is straightforward. Each worker works h hours and produces h units of output. The revenue per worker/household is R and this is split between c and g to maximize utility (with the implication that $U_c = U_g$). If the utility-maximizing values are $c*$ and $g*$, with $c* + g* = R$, the firm would pay its workers a cash wage $c*$ and use its remaining revenues to provide $g*$ units of the collective good per worker/household.

Clearly this solution could be replicated by tax finance of the collective good. If the enterprise were instead to pay its workers a gross wage $w(= R)$, with identical workers, all would vote for a tax of $g*$ on their wages to achieve the optimal combination $(c*, g*)$. Depending on the nature of the collective good, the optimum could also be achieved by privatization. If units of the collective good could be sold, then individual households would choose to spend $g*$ of their wage on the collective good and $c*$ on private goods. The problem here is that, in some cases, the collective good may have the characteristics of a public good so that it cannot be supplied efficiently by the market.

'Exogenous' unemployment outcome

As a first step to investigating different institutional arrangements within this context, we sketch the impact of unemployment on the provision of social services, taking the level of unemployment itself as exogenous. Specifically, we assume that employment is reduced to the level required for revenue maximization, so the enterprise retains a proportion h of the workers in full-time work, while the other $(1 - h)$ become unemployed. The unemployed workers are entitled to a benefit b: they may also continue to receive the collective good at the same level as the workers who remain in work. We consider two assumptions for the finance of benefits. The first is that they are financed locally, by a tax t per worker, with the Employment Fund budget constraint given by:

$$ht = (1 - h)b.$$

The second is that they are wholly financed from central funds. (In reality in Russia, the Employment Fund levies a 1 per cent payroll tax on enterprises, the bulk of which is used to finance unemployment benefits and other expenditure on employment services in the locality where it is collected. Clearly, in a situation of high unemployment, this tax rate would be hopelessly inadequate and either it would have to be raised substantially or else the Employment Fund would need to be supported from central funds. For simplicity we here consider the case where the Employment Fund is 100 per cent financed from central funds.)

With locally funded benefits, the net revenue per worker is:

$$R/h - t = [R - (1 - h)b]/h.$$

The firm continues to finance the collective good for the whole community, so that the remaining income per worker is

$$c = [R - (1 - h)b]/h - g/h = [R - (1 - h)b - g]/h.$$

Hence we replace the previous budget line $(c + g = R)$ by

$$c + g/h = [R - (1 - h)b]/h.$$

This differs from what went before on account of both income effects (positive if $b < c*$) and substitution effects (the relative price of g increases because it has to be provided for the unemployed as well as the employed). To check on the income effect, consider the case where $g = g*$, as previously, and recalling that $R = c* + g*$, we have $c = [c* - (1 - h)b]/h$. If $b = c*$, this gives $c = c*$, and with c decreasing in b it follows that if $b < c*$ we will have $c > c*$.

If the enterprise concerns itself only with the welfare of currently employed workers, it will optimize by maximization of $U(c, g)$ subject to the above budget line. Both income and substitution effects raise c (so $c > c*$) but the effects on g go in opposite directions. In practice, income effects may not be large (b close to $c*$), in which case the enterprise will cut back on provision of the collective good. In any event the outcome is inefficient, because the slope of the budget line no longer reflects relative marginal social cost.

Whether this situation might even in principle be improved by transferring the responsibility for the collective good to local government is unclear. Standard public choice theory would say that the government maximizes the welfare of the median voter, and, if the majority of the workers are still in work, the outcome is just the same as if the enterprise made the decision. On the other hand, if the local government were to choose g to maximize the utilitarian definition of social welfare, the previous optimum might be restored. This would be the case, for example, if the utility function is separable. Writing social welfare as V, the problem is to select g to maximize V subject to the above budget constraint. V is given by:

$$V = hU(c, g) + (1 - h)U(b, g),$$

where c is now the private good consumption of employed workers (and b the private good consumption of the unemployed). The utility function being separable we have:

$$U(c, g) = U^1(c) + U^2(g),$$

so,

$$V = hU^1(c) + (1 - h)U^1(b) + U^2(g),$$
$$= hU^1\{[R - (1 - h)b - g]/h\} + (1 - h)U^1(b) + U^2(g)$$
$$dV/dg = -U_c^1 + U_g^2 = 0.$$

A more redistributive local government would however be inefficient: it would over-provide g as a means of reducing the inequality in private good consumption resulting from unemployment. A completely egalitarian local government would set $U(c, g) = U(b, g)$, which would entail raising taxes until the private consumption of employed workers fell to the same level as that of the unemployed. Since b is assumed to be less than the previous optimum, $c*$, there is under-provision of the private, and equivalently over-provision of the public, good.

Now consider the situation in which unemployment benefits are financed from central funds. The budget constraint for the representative employed worker at the firm is now $c + g/h = R/h$. The income effect is clearly larger than before. Again the substitution effect leads to an inefficiency, with too little of the collective good being produced. With exogenous unemployment, central financing of benefits is a pure lump-sum transfer.

Outcome with endogenous unemployment

A simple, if ad hoc, procedure might be to assume that, first, employment is chosen to maximize total revenue for the town (inclusive of revenue from externally funded benefits) and, second, with given employment, spending on the collective good is chosen by the enterprise to maximize the welfare of employed workers. We first look at the solution using this procedure and then consider other models of employment determination. With internal funding of benefits, the solution is exactly the same as that already discussed. The employment rule will lead to the employment of a proportion h of the workers, and thereafter the analysis is unchanged. But with external finance, the employment rule leads to a lower level of employment.

Writing the employment rate as n, and, for sake of simplicity, taking a linear product demand curve of the form $p = A - aq = A - an$, we have revenue per worker, $R = pq = (A - an)n$. Externally funded benefits bring the town an income $(1 - n)b$. Hence the total income per worker/household in the town is:

$$y = (A - an)n + (1 - n)b.$$

Setting $dy/dn = 0$ gives the optimal value of n for the town:

$$n = (A - b)/2a.$$

Employment falls if the demand for the firm's product falls, or if the unemployment benefit increases. (With internal financing of benefits, the corresponding value of n is $A/2a$.) It may also be noted that, at the optimal level of employment, revenue per worker employed,

$$R/n = A - an = (A + b)/2,$$

which implies $R/n > b$, since $A > b$ is necessary for positive employment. The income-maximizing strategy for the town is to set the marginal revenue product of labour equal to the unemployment benefit. Because of the downward-sloping demand curve, average revenue per worker will exceed marginal revenue and hence be greater than the unemployment benefit.

The budget constraint for employed workers is now:

$$c + g/n = R/n.$$

Since $n < h$, both income and substitution effects are larger than before.

NOTES

We thank Annette Brown, Qimiao Fan, Jeni Klugman, Peter Knight, and Paulo Vieira da Cunha for detailed comments on an earlier version.

1 The survey covered 41 firms in the Moscow area. For a more extended discussion of the results, see Commander et al. (1993).
2 For a full description and analysis of the 1994 survey, see Commander et al. (1996).
3 See Commander et al. (1993) for more details.
4 The bulk of benefits costs have normally been subsumed in Social Fund expenditures. Qimiao Fan has pointed out to us that firms could also write benefits into production costs partly for tax reasons, as also because of restrictions placed on the use of the Social Fund.
5 See Commander et al. (1996) for a fuller discussion.
6 See Commander and Schankerman (1995) for more on this approach.
7 The data set excludes firms in the military–industrial complex and hence may likely understate concentration.

REFERENCES

Alfandari, G., L. Freinkman, and Q. Fan (1996), 'Financial transfers and Russian industrial firms', in S. Commander, M. Schaffer, and Q. Fan (eds.), *Economic Policy and Industrial Restructuring in Russia*, Washington DC: World Bank.
Brown, A., B. Ickes, and R. Ryterman (1993), 'Industrial concentration in Russia', World Bank, mimeo.

Commander, S. and M. Schankerman (1995), 'Enterprise restructuring and the efficient provision of benefits', EBRD/World Bank, mimeo.

Commander, S., U. Lee, and A. Tolstopiatenko (1996), 'Social benefits and the Russian industrial firm', in S. Commander, M. Schaffer, and Q. Fan (eds.), *Economic Policy and Industrial Restructuring in Russia*, Washington DC: World Bank.

Commander, S., L. Liberman, C. Ugaz, and R. Yemtsov (1993), 'The behaviour of Russian firms in 1992: Evidence from a survey', World Bank, Washington DC, mimeo.

Standing, G. (1992), 'Industrial wages, payments systems and benefits', ILO, Budapest, mimeo.

Wallich, C. (ed.) (1994), *Russia and the Challenge of Fiscal Federalism*, Washington DC: World Bank.

6 What comes after enterprise-centred social protection?

The case of East Germany

MARTIN KOHLI

Introduction

In any assessment of the changing welfare mix in the West, social protection at the level of the enterprise turns out to be an especially complex and fluid field. In transitional economies, this is even more the case. There are rapid and massive changes in two dimensions: (1) enterprises are shedding some social protection functions related to the socialist economic system and taking up some new ones related to the market system; (2) a key precondition of enterprise-level social protection is also changing – the question of who is employed, in other words, who is in a position to receive the benefits.

The socialist societies of Eastern Europe[1] were characterized by what I have called an 'enterprise-centred social policy' (Kohli, 1994a) in which labour force participation rates were high and the enterprise was the focus of a large number of social protection functions. The transition process has put both of these features of the social policy regime of 'real socialism' in jeopardy. This has occurred on an especially massive scale in East Germany, where enterprises have been forced to strip down, and where the precondition of enterprise-level social protection – that people remain employed – has turned out to be very far from trivial.

In this paper, I will address both of these dimensions. The shedding of social protection is examined in terms of the change from enterprise-centred social protection to a new enterprise portfolio of welfare functions. Given the lack of appropriate data, the change is described in qualitative terms only. The shedding of workers can be analysed quantitatively by examining how the labour market has evolved in the aggregate as well as which workers remain employed and which are shed.

The key question of the paper is the relation between enterprises and other agents of social protection. Which protection functions are retained by enterprises, and which ones are added in the process of transition? To what extent and by what means do enterprises succeed in passing protection obligations on to other actors, e.g. those in the public sphere? How do the actors cooperate to create a new welfare mix?

In discussing this question, three mechanisms of transition for East German workers can be distinguished:

(1) the transition to new stable jobs where the enterprise in its new form takes over a part of social protection;
(2) the transition to an intermediate organizational framework – a 'second labour market' where workers leave their enterprise but remain employed with special firms funded largely by public subsidies (provided, i.e., by unemployment insurance), and can be recalled by their former enterprise; and
(3) the transition out of the labour force, usually into a social protection pathway such as unemployment or (early) retirement, where the enterprise may bear some of the cost but most of it is typically passed on to actors in the public sphere.

The first mechanism is still the most common in quantitative terms, and probably also the most diverse, but can be treated here only summarily. The second mechanism is much less frequent but represents an interesting new type of local networks between labour market actors ('local corporatism'), which is gaining attention in Western countries as well but is of special relevance in the institutional framework created for the East German transition. The third mechanism is again important quantitatively and needs to be studied in structural as well as institutional terms; it can be hypothesized that labour shedding in the transitional labour markets is heavily structured along the lines of age, gender, and qualification.

As to the latter, I will focus particularly on how the labour force is being reduced along the age dimension. This is an interesting issue because in the West it has been the main dimension of workforce restructuring in recent decades, and also because occupational pensions usually form the major part of enterprise-level social protection. The background of this part of the following argument is the recent studies of early exit from the labour force in Western societies (Kohli *et al.*, 1991; Naschold and de Vroom, 1994). For Western enterprises, early exit has offered them the possibility of downsizing or restructuring their labour force in a relatively 'bloodless' way. This possibility depends on the availability of adequate institutional pathways between work and retirement proper. At the same time, these pathways add to the financial burden of social protection to be shared between enterprises, the state, and in some cases the ageing workers themselves.

Looking at the three mechanisms as a whole, the transition can be seen as a change in the welfare mix, with the state (at the national level but also at the community level) and the 'civil society' taking on a more important role. It should be added here that sociological interest in social protection and the welfare mix goes beyond the purely economic aspects. It is not only about the coverage of risks, or the redistribution of income, but also about the social relations and identities that social protection creates and modifies – relations between individuals and the enterprises or the state, relations between classes, or relations between age groups and generations. Not only do networks of economic exchange produce a distribution of goods and incomes, they also constitute a network of social relations, and locate individuals in social space.[2] Thus, in examining the enterprise, the family, or the civil society as part of the welfare mix, sociological interest is focused not only on their economic potential (e.g. to make up for the deficiencies of public social security), but also on their impact on relations, conflicts, identities, and legitimacies.

East Germany as a special case

In the sociological literature, welfare patterns are now usually differentiated in terms of national regime types. The term 'regime' emphasizes the systematic character of social policy features, i.e. the connectedness of various dimensions in a structured whole (see Ferge, 1992; Kolberg, 1992). The most important point in this respect is the connection between social protection and the social organization of work, i.e. labour markets and labour relations (see Esping-Andersen, 1990).

The appropriate number and identification of regime types, and the grouping of specific countries into them, is of course still a matter of debate. Esping-Andersen's (1990) distinction between conservative, liberal, and social democratic regimes – which itself takes up an earlier distinction by Titmuss – is now widely used, but some authors disagree with these lines of differentiation, or want to add a fourth or fifth regime type. It seems obvious, however, that pre-transition Eastern Europe can be treated as one – by now largely historic – regime type ('real socialism'). This certainly does not do justice to the differences between the countries of Eastern Europe – differences in structure (e.g. level of industrial and service development, or importance of the second economy) as well as in social policy institutions (e.g. age thresholds and replacement levels of pensions). The German Democratic Republic (GDR) was characterized by relatively high age thresholds (65 for men, 60 for women) and a small size of the informal economy, thereby making formal employment –

which was overwhelmingly in state enterprises or large cooperatives – particularly salient.[3] There were of course other differences that relate more to the dimensions of social relations and identities. As an example, in terms of the main sources of legitimacy, Offe (1994) has proposed distinguishing between three types of social integration: integration mainly through economic success (GDR, Czechoslovakia), integration through nationalist identities (Poland, Hungary), and integration through outright repression (Romania, Bulgaria). But in some basic respects, all these societies seem to have been exemplars of a common structural regime type.

For the post-1989 transition period, this is less and less true. East Germany stands out as an immediate transition to a Western institutional pattern (Offe, 1994: 193) where the ownership structures have been largely privatized, where firms are exposed to Western market structures, and where they can use an extensive public social infrastructure to downsize their labour force (see Hare, 1994) – prominent among them being the early exit pathways. It might be concluded that the East German case has nothing to offer for an analysis of other countries where the transition to market structures and institutions is more gradual and where social protection transfers from outside are available only to a much lower extent. But such a conclusion would deny the analytic potential that lies in the observation of a condensed and pure form of transition.[4]

The structure of pre-transition enterprise-level social benefits[5]

Interest in the pre-transition social protection regime may be simply historical, referring to a regime that has now gone out of business. Another interest is along the lines of the 'legacy' argument: the experiences and institutions of 'real socialism' still have and will continue to have a strong impact on the post-communist transformation (see Machonin, 1993). But the most important reason is again analytical: even though such a regime may never again become a reality, it can serve as a model by which to sharpen our perception of today's range of empirical alternatives. It is therefore necessary to review them briefly here (see Kohli, 1994a, 1994b).

The countries of 'real socialism' were above all characterized by a low degree of functional differentiation – between society, economy, and polity as well as within these subsystems. One of the most striking dimensions of this was the extent to which work and social protection were fused. The link between employment and social protection was achieved both by a policy of full employment and by channelling a substantial part of social protection directly through the enterprise.

To be sure, there were other channels as well, above all state transfers and price subsidies. State transfer systems accounted, for example, for old age pensions and family allowances. These systems were less broad in the GDR than in the West because there was no need for social protection against unemployment; on the other hand, pension benefits – the most important piece of enterprise-level social security in the West – were completely provided by the state, in the form of basic pensions as well as complementary pensions for some specific occupations. But the most interesting channel, especially from a sociological perspective, was through the workplace and the enterprise. In social protection, the work nexus took precedence over the cash nexus. Even state transfers such as pensions were to some extent administered and distributed through enterprise-level institutions. Therefore, the usual calculation of the share of overall social protection provided by each institutional actor would not give an adequate measure of the importance of the enterprise.

Much more so than was true for the West, the East European countries were 'work societies' – even though productivity was low and work motivation doubtful. The centrality of work was expressed and maintained ideologically through its symbolic valuation and heroization (the GDR as a 'workers' and peasants' state'). More importantly, it was realized through the two processes just mentioned: high labour force participation, and distribution of resources through the enterprise.

Labour force participation was higher than in the West in two dimensions: for women and for the elderly (see figures 6.1 and 6.2). In the GDR, female labour force activity rates in 1989 – i.e. immediately before the transition – almost reached the male level, whereas in West Germany they still lagged substantially behind, and also still showed a slight bimodal distribution, indicating the persistence of the three-phase model of female formal work careers. The available data on the evolution up to 1989 show that female labour force participation had started at much lower levels in the first decades of the socialist economy, and had only later risen to the level of full employment. Thus, the current female retirement cohorts in large part have not had a full work life, which is significant in terms not only of cohort experience but also of pension claims. For the elderly, the drop in labour force participation started later than in the West. Of the five-year group just before the public pension age (60–64 for men, 55–59 for women), more than three-quarters were still in work, whereas for West Germany the corresponding figures were around one-third.[6]

The data on the labour force participation of retirees – available only

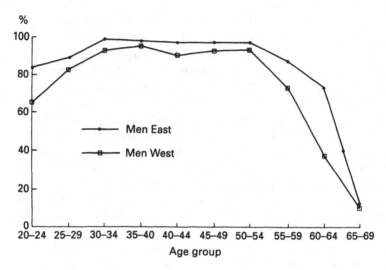

Figure 6.1   Labour force activity rates for men, by age group: East and West Germany, 1990 (%)
Source: Wagner and Schupp (1991: 192).

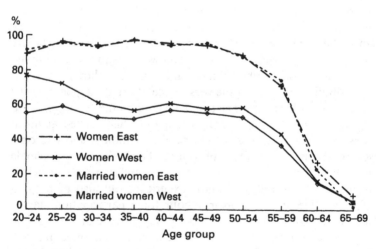

Figure 6.2   Labour force activity rates for women, by age group: East and West Germany, 1990 (%)
Source: Wagner and Schupp (1991: 192).

Table 6.1. East Germany: labour force participation rates in retirement, 1972–88 (%)

Year	Total	Men[1]	Women[2]
1972	22.7	29.2	15.3
1975	18.1	24.7	15.2
1980	13.0	16.6	11.5
1986	10.3	11.8	9.8
1988	9.9	11.0	9.5

Source: Winkler (1990), vol. 2, p. 324.
1 Percentage of total population 65 + .
2 Percentage of total population 60 + .

for the entire population in retirement, i.e. from age 60 for women and age 65 for men – present an interesting special angle on the labour regime. They show that there was also a (modest) trend towards earlier exit (see table 6.1). Employment of retirees was usually with their former enterprise. In a context of chronic labour shortages and with soft budget constraints, it was advantageous for enterprises to retain their retirees, especially as a 'reserve army' to cope with the frequent production breakdowns due to equipment failure or inadequate supplies. That retirees should be kept in the workforce was part of the 'right to work' written into the GDR constitution. In addition, GDR gerontology produced a number of studies showing that work was favourable for personality development. From the point of view of the retirees, motivation to work was helped along by rather low pension levels.

The fact that in spite of these reasons the labour force participation of retirees decreased over time has been attributed by some authors (e.g. Rys, 1993) to the same structural factors as in the West: in a period of decreasing demand for work, early exit made it possible to evade (open or hidden) unemployment. For the GDR, accounts by participants (see Ernst, 1995) shift the explanation to the supply side. Whereas demand for work remained high, attempts to recruit retirees were increasingly less effective. One of the factors for this was an increasing preference for leisure. Another was that, although pensions were low, many pensioners had the possibility of topping them up through their visits to (and transfers from) Western relatives. And, finally, even non-working pensioners retained the right to participate in many aspects of the enterprise network of distribution.

The distribution of resources through the enterprise was the second feature of the 'enterprise-centred social policy'. In the GDR, the enterprise was a centre of sociation in a very broad sense. It was a political unit, with the state party being organized more through firms than through local communities. The enterprise was a cultural unit, with many cultural activities (including theatres and concerts) being sponsored by it. And it was above all a material unit: a distributor of scarce goods and services ranging from housing and vacation places to medical and child care. Such distribution was especially important in an economy where markets were highly restricted – where money did not generally give access to goods but gave only the right to queue up for goods.[7] As mentioned, even the non-working elderly remained partially integrated into this form of sociation. They could participate in what the union – in a telling reference to the militarization of work – called its 'veterans' organizations', which made them eligible for the same benefits as active workers. But the salience of these organizations went beyond material aspects alone; they also provided the 'veterans' with a social link that seems to have been valued in its own right (see Teipen, 1992).

It is not yet, and may never be, possible to quantify the social benefits channelled through the enterprise, especially if one includes the various forms of indirect benefits. The same is true for their structural significance. Although the structural potential of the enterprise-centred social policy is obvious, the questions about its precise level of effectiveness remain open. (The social policy studies published in the GDR failed even to identify these questions, much less to answer them.) There are four main questions that would need to be addressed, the first two regarding the size of enterprise-level social benefits, the last two regarding their incentive function:

(1) To what extent did enterprises also control benefits that were not directly their own (e.g. by being gate-keepers for access to higher education)?

(2) To what extent did enterprises indirectly and unwillingly provide social benefits to their workers in the form of goods, qualifications, and working time that workers appropriated for their own use, or for their private networks of reciprocal exchange that were so essential to survival in an economy of scarcity? It seems clear that the size of enterprise social benefits is seriously underestimated if they do not include these indirect benefits, and that some occupations (e.g. construction and repair work) provided especially favourable conditions in this respect.

(3) To what extent did enterprise social benefits function as an incentive to attract workers in the competition between enterprises in the external labour market?

(4) To what extent did enterprise social benefits function as an incentive in the internal labour market in the sense of a means of control over workers' performance?

The aspect of performance control was especially important in a situation – typical of socialist enterprises – in which wage differentiation was low, the threat of dismissal practically non-existent, and control at the shop-floor level rather tenuous. As a whole, the enterprise-centred social policy appears to have been a key part of the functioning of the socialist economy as analysed, for example, by Kornai (1980), and of its social networks of exchange and clienteleship ('communist neo-tradition-alism'; see Jowitt, 1983; Walder, 1986).

The transition process: labour market change

The most dramatic overall feature of the transition process in the GDR has been the near-collapse of the labour market and the resulting loss of employment. The evolution (or rather involution) of the East German labour market can be documented by some aggregate data (table 6.2). In May 1989, the labour force comprised a total of 9.8 million employed persons. By May 1993, this number had shrunk to 6.2 million. Since then, there has been a slight increase again, to 6.4 million in May 1995, but this still amounts to less than two-thirds of the 1989 level.[8] Although GDP growth in the East has picked up again, with growth rates of between 6 per cent and 9 per cent since 1992, job creation has lagged behind. About 1 million persons (in net terms, as of May 1995) have moved and more than half a million commute to West Germany. One million are registered as unemployed, and another million take part in various publicly funded labour market measures: direct job creation ('ABM', usually on full wages), wage subsidies (at a somewhat reduced level), full-time requalification programmes ('further training'), 'short-time work' (a programme of temporary and/or partial unemployment compensation), and early retirement.

This labour force involution has been managed through large-scale social transfers under the West German regime of social insurance and social assistance that has now been extended to the East. There is a range of programmes with varying and changing eligibility rules and replacement levels, and one can observe a great deal of programme switching and institutional 'bricolage', resulting in a policy process of muddling through. Many programmes (e.g. pre-retirement) had deadlines that were extended several times in line with the labour market data showing that,

Table 6.2. Labour market evolution, 1989–95

	1st half-year 1989	2nd half-year 1989	1st half-year 1990	2nd half-year 1990	1st half-year 1991	2nd half-year 1991	1st half-year 1992	2nd half-year 1992	1st half-year 1993	2nd half-year 1993	1st half-year 1994	2nd half-year 1994	1st half-year 1995
4. Working-age population ('000)	10,721	–	–	10,618	–	10,527	–	10,465	–	10,505	–	10,540	–
4.1 Migrations to West Germany ('000)	49	339	257	138	102	148	94	106	78	95	73	–	–
4.2 Migrations from West Germany ('000)	1	4	12	24	34	47	51	61	54	65	60	–	–
4.3 Commuters to West Germany ('000)	–	–	–	206	446	541	451	506	–	607	–	550	–
5. Total employment ('000)	9,836	9,610	9,076	8,060	7,462	6,903	6,423	6,298	6,183	6,259	6,237	6,433	6,411
5.1 Share of female employment (%)	49	–	49	47	46	46	46	46	45	44	–	45	–
5.2 Employees in *Treuhand* companies ('000)	–	–	4,100	2,979	2,115	1,404	1,070	458	296	187	132	119	–
6. Employment by sector ('000)													
6.1 Agriculture and forestry	977	971	804	651	469	385	291	255	234	225	223	230	228
6.2 Energy and mining	349	351	345	320	244	208	181	164	146	134	120	116	106
6.3 Manufacturing	3,509	3,254	3,092	2,658	2,171	1,727	1,336	1,210	1,120	1,085	1,047	1,053	1,032
6.4 Construction	629	622	620	640	702	728	792	840	883	963	986	1,056	1,063
6.5 Trade and transport	1,500	1,535	1,446	1,288	1,251	1,205	1,149	1,133	1,116	1,136	1,117	1,165	1,123
6.6 Services	617	622	649	771	919	969	999	1,039	1,075	1,133	1,161	1,230	1,244
6.7 Government (incl. *ABMs*)	2,040	2,040	1,965	1,672	1,505	1,452	1,436	1,412	1,360	1,322	1,303	1,299	1,303
7. Employment in labour market measures ('000)													
7.1 Employed in job creation measures (*ABMs*)	–	–	–	20	148	390	402	355	237	177	198	226	213
7.2 'Wage-cost subsidies East' (§ 249h AFG)	–	–	–	–	–	–	–	–	14	63	91	103	109
7.3 Short-time workers	–	–	656	1,794	1,899	1,035	417	233	201	125	105	59	72
7.4 Full-time equivalent of loss of working hours in case of short-time working	–	–	–	866	1,078	594	223	109	89	56	46	29	36
8. Non-active population in labour market measures ('000)													
8.1 In full-time further training measures	–	–	–	45	170	310	442	434	368	271	234	264	255
8.2 In early retirement	–	–	–	460	521	705	806	834	857	778	643	569	370
9. Total persons in labour market measures (7.1 + 7.2 + 7.4 + 8.1 + 8.2) ('000)	–	–	–	1,391	1,917	1,999	1,873	1,732	1,565	1,346	1,212	1,191	984
9.1 As % of potential labour force (11.)	–	–	–	15	22	23	21	20	18	15	14	14	11

10. Total unemployment ('000)	142	642	843	1,038	1,123	1,101	1,100	1,175	1,117	1,015	1,003
10.1 Unemployed women ('000)	69	352	482	635	715	704	708	754	734	660	639
10.2 Unemployed women (%)	54.6	55.2	59.5	61.6	63.6	63.9	64.4	64.1	65.7	65.0	63.7
10.3 Long-term unemployed ('000)	–	–	–	–	–	271	–	356	–	361	–
10.4 Long-term unemployed (as % of unemployed)	–	–	–	–	–	24.4	–	30.7	–	34.7	–
10.5 Women proportion of the long-term unemployed (%)	–	–	–	–	–	68.9	–	74.4	–	77.0	–
10.6 Unemployment rate (%)	1.6	7.3	9.5	11.8	14.2	13.9	15.1	16.2	15.7	14.2	14.3
10.7 Male unemployment rate (%)	–	6.4	8.0	8.9	10.0	9.7	10.4	11.2	10.4	9.6	10.1
10.8 Female unemployment rate (%)	–	8.2	11.2	14.7	18.9	18.6	20.2	21.5	21.3	19.2	18.7

Source: Employment Observatory East Germany, No. 16/17, November 1995.

contrary to predictions, the 'floor' of the downswing had not yet been reached.

With most of the registered unemployed receiving compensation in addition to all those in the special programmes just mentioned, about 2 million people in May 1995 were living fully or partially on incomes paid by the public labour market agencies (the peak had been reached in May 1991 with more than 3.5 million). Some of these income transfers – the requalification and wage subsidy programmes – can be considered as active labour market policy, whereas the others are passive: they compensate people for not working. Women – who comprised 49 per cent of the 1989 labour force – have a disproportionally low share in active labour market programmes, and a disproportionally high share in unemployment (64 per cent). As for the elderly, those taking – or having already taken – early retirement are added to by those of retirement age who were still working in 1989 and who practically disappeared from the labour market. All in all, early exit has reduced the 1989 workforce by about one-tenth.

These data show how strongly the removal of workers from the workforce has been structured along the lines of gender and age. However, qualification level also has a strong effect, as demonstrated most convincingly by longitudinal data on the 'working-age' population (i.e. age 16–59) from the German Socio-Economic Panel analysed in terms of changes between 1990 and 1994 (Holst and Schupp, 1995: 404). Of all men employed in 1990, 71 per cent were still employed four years later; for women, the figure was 60 per cent. Hardest hit were the unskilled workers, among whom only 50 per cent of the men and 37 per cent of the women remained employed. For skilled workers, the respective proportions were 77 per cent (for men) and 48 per cent (for women), and, for qualified white-collar employees, 68 per cent (for men) and 69 per cent (for women). This is not to say that all those not employed any more were completely lacking any enterprise social protection; it is likely that some of them received, for example, occupational pensions or some form of severance pay. But, by and large, these former workers had moved into the care of the state, or of their own family and savings.

The transition process: mechanisms

The transition to new stable jobs

As mentioned before, in spite of this massive downsizing of the labour force, the first transition mechanism – remaining in employment – is still the most frequent one. Here, the question of which social protection functions are shed by the enterprise in the transition process, which ones are retained, and which ones are added has its most direct relevance.

A natural approach to the study of changes in the enterprise portfolio of social protection functions for those who remain employed would be to quantify the input (in terms of the share of the 'social wage' in enterprise budgets, or of the proportion of enterprise to public social protection spending) and the output (in terms of what workers receive) at an aggregate level, either for the whole economy or for a representative sample of enterprises. Owing to a lack of the relevant data, this is at present not possible for the GDR. Moreover, such an aggregate approach would necessarily give only a rather crude picture and needs to be complemented by enterprise-level case-studies.

A recently completed study (Kohli, 1995) can provide an example of the latter (see also the cases presented by Schuster and Stieler, 1994). The case is one of a railway security equipment enterprise that in 1989 had 2,800 workers, with products that were advanced enough to go partly for export (mainly to Eastern Europe, but to some extent also to the West) but were produced at low levels of productivity with out-of-date capital stock. As early as the end of 1989, the management had made contact with S. (its major West German competitor and one of the traditional mainstays of the West German electrical engineering industry) with a view to acquiring new capital and technology. After a period of increasing cooperation, the Treuhandanstalt sold the enterprise in January 1991 to S., which had to guarantee a minimum of 1,200 jobs and DM 145 million investments; and in 1992, the enterprise was fully integrated into the S. corporation. At the time of our study (the end of 1993), the enterprise still employed 1,300 workers. They earned the industry-wide standard of 80 per cent of the West German wage level, but, including some enterprise bonuses, the real wage was about 86 per cent.

In terms of the portfolio of social protection, the main process is one of massive reduction. Most of the social benefits that the GDR enterprise had provided for its workers were shed. The policlinic was sized down to a small ambulance for work-related health problems and accidents, the kindergarten was divested to the city (which took over its employees), and the dentist became self-employed. A similar pattern was put into effect with auxiliary production functions such as transport. Several former employees became self-employed and took over these functions, with some capital support by the enterprise (e.g. for buying the former enterprise-owned trucks) and some guarantee that they would keep the business from the enterprise at least in their start-up phase. Thus, a strategy of out-sourcing was followed for both production-related and welfare functions.

On the other hand, there has been one main addition to the portfolio of social protection functions, namely, enterprise-level occupational pensions (to complement public pension insurance). Like most large West German enterprises – and especially the more traditional ones – S. has an extensive enterprise-specific plan that is an important part of the social wage, and as such can be an issue in wage negotiations. A key question for the East German workers has been whether seniority status attained in the former GDR enterprise would be honoured under the new ownership, in terms both of direct wage bonuses and of enterprise pensions. (Moreover, seniority status has a direct bearing on a range of other dimensions of the work contract and work situation of the individual, including, for instance, eligibility for job protection, early retirement, and severance pay.) S. has decided on a compromise: to base the bonuses for long-term enterprise membership on the real tenure in the old enterprise, and to set October 1992 as the base point for enterprise pension claims (which had not existed in the GDR).

The transition to an intermediate organizational framework

The second transition mechanism is of a very different nature. It is a departure from 'normal' employment in enterprises, being contingent on a special institutional framework that is only rarely found but that may be of interest much beyond its present low frequency as a model for future possibilities. In East Germany, the transition of workers from their former enterprise to an intermediate organization in a 'second labour market' mostly occurs in the framework of the 'wage-cost subsidies' programme, one of the active labour market programmes funded as part of the federal Labour Promotion Act. It currently comprises slightly more than 100,000 workers. While the larger and more traditional job creation programme ('ABM') consists of wage subsidies or wage replacement for workers employed in normal enterprises, the 'wage-cost subsidies' are usually given to special organizations in which several actors – private enterprises as well as public and third-sector ('civil society') agencies – cooperate. Workers are employed to perform tasks – for example in environmental clean-ups, social services, or cultural work – and benefit from the normal range of employment-related social protection. Cooperation between different institutional actors is even necessary in terms of financing; the public 'wage-cost subsidies' programme pays only the average level of unemployment benefits, so that pay needs to be supplemented by other sources.

Interest in these intermediate organizational forms comes from two sides: from the field of labour market policy and from that of industrial relations (see Teipen and Willisch, 1995). In labour market policy, it is expected that these organizations will perform a bridging function. Workers who would otherwise almost certainly be shed from the labour force are retained in productive activities in an enterprise setting close to their former work, and can be recalled by their former enterprise if the need arises. 'Flexible coordination' (Schmid, 1991) in this sense is easier in decentralized local settings where actors can organize cooperation according to their specific conditions and potentials. In studies of industrial relations and governance, the flexibility gains provided by decentralization and regionalization are stressed as well. Networks of actors such as enterprises, local unions, associations, communes, and local branches of state or federal agencies can create a framework of 'local corporatism' (Hernes and Selvik, 1981) that is more flexible as regards employment and production than corporatism at the national level.

For enterprises, these intermediate organizations offer the possibility of farming workers out into 'waiting' positions or 'qualification loops' where some social protection functions are externalized to other actors but where the enterprise is institutionally and financially implicated as well, and retains a hold on the workers in order to be able to reactivate them for its own production. In East Germany, the extensive framework of labour market policy and social transfers has engendered a substantial number of agencies and associations in which much depends on local initiative and a willingness to cooperate. Local branches of the labour administration, of the Treuhandanstalt, and of the large voluntary associations through which some social transfers are distributed cooperate with enterprises, employers' associations, and union representatives to create a highly diversified 'second labour market'. It is too early to say to what extent it is achieving its goals, e.g. in terms of bridging functions, and to what extent it is simply a new and somewhat fancier pathway out of the labour force. But it is likely to create at least some promising and durable intermediary forms.

The transition out of the labour force

The transition out of employment is discussed here with a focus on early exit from the labour force. It provides an especially good example of how enterprises try to pass on (most of) their social costs to other actors. The aggregate data presented earlier highlighted the salience of the age dimension (alongside the dimensions of gender and qualification) in the

Table 6.3. Labour force activity rates by age and sex, 1989–92 (%)

	Age		
Year	55–59	60–64	65+
Men			
1989	93.7	77.2	12.5
1990	86.7	71.0	8.3
1991	69.9	29.9	4.9
1992	45.5	19.7	2.7
Women			
1989	77.8	29.7	4.6
1990	71.5	26.1	4.0
1991	35.6	7.3	1.0
1992	24.6	4.3	1.0

Source: Kohli (1994b), based on Socio-Economic Panel (East) (for 1989: retrospective data from the 1990 Panel), and own calculations.

process of labour force involution. The extent of early exit is visible in more detail in table 6.3 (with the more realistic labour force activity rates instead of participation rates).[9] In 1989, men aged 55–59 were still almost fully engaged in the labour force, and for those aged 60–64 the figure was over three-quarters. In 1992, their activity rates had decreased to less than one-half and less than one-fifth, respectively. For elderly women, the decrease was even more dramatic. Within three years, the labour market lost most of the women over 60, and a majority of those aged 55–59. Never before has the use of early exit to control unemployment been put into focus so sharply. In addition to this issue of the quantitative labour market balance, there are also qualitative issues involved – with regard to 'weeding out' those deemed unfit for the new market economy and those who are politically incriminated.[10]

A picture of how this has been achieved at the level of the enterprise is again provided by our case-study. In the railway security equipment enterprise, cutting the labour force by half has been brought about to a large extent by shedding working pensioners, by putting elderly workers into pre-retirement, and by externalizing auxiliary and social protection functions. In this process, the mean age of the workforce was reduced from 43 years (in 1989) to 39.8 (in 1993). For workers who went into pre-retirement, S. developed a rather generous enterprise-specific social plan parallel to the one in effect in its West German plants. It provided for a topping up of the 'age transition money' paid by the public unemployment fund (set at 65 per cent of final net salary) to 100 per cent for 1991 and 90 per cent for 1992. Thus, S. certainly did contribute to the social protection pathways out of the labour force that it used as a legitimate way of shedding its workers; but it also relied heavily on the social protection infrastructure put in place and financed by public actors.

On the whole, there are major quantitative but few qualitative differences compared with the Western experience in terms of the procedures by which the shedding of elderly workers has occurred (see Kohli, 1994b). These procedures consist of (a) eclectic use of social policy instruments to construct pathways of early exit ('bricolage'), (b) cooperation among the relevant actors – management, unions, the state, and the elderly workers themselves – in producing early exit, and (c) conflict among the actors (especially between enterprises and the state) over who has to bear the costs. The enterprises try to externalize the costs by creatively using the social protection instruments that had been developed to cover specific risks such as unemployment or disability, and the state tries to change the rules in order to make the enterprises shoulder a larger part of the costs. A case in point is the West German conflict over the '59er rule', whereby firms have used a special provision of early retirement (at age 60) for the long-term unemployed by agreeing with elderly workers to make them unemployed at age 59 or earlier so that they then become eligible for this special provision (see Jacobs et al., 1991). This conflict is a telling example of the style of bargaining between the state, capital, and labour typical of corporatist regimes of industrial relations and economic coordination. It has dragged on for almost two decades now, and is at present again the centre of a heated political debate.

In East Germany, the state has shouldered a much larger part of the costs of early exit. The costs in terms of personal income are to a large extent covered by institutions at the national level (mostly by the public pension and the public unemployment systems). The main exceptions are special schemes of severance pay ('Sozialpläne'). However, in addition to personal income there is the issue of the social benefits and the social links originally provided by the enterprises – including those for retired 'veterans'. Some of the social benefits are turned over to the local communities or to the large private (but mostly publicly funded) welfare associations. Others are turned over to the market, or simply disappear (e.g. crèches, policlinics, youth clubs, or veterans' circles).

Conclusion

As shown here, East Germany has suffered a labour market involution that has dramatically reduced the share of the population that is able to benefit from enterprise-level social protection. Labour shedding has been especially heavy at the upper end of the normal work biography, duplicating the trend towards early exit from the labour force that has also been observed in the West but in a much more massive fashion. Moreover, the enterprises have also dramatically reduced their portfolio of social benefits for the workers who remain employed, while at the same time adding important new benefits such as occupational pensions.

This has created a new pattern of social protection that relies heavily on the institutional mechanisms and transfers provided by the West German system but with a somewhat different welfare mix. In terms of income replacement, East Germans shed from the labour force have to bear more of the costs themselves than would be the case in West Germany, except where an enterprise (such as in our case-study) provides additional benefits. In terms of the broader sociological interest in social relations and social participation, the new welfare mix also has obvious shortcomings. On the other hand, there is a range of new welfare institutions, organized partly by the community and partly by the large quasi-public welfare associations imported from West Germany. It remains to be seen to what extent these new institutions of civil society will be able to make up for what enterprises are shedding. But much of what had been provided by the enterprise is now likely to devolve onto the primary networks of family and neighbourhood.

NOTES

This chapter was completed while the author was a Fellow at the Collegium Budapest Institute for Advanced Study.

1 I use this term for what in English parlance is often called 'Central and Eastern Europe', i.e. all the European socialist countries east of the former 'iron curtain'.
2 This is what in the English rendering of Simmel's (1908) term '*Vergesell-schaftung*' is usually called 'sociation', or, in a more common but somewhat problematic term, 'social integration'.
3 A very special feature was the systematic link with the West whereby the D-Mark became a second currency, and pensioners were given the privilege of visiting their Western relatives.
4 Moreover, the East German case offers particularly good data possibilities, e.g. with data sets such as the German Socio-Economic Panel (SOEP) or the Berlin Life History Study that span the entire transformation period and comprise large amounts of retrospective data.
5 See Kohli (1994a) for a more extensive overview.
6 The same patterns hold for the other countries, with some differences due to the much larger size of the informal sector, e.g. in Hungary and Poland, where the available data on labour force participation rates (which pick up

participation in the formal economy only) give the impression of much earlier exit (see Keyfitz, 1992).

7 Moreover, the communes, with their very limited budget resources, depended on the large enterprises for their social and cultural institutions (sports facilities, leisure centres, theatres, etc.) as well as for their resources for constructing and maintaining the communal infrastructure (roads, housing, etc.).

8 The employment loss has been especially dramatic not only in the primary sector (agriculture and energy/mining), where Eastern levels were much higher than in typical Western economies, but also in the manufacturing sector: from 3.5 million in May 1989 to 1 million in May 1995. The situation today is one of large-scale de-industrialization of East Germany.

9 The data are cross-sections from the German Socio-Economic Panel. Its first wave of data in East Germany was collected in June 1990 (i.e. immediately before the economic union of 1 July) and included some retrospective questions on the situation one year before.

10 In his 'Song on the corrupted old men' – a bitter indictment of GDR gerontocracy, which had forced him into exile several years ago – Wolf Biermann's plea has been 'not revenge – retirement!'.

REFERENCES

Ernst, J. (1995), *Frühverrentung in Ostdeutschland*, Frankfurt/M: Lang.

Esping-Andersen, G. (1990), *The Three Worlds of Welfare Capitalism*, Oxford: Polity Press.

Ferge, Z. (1992), 'Social policy regimes and social structure', in Z. Ferge and J. E. Kolberg (eds.), *Social Policy in a Changing Europe*, Frankfurt/M: Campus, pp. 201–222.

Hare, P. (1994), 'Social protection and its implications for enterprise restructuring', CEPR/IAS conference on Social Protection and the Enterprise in Transitional Economies, Vienna, 25–26 March.

Hernes, G. and A. Selvik (1981), 'Local corporatism', in S. Berger (ed.), *Organizing Interests in Western Europe*, Cambridge and New York: Cambridge University Press, pp. 103–119.

Holst, E. and J. Schupp (1995), 'Aspekte der Arbeitsmarktentwicklung in Ostdeutschland', *DIW Wochenbericht* 23/95, 401–410.

Jacobs, K., M. Kohli, and M. Rein (1991), 'Germany: The diversity of pathways', in M. Kohli, M. Rein, A.-M. Guilllemard, and H. van Gunsteren (eds.), *Time for Retirement: Comparative Studies of Early Exit from the Labor Force*. Cambridge and New York: Cambridge University Press, pp. 181–221.

Jowitt, K. (1983), 'Soviet neotraditionalism: The political corruption of a Leninist regime', *Soviet Studies* 35, 275–297.

Keyfitz, N. (1992), 'Retirement in industrial societies: East and West'. Paper prepared for Workshop on Social Protection and Economic Transformation, Laxenburg (Austria), 11–13 June.

Kohli, M. (1994a), 'Die DDR als Arbeitsgesellschaft? Arbeit, Lebenslauf und soziale Differenzierung', in H. Kaelble, J. Kocka, and H. Zwahr (eds.), *Sozialgeschichte der DDR*, Stuttgart: Klett-Cotta, pp. 31–61.

(1994b), 'Work and retirement: A comparative perspective', in M. W. Riley, R. Kahn, and A. Foner (eds.), *Age and Structural Lag: Society's Failure to Provide Meaningful Opportunities in Work, Family, and Leisure*, New York: Wiley, pp. 80–106.

(ed.) (1995), *Möglichkeiten und Probleme einer Flexibilisierung des Übergangs in den Ruhestand*, Berlin: Freie Universität (project report).

Kohli, M., M. Rein, A.-M. Guilllemard, and H. van Gunsteren (eds.) (1991), *Time for Retirement: Comparative Studies of Early Exit from the Labor Force*, Cambridge and New York: Cambridge University Press.

Kolberg, J. E. (ed.) (1992), *The Study of Welfare State Regimes*, New York: Sharpe.

Kornai, J. (1980), *Economics of Shortage*, Amsterdam: North-Holland.

Machonin, P. (1993), 'The social structure of Soviet-type societies, its collapse and legacy', *Czech Sociological Review* 1, 231–249.

Naschold, F. and B. de Vroom (eds.) (1994), *Regulating Employment and Welfare: Company and National Policies of Labour Force Participation at the End of Worklife in Industrial Countries*, Berlin and New York: de Gruyter.

Offe, C. (1994), *Der Tunnel am Ende des Lichts*, Frankfurt/M: Campus.

Rys, V. (1993), 'Social security reform in Central Europe: Issues and strategies', *Journal of European Social Policy* 3, 163–175.

Schmid, G. (1991), 'Flexible Koordination: Instrumentarium erfolgreicher Beschäftigungspolitik aus internationaler Perspektive', WZB Discussion Paper FS I 91–8. Berlin: WZB.

Schuster, M. and B. Stieler (1994), 'Former East Germany: From plan to market and the dramatic effect on exit', in F. Naschold and B. de Vroom (eds.), *Regulating Employment and Welfare: Company and National Policies of Labour Force Participation at the End of Worklife in Industrial Countries*, Berlin and New York: de Gruyter, pp. 309–362.

Simmel, G. (1908), *Soziologie*, Leipzig: Duncker & Humblot.

Teipen, C. (1992), 'Von der Veteranenbetreuung zur Seniorenarbeit: Gewerkschaften und Rentnerinnen in den neuen Bundesländern', Berlin, Freie Universität, unpublished diploma thesis.

Teipen, C. and A. Willisch (1995), *Dezentralisierung von Großunternehmen und regionale Verflechtungen von arbeitspolitischen Akteuren: Die Auswirkungen institutioneller Reorganisation auf den Übergang in den Ruhestand*, Forschungsgruppe Altern und Lebenslauf (FALL), Forschungsbericht 52, Berlin: Freie Universität.

Wagner, G. and J. Schupp (1991), 'Die Sozial- und Arbeitsmarktstruktur in der DDR und in Ostdeutschland – Methodische Grundlagen und ausgewählte Ergebnisse', in Projektgruppe 'Das Sozio-ökonomische Panel' (eds.), *Lebenslagen im Wandel: Basisdaten und -analysen zur Entwicklung in den neuen Bundesländern*, Frankfurt/M: Campus, pp. 178–197.

Walder, A. (1986), *Communist Neo-traditionalism*, Berkeley: University of California Press.

Winkler, G. (ed.) (1990), *Sozialreport 90: Daten und Fakten zur sozialen Lage in der DDR*, Berlin: Verlag Die Wirtschaft.

7 Enterprise social benefits and the economic transition in Hungary

MARTIN REIN and BARRY L. FRIEDMAN

Introduction

In Hungary as in other Eastern bloc countries, enterprises have given a variety of non-wage benefits to their workers, sometimes called the 'social wage'. We explore what has happened to non-wage compensation during the economic transition that began in 1989. During this period, the real wage has fallen and many aspects of enterprise operations have undergone change. This paper considers three broad questions. (1) How has total compensation and its composition changed during this period of restructuring? Have changes in non-wage compensation offset or reinforced changes in wages and which elements have been increasing, which decreasing? (2) What factors can account for the change? (3) Have enterprise non-wage benefits in fact served social functions in addition to their business functions, and, if so, has the social role of benefits changed during this period? This paper offers an exploratory investigation of these questions.

We have assembled several sources of data on non-wage compensation in Hungary. The data are generally aggregative. We supplemented these with six case-studies of individual enterprises.[1] These data are not sufficient for a rigorous investigation of our questions, but they help suggest aspects of these issues. Moreover, they help identify complications relevant to a full analysis and the data that would be required to deal with them. The paper is basically an initial exploration of the available data and of a framework that could help analyse them.

We first suggest a framework for thinking about the determinants of non-wage compensation and its possible social functions. Then, we use our framework to explore our questions using the various data sources. Finally, we consider the requirements for a more complete analysis.

Framework for analysis

The determinants of non-wage compensation

The primary actors whose behaviour determines non-wage compensation are employers, workers, and government. Enterprises can choose different packages of wages and benefits based on what they consider useful in attracting and keeping the kinds of workers they want. Thus, anything that changes the cost of benefits to employers could affect the design of packages. However, employers may not be able to set packages unilaterally and expect them to hold. Benefits affect workers in ways that influence their choice of where to work based on their own needs and tastes. In designing benefits, employers need to consider not only their direct costs but also the influence of benefit packages on their ability to attract and retain the kinds of workers they need. Finally, the interplay between enterprises and workers around benefits is also influenced by government. Government may affect the cost of benefits to employers and the value to workers through tax incentives. It may also affect the design of packages through regulation and mandating.

During the transition period, the changes in government policy may have contributed to an increase in the variability across enterprises as a result of the removal of government mandates. To simplify the issue, suppose that in the socialist system the government mandated all benefits. In this pre-reform setting, we would expect a high degree of uniformity in benefit packages across enterprises. Suppose then that the reform government rescinded its mandate. Left on their own, some enterprises would drop the benefits (or some of them) while others might find them valuable in attracting or keeping suitable workers. In other words, we would expect increasing variability across enterprises in benefit packages during the period of reform.

In fact, government policy in Hungary has been more complicated. Although old rules and expectations have dwindled, the government has actually introduced some new mandates during the reform period. But increased variability is still a possibility. First, in some benefit areas there may, indeed, be less regulation. Second, the government may not enforce its mandates or do so only selectively. Third, some new government initiatives are in the same areas as old benefits but allow enterprises more flexibility on how the benefits are delivered. As already indicated, some of the new regulations still try to encourage particular benefits, but allow enterprises more flexibility in the way they are delivered. Although variability may be expected in any case, the changing government policies could increase it across enterprises, either in kinds of benefits or, for a given kind, in the form of delivery.

Government policy is both active and reactive. Not only does government have its intentions, which may change for exogenous reasons, but it also reacts to the behaviour of enterprises, at least when it discovers what this behaviour is. Over the long run, this may result in cycles of action and reaction in policy. This paper, however, is concerned primarily with the transition in Hungary since 1989. This period has probably been too short for complicated cycles.

Our aggregate and case data sources do not permit a statistical test of the contributions of specific factors to the change in non-wage compensation. Rather, the discussion suggests issues to consider in our preliminary exploration of Hungarian data. On the outcome side, we should look for changes in the mix of benefits and the forms in which they are delivered as well as for signs of increased variability in these across enterprises. Concerning determinants of change, these may include the mandates, tax incentives, and regulations of government as well as reactions by government to changes in enterprise behaviour; the cost of benefits to enterprises and the rights of enterprises to control cost items such as infrastructure; the needs or tastes of workers; disequilibrium pressures such as those leading to the shedding of workers and its implications for benefits.

The social function of non-wage compensation

In discussing the determinants of benefits, government policies played a central role. Government, however, is one of the main interpreters of what is social, and its actions are likely to change as thinking about social responsibilities changes. It is beyond the scope of this paper to explore the mind of policy-makers, and there may not be a unified view on social needs and standards. Our concern is with what is done rather than what is said. We will examine benefits that could fit several possible social rationales. In particular, we will look for benefits that are a form of social protection, those that involve the delivery of social services, commodity benefits, and benefits that do not fit any of these categories. Enterprise involvement is changing in each of these areas in directions that give insights into the concerns driving policy.

The social rationale for commodity subsidies is perhaps the least clear, but in view of their extensive use we allow the possibility that countries might consider them to be social. As one possible rationale, in the socialist economy fixed prices created shortages in which some goods were not available at all in markets and others were in chronically short supply. Enterprise commodity benefits could serve the social function of making goods available. Enterprises were generally not the sole source of a commodity, but provided a convenient supplement to what could be purchased in stores. With the opening of markets, it might be expected that the need for commodity benefits from enterprises would diminish. On the other hand, the period of transition in Hungary has become one of rapid inflation. Although markets may be working, not all people can keep up with the price increases. The government might decide to offer commodity subsidies once more to protect people against the uncertain consequences of inflation (even though the hedonic wage theory of benefits suggests that, if real benefits go up, real wages may go down). Since these two tendencies work in opposite directions, we may be able to observe only the net outcome – that is, the extent of commodity benefits.

Turning to the role of enterprises in social services, in the socialist era enterprises were responsible for a range of social services such as kindergartens and nurseries that might be provided by other agencies in other countries. Sometimes these services were limited to employees of the firm. In other cases, they were available to the whole community, in line with the view that the enterprise was a social entity. 'The enterprises were not regarded as mere producers of goods ... but rather a place where people were brought together to participate in the process of socialization and to create a "new man"' (Kameniczky, 1984). If this view should recede with the progress of reform, enterprise obligations may also diminish.

Finally, enterprise benefits may include some that are forms of social protection. Social protection benefits tend to share the common feature that they protect people against risks of income loss. Of course, the fact of income loss on its own is not sufficient to establish the social need for protection. There are many cases of income loss for which countries offer no protection. Generally, the feature distinguishing income losses deserving social protection is that there is some form of market failure – generally an insurance problem. There may also be a distribution problem. Although government programmes are one way to provide social protection, many countries also rely on enterprises to perform similar functions in areas such as pensions, disability insurance, and health insurance.

We will examine the extent to which enterprise benefits in Hungary serve a social protection function. There are reasons to expect increases in the extent of social protection in enterprises during the period of transition. First, in the process of restructuring, enterprises have sought ways to shed workers, but this has resulted in an increase in some forms of enterprise social protection. Enterprises might have tried to shift workers to social protection programmes, a combination of their own and those of government. Or the government might have mandated that enterprises provide some form of social protection in exchange for being able to dismiss a worker. Second, fiscal pressures might have induced the state to cut benefits in its own programmes or shift responsibilities to enterprises. The changes may have affected the overall availability of social protection benefits as well as the relative roles of enterprises and government.

We have suggested several rationales for social involvement with enterprise benefits. These suggest a classification of benefits in terms of their possible social functions, those that are a form of social protection, commodity benefits, social services, and those that serve no social function. The extent of enterprise involvement in each of these areas may change, and we have suggested a number of reasons to expect changes. We will examine whether actual changes correspond with these expectations. The changes give an insight into the evolving social roles of enterprises.

Trends in compensation

To provide an overview, tables 7.1–7.3 present the trends in Hungary in overall compensation and its breakdown. The data were assembled by the Hungarian Central Statistical Office from the combination of 'balance sheet reports' submitted by enterprises and information from government on its employees. The coverage is thus all employees. Data are presented for 1987 to 1992 to facilitate comparisons with subsequent data, but care is needed for the period before 1989. Following the introduction of an income tax, wages were increased in 1987 and 1988. The apparent increase in real wages for 1988 reflects only this one-time compensatory policy and not a trend.

Table 7.1 shows that from 1989, when the transition began, there was a sharp drop of 23 per cent in the real wage bill because of rapid inflation. However, overall non-wage compensation went up during this period by 36 per cent, offsetting some of the decline in real wages. The net decline in total compensation was thus only 17 per cent. Table 7.2 breaks down the change in the real wage bill into the change in employment and the change in real wages per worker. It turns out that employment fell substantially during this period, declining by 13 per cent between 1989 and 1992. Thus, much of the decline in the real wage bill reflects the shedding of workers. For an individual who remained employed, the decline in the real wage was only 12 per cent. Moreover, the increase in non-wage compensation per worker was larger, 56 per cent. Thus, the decline in total compensation per worker was only 5 per cent.

It is risky to draw conclusions on the market offer curve of employers

Table 7.1. The structure of labour costs in Hungary: enterprise and government employees, 1987–92 (1987 Ft billion)

	1987	1988	1989	1990	1991	1992	Change (%) 1987–1992	Change (%) 1989–1992
Wages	301.80	439.21	434.60	415.52	357.24	333.31	10	−23
Benefits in cash	3.90	2.77	1.70	1.38	1.02	2.52	−35	48
Benefits in kind	10.70	8.05	6.22	5.17	4.55	3.80	−64	−39
Other wage-like income:								
from government	–	–	5.70	4.59	4.59	8.16		43
from enterprises	–	–	36.93	49.84	52.82	54.29		47
Total, other wage-like income	55.00	50.64	42.62	54.43	57.41	62.45	14	47
Total, non-wage	69.60	61.46	50.54	60.98	62.99	68.78	−1	36
Total compensation	371.40	500.67	485.14	476.50	420.23	402.09	8	−17

Sources: compensation data – *National Accounts, Hungary 1991*, Hungarian Central Statistical Office, Budapest, 1993; employment data – *Statistical Yearbook of Hungary*, Hungarian Central Statistical Office, Budapest, 1993.

Table 7.2. Real labour costs per worker, 1987–92 (1987 Ft)

	1987	1988	1989	1990	1991	1992	Change (%) 1987–1992	Change (%) 1989–1992
Active earners ('000)	5,589	5,548	5,505	5,472	5,304	4,796	−14	−13
Wages	53,999	79,166	78,947	75,937	67,354	69,495	29	−12
Benefits in cash	698	499	309	252	192	526	−25	70
Benefits in kind	1,914	1,451	1,129	944	858	793	−59	−30
Other wage-like income	9,841	9,127	7,743	9,947	10,825	13,021	32	68
Total, non-wage	12,453	11,078	9,181	11,143	11,875	14,340	15	56
Total compensation	66,452	90,244	88,128	87,081	79,230	83,835	26	−5

Sources: compensation data – *National Accounts, Hungary 1991*, Hungarian Central Statistical Office, Budapest, 1993; employment data – *Statistical Yearbook of Hungary*, Hungarian Central Statistical Office, Budapest, 1993.

Table 7.3. Labour costs as a percentage of total compensation, 1987–92

	1987	1988	1989	1990	1991	1992
Wages	81	88	90	87	85	83
Benefits in cash	1	1	0	0	0	1
Benefits in kind	3	2	1	1	1	1
Other wage-like income:						
from government	–	–	1	1	1	2
from enterprises	–	–	8	10	13	14
Total, other wage-like income	15	10	9	11	14	16
Total, non-wage	19	12	10	13	15	17
Total compensation	100	100	100	100	100	100

Sources: compensation data – *National Accounts, Hungary 1991*, Hungarian Central Statistical Office, Budapest, 1993; employment data – *Statistical Yearbook of Hungary*, Hungarian Central Statistical Office, Budapest, 1993.

without holding other variables constant. Although we are unable to do so, our numbers are at least suggestive about the adjustment process. The disequilibrium was addressed mainly by the shedding of workers. For workers who were retained, there was only a 5 per cent fall in total compensation. However, there was a shift in the form of compensation from wages toward benefits. One of the limitations of this argument is that the increased non-wage benefits included some that went to support the workers who were shed; compensation per retained worker probably did go down more than indicated here, although the table does not have a breakdown of benefits between shed and retained workers.

The percentage breakdown of total compensation is shown in table 7.3. Wages as a percentage of compensation declined from 90 per cent in 1989 to 83 per cent in 1992 because the non-wage component accounted for a larger share. Table 7.1 also shows that non-wage compensation was not a monolithic whole. It divides non-wage compensation into three parts. Cash benefits include items such as sick pay or leave and scholarships. Benefits in kind include crèches, kindergartens, sports, medical care, and recreation facilities. Benefits not in these categories are called 'other wage-like income'. This classification is not too informative, but it does show the sharply divergent patterns in specific benefits. Separate data for government and enterprise workers are available in the 'other wage-like' category, but not for cash or in-kind benefits. Given these categories, cash and other wage-like benefits increased by nearly 50 per cent after 1989, and benefits in kind declined by nearly 40 per cent.

The structure of labour costs in Hungary can be compared with that in

Table 7.4. The structure of labour costs for manual and non-manual workers in firms of 20+ employees in manufacturing, selected EC countries, 1988, and Hungary, 1992 (% of total labour costs)

	Germany	France	Holland	UK	Hungary
Earnings	56.3	52.2	55.1	73.1	45.0
Bonuses	9.1	6.5	7.7	1.4	7.1
Days not worked	11.5	9.7	10.9	11.4	4.7
Total, direct remuneration	76.9	68.4	73.6	85.9	56.8
Statutory costs	16.5	19.2	15.8	7.3	29.0
Total, direct & statutory	93.4	87.6	89.4	93.2	85.8
Customary expenditures	6.5	12.0	10.6	6.8	14.2
Social	4.3	8.5	7.1	4.2	7.3
Other	2.2	3.5	3.5	2.6	6.9[1]

Sources: *Labour Costs Survey: Initial Results, 1988*, Eurostat, Luxembourg, 1991; and *Labour Cost Survey 1992*, Hungarian Central Statistical Office, Budapest.
1 These include customary expenditures for travel, payment for special tasks, in-kind honorariums, vocational training, jubilee gratuities, payment for persons such as members of the board who are not on the normal payroll, and others.

European Community countries because the Hungarian Central Statistical Office in 1992 conducted an enterprise-based survey of the cost of labour, following closely the Eurostat survey carried out by the European Community. However, Eurostat data are available only for firms in manufacturing for 1988. Table 7.4 shows the structure of labour costs for firms with 20 or more workers in manufacturing for four EC countries in 1988 and for Hungary in 1992. Table 7.4 is thus more limited in coverage than tables 7.1–7.3 in that it excludes workers in general government, community and personal services, agriculture, the military, unpaid family members, and enterprises of fewer than 20 persons, covering somewhat less than 70 per cent of active earners. It also classifies costs differently, following the EC convention of distinguishing direct remuneration, compulsory or statutory benefits, and benefits that are customarily or voluntarily provided by enterprises.

Table 7.4 shows that total direct remuneration in Hungary is a substantially lower fraction of total compensation than in all the EC countries. However, statutory costs are substantially higher in Hungary. These include enterprise contributions to public social insurance programmes. Combining these, Hungary is only a little lower. On the other hand, Hungary is the highest in terms of customary benefits. In this category, Germany and the UK are lowest, while France is slightly behind Hungary. Customary benefits include some that serve only business purposes and others that may serve a social function as well. To

Table 7.5. Enterprise social benefits: all industries and manufacturing, 1992
(expenditures as % of customary expenditures)

Type of social benefit	All industries[1]	Manufacturing
Cost of welfare services	19.7	18.6
Grants to credit unions	0.8	0.5
Contributions to disability insurance	0.4	0.3
Contributions to early retirement	4.9	7.3
Severance pay	8.0	11.5
Sickness benefits	4.6	5.2
Cost and reimbursements of fares for travelling to work	6.2	7.0
Contributions to private insurance	0.8	0.7
Totally customary expenditure as % of total compensation	14.1	14.2

Sources: *Labour Cost Survey 1992*, Hungarian Central Statistical Office, Budapest.
1 Excludes general government, agriculture, small enterprises.

get a rough estimate of the breakdown, we assume as strictly business expenses items such as honorariums or payments to members of the board of directors of firms, travel expenses when at work, grants to cover the expenses of celebrations on festive occasions, and payments for performing special tasks. The remaining customary expenditures we label as 'social'. By this admittedly arbitrary standard, French enterprises offer the most social benefits, Hungary a little less, and Germany and the UK the least.

The customary benefits in table 7.4 are probably close to the total non-wage compensation in tables 7.1–7.3, although we lack information on the specific components in tables 7.1–7.3. One discrepancy is that sick pay or leave is included as a cash benefit in tables 7.1–7.3 but is a form of direct compensation in table 7.4. Another source of difference is that tables 7.1–7.3 cover all workers whereas table 7.4 covers those in manufacturing enterprises with more than 20 employees. The figures in the tables are close, but not identical as might be expected, given these discrepancies. Concerning days not worked, table 7.4 shows that Hungary ranks lowest among the countries in the table. In the UK, Germany, and most recently Holland and Hungary, the first days of sick leave are paid by the enterprise. In Hungary, the enterprise obligation has recently been raised from three to ten days, but it is as high as six weeks in Germany.

In view of the differences in coverage between tables 7.1–7.3 and table 7.4, table 7.5 presents a comparison of benefits between manufacturing and all industries for 1992. This table shows a number of specific benefits that are included in customary expenditures. We chose ones that might be considered to have social functions. They are expressed as percentages of total customary expenditures.

Total customary expenditures are about the same percentage of total compensation in both manufacturing and industry as a whole. This suggests that differences in coverage should not be the source of major differences between tables 7.1–7.3 and 7.4. On the other hand, there are differences in specific benefits. The biggest differences are in early retirement and severance pay. This probably reflects a greater willingness by enterprises in manufacturing to rely on exit strategies than other enterprises. Tables 7.1–7.3 and 7.5 all suggest · the importance of examining specific benefits because they may have diverging patterns over time or across industries.

We found limited data on the changes in specific benefits over time, which are presented in table 7.6. The data for 1987 were collected by the Ministry of Finance from the enterprise 'balance sheet' reports as well as from the accounting reports of cooperatives and public institutions. The data for 1992 are based on estimates made by experts drawing on sources such as preliminary tax information, banks, and social security reports.[2] The data source for table 7.6 has classified non-wage benefits into two categories: 'social wages in kind' and 'social wages in cash'. Both categories, however, include benefits that serve only business purposes with no clear social function. We tried to identify such business benefits, denoted by an asterisk and placed at the bottom of each category. We distinguish them from the other benefits that might have a social function and that we call 'enterprise social benefits' in each category. The total in each category we call the 'social wage', following Hungarian usage. All of these categories are in some degree arbitrary, but they help illustrate some of the differences among benefits.

The nominal data for 1992 seem to show substantial increases in most categories, but this was a period of rapid inflation, the consumer price index for 1992 being 2.89 times its 1987 value. When all values are expressed in 1987 prices, it is clear that many of the items have declined in real value, sometimes substantially, while others have gone up. Total real enterprise social benefits *in kind* went down by 16 per cent. In contrast, total enterprise social benefits *in cash* went up by 19 per cent. This left the combined total of enterprise social benefits of both kinds up slightly by 3 per cent. In other words, the total of social benefits originating in enterprises was fairly stable, but there was a large adjustment in the composition of benefits away from benefits in kind and toward cash benefits. If we had relied on the official categories involving

Table 7.6. Social wages in cash and in kind, 1987–92 (Ft million)

	1987	1992		Percentage change
	Current Ft (1987 prices)	Current Ft (1992 prices)	Real Ft (1987 prices)	(1987 prices)
Social wage in cash				
Sick pay	2,450	600	208	−92
Sick leave	–	10,000	3,460	na
Early retirement, disability	–	3,500	1,211	na
Social aid	970	750	260	−73
Travel disbursement	9,000	21,000	7,266	−19
Rent compensation	800	4,000	1,384	73
Food coupons	1,500	6,000	2,076	38
Clothing	300	1,900	657	119
Grants for the needy	430	650	225	−48
Earnings supplement, disabled	–	400	138	na
Subtotal: enterprise social benefits in cash	15,450	53,300	18,443	19
*Wages paid for holidays	28,000	70,000	24,221	−13
*Private car compensation	250	1,200	415	66
*Payments for foundations	–	6,000	2,076	na
Total: social wage in cash	43,700	130,500	45,156	3
Social wage in kind				
Nursery	320	480	166	−48
Kindergarten	400	630	218	−46
Recreation	2,900	4,800	1,661	−43
Culture	850	1,300	450	−47
Sport	1,500	2,400	830	−45
Social care	720	1,300	450	−38
Medical care	300	500	173	−42
Subsidized housing loans	200	3,000	1,038	419
Subsidized rent	1,500	2,500	865	−42
Uniforms	1,500	4,500	1,557	4
Subsidized canteens	2,800	8,000	2,768	−1
Private insurance premiums	–	2,000	692	na
Subtotal: Enterprise social benefits in kind	12,990	31,410	10,869	−16
*Training	700	1,100	381	−46
*Company cars	–	4,000	1,384	na
*Free shares	–	3,000	1,038	na
*Bonuses	8,000	14,000	4,844	−39
Total: social wage in kind	21,690	53,510	18,516	−15
Combined totals				
Enterprise social benefits	28,440	84,710	29,311	3
Enterprise social wage	65,390	184,010	63,671	−3

Sources: 1987 data – unpublished analysis of data in Ministry of Finance summary balance sheet reports; 1992 data – expert estimates based on detailed balance sheet reports from a report commissioned by the Central Statistical Office.

the 'social wage', this result would have been partly obscured. The combined social wage is fairly stable, down by only 3 per cent; the social wage in kind is down by 15 per cent, which is similar to the enterprise social benefits in kind; but the social wage in cash barely grew in contrast to the enterprise social benefit.

The finding of stability in overall benefits is probably a result of the time period. In tables 7.1–7.2 too there was little change in total non-wage compensation between 1987 and 1992 even though there was a big increase between 1989 and 1992. Unfortunately, the detailed breakdown of benefits is available only for 1987 and 1992. The important point, however, is that data on non-wage compensation as an aggregate do not reveal the divergent trends in specific benefits.

Looking at the detailed benefits, there are several items such as food, clothing, and rent that are subsidized both in kind and in cash. Whereas the real cash subsidies for these went up substantially, the in-kind subsidies either went down or, in the case of uniforms, rose much less. It seems that, rather than give up benefits during this period of reform, enterprises have shifted toward cash and away from in-kind delivery.

The balance sheet data are accompanied by estimates of public spending, termed 'social income', both in cash and in kind, although there is no breakdown on the public side. These figures can provide an estimate of the share of enterprise social benefits in total social spending, shown in table 7.7. The top of the table presents the calculations using the entire social wage as the enterprise contribution. The bottom uses only the enterprise contribution to social benefits, which in principle is more appropriate but in practice is limited by our ability to distinguish benefits that have a social function. Thus, our discussion should be considered only suggestive, based as it is on our particular designation of which benefits are social. Enterprise social benefits contribute close to 10 per cent of the total. For cash benefits, enterprise and public shares remained constant in 1987 and 1992, indicating that the public benefits increased at the same rate as those of the enterprise. For in-kind benefits, the public share rose: public spending in kind increased 15 per cent in real terms whereas enterprise spending declined. While the public sector was substituting for enterprise in-kind benefits, the data do not show which public benefits went up. Because of the decline in enterprise benefits in kind, the overall enterprise contribution went down slightly from 10 per cent to 9 per cent. Total public spending increased by 18 per cent in real terms. Although the majority of social spending comes from government, enterprises play a role that, though limited, may not be negligible.

Table 7.7. Employer and public contributions to total social spending, 1987–92 (current Ft million)

	1987		1992	
	Ft	%	Ft	%
(a) Social wage and social income				
Cash				
Enterprise social wage	43,700	22	130,500	19
Public spending	158,900	78	549,500	81
Total	202,600	100	680,000	100
In kind				
Enterprise social wage	21,690	17	53,510	14
Public spending	102,310	83	341,090	86
Total	124,000	100	394,600	100
Combined				
Enterprise social wage	65,390	20	184,010	17
Public spending	261,210	80	890,590	83
Total	326,600	100	1,074,600	100
(b) Social benefits and social income				
Cash				
Enterprise social benefits	15,450	9	53,300	9
Public spending	158,900	91	549,500	91
Total	174,350	100	602,800	100
In kind				
Enterprise social benefits	12,990	11	31,410	8
Public spending	102,310	89	341,090	92
Total	115,300	100	372,500	100
Combined				
Enterprise social benefits	28,440	10	84,710	9
Public spending	261,210	90	890,590	91
Total	289,650	100	975,300	100

Sources: 1987 data – unpublished analysis of data in Ministry of Finance summary balance sheet reports; 1992 data – expert estimates based on detailed balance sheet reports from a report commissioned by the Central Statistical Office.

Evidence on the determinants of benefit changes

We suggested above several kinds of variables that might be expected to affect benefits, including their cost to enterprises, the needs or tastes of workers, the pressure to shed workers, and the array of government policies that affect benefits. Unfortunately, we lack the quantitative data on costs and needs that would permit a full evaluation of the determinants of change. Instead, we first examine government policies that have played a major role in stimulating changes. Second, we focus on the hypothesis of increased variability across enterprises, suggesting the cost, need, and policy factors that might account for the observed pattern.

Government policy and benefits

Even in the socialist era, Hungarian benefit policy did not fit the simple model of the government mandating uniform standards for all enterprises. The Fajth and Lakatos paper (ch. 8 in this volume) provides details on institutional arrangements before and after the transitions. Before 1968, planners did determine benefits in considerable detail. After 1968, however, the planners specified a minimum welfare fund and enterprises had more discretion over how it was used. It is likely that enterprises took advantage of this to get around restrictions on wages; wages apparently were more tightly monitored than benefits, which became the easier channel for increasing total compensation. Although these employer practices may have increased the variability of benefit packages across enterprises, there were also elements of a social philosophy relating to benefits that might have encouraged a degree of uniformity.

Even in socialist countries, the link between general philosophy and practical policy may be sufficiently weak that there can be variations in the implementation of policy. Nevertheless, there were some prevailing attitudes concerning policy that may have influenced the direction of benefit practices. There was, for example, a view that benefits – both in general and specific types – enhanced worker productivity. In other words, there was a theory of motivation relating to benefits, and planned economies tried to encourage managers to follow the same theories. There was also a view that certain social functions were the responsibility of enterprises and that enterprises should play a central role in the development of a socialist society. These ideological views could have helped shape conventions concerning the appropriate design of benefit policy and so could have contributed to uniform practices.

We lack the evidence to distinguish the forces toward uniformity and those toward diversity in their effects on enterprise benefit policies in the period before 1989. However, the transition beginning in 1989 brought another major change as the obligation by enterprises to maintain welfare funds was eliminated altogether. Moreover, the ideological underpinnings that might have contributed to the old conventions for benefit policy may have weakened. There is thus reason to believe that enterprises may have acquired more freedom to design their own policies. On the other hand, they are not totally free. A series of new government regulations has influenced their actions. There are some explicit new mandates. In many cases, however, the new policies offer incentives that allow enterprises an element of choice. Consider some examples of government policies:

Mandates
- The state itself contributes toward payments for sickness, but also mandates enterprise contributions. In 1985–91 the enterprise was required to cover sick pay for the first three days of sickness. Since 1992, the government has been shifting the burden of payments toward enterprises by requiring sick leave for the first ten days of sickness.
- The state has mandated that 85 per cent of the cost of travel to work be financed by the enterprises for workers who commute to work from outside the city limits.

Incentives
- There is an incentive for food benefits in the form of a provision for tax exemption for food amounting to Ft 1,200 per month per worker. Enterprises take advantage of the exemption in more than one way. Many firms opt to provide their employees with food coupons that permit them to purchase food items in the chain store, Julius Meinl. Other enterprises invest in a highly subsidized canteen. Some do both.
- In the case of clothing there is an allowance that is tax exempt, but there is also a subsidy for uniforms. The government has sought to reduce the spending on uniforms by imposing more stringent standards for the items to be allowed as work clothing, but enforcement has been difficult. Itemized reimbursement invoices have been required, but, as table 7.6 shows, real spending on uniform subsidies continued to rise slightly.
- In 1991 there was a general household energy subsidy for electricity, gas, and central heating, but it was phased out.

The government has also been involved with the issue of shedding workers. On the one hand, there is an interest in encouraging enterprises to become more efficient even if this means shedding workers. On the other hand, dismissed workers may be eligible for unemployment insurance, increasing the burden on that system. To discourage dismissals, the government in 1991 mandated severance payments. An enterprise is required to pay from three months to one year of severance pay, depending on the years of service of the dismissed worker. As an alternative to outright dismissal, the government has also encouraged the use of early retirement. When enterprise reorganization requires a substantial reduction in employment, workers with three years to go before retirement can be offered early retirement benefits. The benefits are paid out of the public pension system, but there is a cost to the enterprise. It must pay 50 per cent of the early retirement pension and the state pays the rest. The state thus has been imposing costs on enterprises for dismissing workers while also opening new choices concerning forms of dismissal.

The extent of benefits and their variations

Changes in government policy and in enterprise costs have tended to affect all enterprises. However, the hedonic wage model of benefits suggests that different enterprises will respond differently to the same stimuli. One of the important features of the new regulatory environment is that in many areas enterprises have more choices. Government policy relies more on incentives than on outright mandates, although mandates do remain. Thus, we expect that the transition period should be characterized by more variations in benefits across enterprises. Unfortunately, our detailed benefit data in table 7.6 show only aggregate expenditures for each benefit type. From these data, we cannot distinguish changes that result because all enterprises change their benefits in the same proportion from those that result because some enterprises change while others do not. Instead, we rely on our case-studies for evidence on specific benefits. We look at the response of benefits to a changing environment, the factors producing the change, and whether the responses are common across enterprises or whether they vary.

Food

Food benefits are one of the largest benefit areas. At Ikarus, a bus manufacturing company, nearly 40 per cent of benefits were for food. Food benefits include both coupons and company canteens. From table 7.6 it is clear that the combination of these two for enterprises as a whole is a large benefit, but on average not as large as at Ikarus. It is also clear from table 7.6 that in the aggregate there has been a substantial shift to increased use of food coupons and a small real decline in canteens. On the other hand, the case-studies show that the shift has not been uniform across enterprises.

Given that enterprises now have a degree of choice between providing food benefits through canteens, subsidized coupons, or not at all, it is not *a priori* clear which option an enterprise will choose. Because of the tax subsidy, it is cheaper for an enterprise to give workers food coupons rather than wages, up to the limit of the subsidy. The choice between coupons and canteens should also depend on the relative cost, but this is more difficult to estimate. There are not only the direct costs of the food in both cases, but also indirect costs. For example, the availability of restaurants near the enterprise may affect the time required for lunch, which is a cost to it. Enterprises will choose the form of food benefit based on its full cost. But enterprises will also choose benefit packages in order to appeal to the desired kind of worker. Three examples illustrate the variety of responses among enterprises.

Ikarus allows workers choice. Individuals can apparently choose the subsidized canteen or individual food coupons. In contrast, Guns-Ansaldo enterprise, a producer of heavy electrical equipment, relies exclusively on its canteen. Guns is the Hungarian partner of an Italian enterprise for which high-quality food has symbolic and instrumental consequences. It tried to eliminate as many social benefits as it could. The canteen, however, was not only kept but improved. A three-course, high-quality meal is available for only Ft 40. The tax-exempt value of the food coupon is absorbed in the cost of the canteen and the firm adds a subsidy. This means that the food coupon option is not available as a direct benefit to workers. The third example is Dunaferr, a state-owned enterprise producing steel sheets and metal products such as radiators. It is a large factory outside of Budapest employing about 30,000 workers. It provides a canteen, but seeks to limit its use through an indirect form of rationing. Only half the workers use it owing to shift work. The meal is served only at lunch time, and the transportation schedule of returning workers to their homes by the company bus is not integrated with the timing of the mid-day meal. As these illustrations show, there is variation across enterprises relating not only to the cost of the benefits but also to the kinds of workers the enterprise seeks to attract.

Kindergartens

There has been a sharp reduction in enterprise real spending on kindergartens and crèches, as seen in table 7.6. A UNICEF report concluded that the reduction 'is fueled by financial difficulties facing most firms and by privatization of the sector which strengthens the profit motive and tends to reduce the average size of firms. Terminations of government regulations requiring enterprises to provide these services, and easing of public expectations have also contributed to their decline. In addition, with increases in short term supply of labor, enterprises no longer find it necessary to supply child care facilities to attract workers' (1993: 70). The argument about financial difficulties is not convincing because other benefits are increasing nonetheless. However, changes in government regulations and declining need seem to be relevant determinants of the changes.

According to the hedonic wage model, workers' preferences are important determinants of benefits. When workers no longer need a benefit – when it no longer has value to them – the benefit also loses its value to enterprises, which want to use benefits to attract and retain workers. Government policy is relevant to the extent that it allows enterprises to reduce the provision of the benefit.

In Hungary, there has been a clear trend toward an ageing labour force, and there has been a general decline in fertility. The crude birth rate per 1,000 population declined from 140 in 1980 to 110 for the first six months of 1993. The decline in enterprise provision of kindergartens and nurseries has been proportionately greater. In 1991, enterprises accounted for only 4 per cent of all the children enrolled in kindergartens and nurseries, and by 1993 only 1 per cent (UNICEF, 1993: 58). These numbers can be compared with the figures in 1970 when 10.3 per cent of children attending pre-school education received the service from the employer. On the one hand, this shows that, even in the socialist period, the workplace was not the primary vehicle for the provision of child care. On the other hand, enterprises have responded to the demographic change by sharply cutting back their involvement in this area. There has been a pronounced shift from enterprises to regional governments and more recently to non-profit organizations as sponsors of child care.

Benefits requiring physical infrastructure
A number of the traditional benefits of Hungarian enterprises required substantial physical investment including housing, vacation homes, and healthcare facilities, as well as the kindergartens and canteens already discussed. There is a general movement away from benefits relying on enterprise infrastructure investments, although the details differ by benefit and by enterprise. It is plausible to argue that the costs of providing benefits based on enterprise infrastructure investments are higher than alternative forms of delivery, although we do not have direct evidence to confirm this. However, the observed pattern of enterprises seeking to cut back such investments is consistent with the idea that these are perceived as high-cost ventures that profit-driven enterprises can no longer afford. Consider the adjustments enterprises have made with respect to infrastructure in several areas.

Housing. It used to be common for enterprises to build and then own dormitories for its workers. The dormitories accommodated primarily relatively unskilled workers who came in from the countryside to work. In the case of Ikarus, most of these workers were let go and the infrastructure sold off or put to other uses. This happens to be a case of substantial infrastructure but where it is not clear that the cost of the investment was the decisive factor in the change. The infrastructure was originally needed to attract and retain the rural workers. But since the enterprise shed its unskilled commuters, the dormitories were not needed.

Interestingly, enterprises did develop new housing subsidies, which seem to be targeted at keeping selected kinds of workers. Enterprises have subsidized middle-level workers by reimbursing their rental costs in the community where the company was located. There is also a programme to reimburse housing loans, but the funds involved are generally limited and appear to be targeted at upper-level workers. Enterprises seem to have avoided direct infrastructure investments in the case of these new types of housing benefit.

Vacation homes. There is a long tradition of subsidizing holiday homes for weekends and for summer and winter vacations. Almost all firms have these vacation homes and many have tried with varying degrees of success to get rid of some or all of them. There was an effort to replace this form of benefit with vacation subsidies. This is an area where the infrastructure cost may have been a dominant reason for the transition, but even here there were also considerations of how to use this benefit to attract and retain workers.

The move away from infrastructure in this area has been limited by practical considerations. The initial effort of enterprises was to sell their vacation homes. But this crowded the market with surplus hotels and a very limited number of buyers. This lowered their price and made the option of selling off the property less attractive. This led to a search for new alternatives. Contracting was one option, where the contractor would charge market-level rents. Another was to retain the property but to use it for other purposes such as training centres. These are apparently adjustments that may eventually lead to the sale of the property if market conditions permit.

As enterprises took away this traditional subsidy, it seems that many of them compensated workers by introducing cash vacation subsidies. This part of the story is consistent with the idea that cash subsidies are a cheaper way of providing vacation benefits than are company hotels, although this depends, of course, on the level of subsidy provided. There is, however, an indication that the old form of subsidy was targeted rather narrowly. The Tarki data show that only 6–13 per cent of workers nationally made use of the facilities. We found similar levels in our case-study at Dunaferr. The cash subsidy may be targeted at a different group and in this way may more effectively help the enterprise retain and attract the kinds of workers it wants. Additional data and tests would be needed to distinguish the roles of infrastructure costs and appeal to workers as factors explaining the movement away from enterprise-run hotels toward vacation subsidies.

Health clinics. Enterprises have frequently sponsored health clinics. There is a clear rationale for having a facility to deal with accidents or illnesses that originate at work, in other words with the health externalities of the work environment. Once the facility is in place, it may have a capacity greater than needed just to cover occupational injuries. Indeed, some enterprise clinics provided a broad range of general health services. However, it was also common for enterprise clinics to be run as a kind of joint venture with the local government: the enterprise created the clinic and paid for the facilities and equipment, but the local government paid the wages of the doctors, nurses, and medical personnel. A study using the Hungarian Household Panel data reports that enterprise health benefits have been the second most common benefit after meals. It found that 34 and 38 per cent, respectively, of public and mixed sector workers receive it, compared with 20 per cent in the completely private sector (Kollo, 1993).

In the new market-oriented environment, a tendency may be emerging toward buying health services rather than providing them directly. In 1993 new legislation was passed making it possible to purchase individual health care. If individual purchases become widespread, enterprises may decide to divest their health facilities, selling perhaps to private health providers or perhaps for different functions altogether. The national data from Tarki show that 20–38 per cent of workers receive health services through the enterprise. However, the data from Ikarus show that only 4 per cent of its welfare costs go on health, compared with 12 per cent for vacation houses.

There is some evidence that firms are providing workers with health insurance benefits, which supplement the health care covered by the public scheme. The future role of the enterprise in this area will depend on the nature of what is covered in the public insurance scheme. The less generous the public coverage, the more intense the pressure for enterprises to cover the cost. Moreover, as with food and clothing coupons, tax exemption will be an important determinant of the role of the enterprise.

Finally, local government may play a role in the evolution of benefits. If a company owns a health clinic (or sports stadium or swimming pool), the value of the asset is in part determined by whether the new owner can get a variance to use the property as it wants. This puts the local government in a strategic bargaining position to deal with the enterprise facility. For example, the government may impose restrictions on the use of the facility. We were told of a hotel in Budapest that could not privatize because the swimming pool had been open to the community and the potential new owners wanted the facility to be limited to the hotel's clientele. Historically, enterprises served their own clientele in Budapest, whereas in Berlin they were more likely to serve the general community, but there are exceptions. There have been other cases where local governments have invested in facilities that enterprises wanted to divest.

Benefits for dismissed workers

There has been a growth in benefits such as severance pay and early retirement. The determinants of these will be discussed together with their social functions in the next section.

The social functions of non-wage compensation

In this section, we examine benefits in terms of several possible social rationales. In particular, we look for benefits that are a form of social protection, those that involve the delivery of social services, commodity benefits, and benefits that do not fit any of these categories. The tendencies associated with these groupings offer insights into the concerns driving policy. We found data on the change in particular benefits between 1989 and 1992 for one large company, GE-Tungsram, which are shown in table 7.8. This offers a one-case illustration of developments in these categories.

Social protection

During the socialist period, social protection in Hungary was the responsibility primarily of government. Enterprises made social insurance contributions to the government, but the government was responsible for delivering most benefits. Since 1989, there has been rapid growth in enterprise benefits that could be considered as social protection. The new benefits, however, are used largely in conjunction with the shedding of workers. Social protection is generally defined as protecting people against the risk of income loss, and that is what these benefits are doing. Early retirement and severance pay have been rapidly growing enterprise benefits, and these are used primarily for workers who are being dismissed. As discussed earlier, severance pay has been mandated by

Table 7.8. GE-Tungsram compensation (% of total compensation)

	1989	1993
Wages	65.38	57.18
Social security contributions	29.10	30.03
Benefits		
1. Social protection		
Early retirement	–	4.35
Severance pay	–	2.61
2. Social & health services		
Child care	0.32	0.12
Medical care	0.57	0.22
Social support	0.27	0.14
3. Commodity subsidies		
Meal allowances	1.23	2.10
Housing support	0.02	0.16
Vacation support	0.09	0.03
4. Miscellaneous		
Scholarship support	0.11	0.01
Retraining costs	–	0.02
Sick pay	0.30	0.73
Legal services	0.04	0.04
Other	2.57	2.26
Total benefits	5.52	12.79
Total compensation	100.00	100.00

government, and the government allows pensions to be paid three years early when workers are shed in a reorganization, but the enterprise must pay half the cost. This is an area where government policy initiated the benefits, but enterprise decisions determine the extent of their use. The government has in effect set a price for dismissing workers in terms of benefits that must be given. Each enterprise then can evaluate the trade-off between the costs of keeping workers and the costs of dismissing them, where different enterprises may make different choices.

In the case of GE-Tungsram, these two benefits in 1993 amounted to nearly 7 per cent of total compensation and over half of benefits, although they did not even exist in 1989. It is noteworthy that Tungsram does not consider these two items to be 'social benefits', although it does report their amounts. Indeed, there are other benefits that it also does not consider to be social, such as supplementary pensions and supplementary death and disability benefits, which it does not even report explicitly as part of its compensation costs. We have data from Ikarus for just one year, but the only one of these enterprise social protection costs reported is pensions. There apparently are not standard procedures for identifying the social components of benefits, and the social protection benefits provided by enterprises are often overlooked altogether.

The high severance pay and early retirement benefits are reflections of the shedding of workers during the period of transition and are thus likely to be temporary. However, other developments may produce long-run changes in enterprise social protection benefits. In December 1993 the Hungarian parliament adopted an Act of Mutual Supplementary Pension and Health Insurance. The preamble of the bill provides a statement of the general purpose:

> It has become increasingly clear over the course of the past decade that the State budget is unable to cover the ever growing expenditures of the uniform compulsory social security system ... It has become clear that in the future only that system will be viable, which takes into account the principle of self-reliance ... financed by fees from the membership and by other contribution supplements ... the goal is the reform of the social security system ... by reducing the excessive role undertaken by the state.

Whereas the state has initiated increases in the social protection benefits to assist workers in the case of dismissal, the reforms in the case of regular pensions and health care do not seem to aim at an increase. Rather, the goal is apparently to shift responsibilities from itself to enterprises.

Social services

In contrast to social protection benefits, where certain enterprise responsibilities have been increasing, enterprise involvement in social services has been declining. Although health insurance is often considered a form of social protection, we classified it here along with social services, because the focus is on the delivery of health services. Insurance is social protection to the extent that it meets unexpectedly high medical expenses. Hungarian enterprise clinics began with a focus on work-related services. Even when they have expanded coverage, the government has shared in the expenses. Thus, we treat this sector as if the government meets the unexpected insurance needs, while the enterprise provides ongoing services.

In the case of Tungsram, all three of the items we list under social services have declined. Similarly, in table 7.6 nursery, kindergarten, social care, and medical care went down substantially. Child care has already been discussed; with the decline in fertility, enterprises no longer find it necessary to appeal to workers by offering this benefit. However, the enterprise reductions are greater than the overall decline in the level of these services. Rather, the enterprise reductions are part of a shift in responsibilities to other sectors – local governments and non-profit organizations. This is true of health clinics as well. Enterprises are selling their clinics or sharing them with local governments. There is a shift away from enterprise health clinics, but not necessarily away from health altogether, because other entities are substituting for enterprises.

With the 1993 legislation to encourage health insurance, the role of enterprises in health insurance, which is a social protection benefit, may eventually increase. But the change that has already taken place is in the area of enterprise-provided health services, and these have declined.

Commodity benefits

Certain commodity benefits have been big growth areas. Table 7.6 showed big increases in spending on food and clothing benefits, at least in the form of cash rather than in kind. The Tungsram case shows a big increase for food, but there is not a separate entry for clothing. A study using the Hungarian Household Panel data reports that subsidized meals are the most common benefit, received by about 68–69 per cent of public and mixed sector workers and 53 per cent of those in the private sector (Kollo, 1993).

The social significance of commodity benefits is not completely clear. We suggested that they may have been intended to assist workers facing market shortages. More recently, they may have served as protection against inflation. But they are large not simply because of enterprise business policy. The state has been actively involved in setting regulations and designing tax incentives to encourage their use. Whatever the underlying social rationale, they are a part – and a relatively large one – of enterprise social benefits.

Miscellaneous benefits

There are many benefits that do not fit neatly into any of the above categories. Sick pay in its original conception is social protection in that it provides income support in the case of income losses from short-term sickness. However, it is often used by workers simply as support for days not worked. In view of the extent of the moral hazard problem, we did not classify it as social protection. On the other hand, the government has been actively involved in financing this benefit. The increase in enterprise sick pay expenses reflects the government policy of transferring more of the responsibility for this benefit to enterprises by requiring them to pay for ten days instead of the previous three days of sickness.

Other miscellaneous benefits in the Tungsram case declined, as have many for enterprises as a whole.

Distributional impacts

One area where benefits may have social consequences relates to their distribution. We did not examine the distribution of benefits, but a recent study by Newbery (1994) produced a surprising finding. His focus was actually on prices and their decontrol rather than on benefits. He asked 'whether the price changes that have taken place since the tax reforms of 1988 have had an adverse effect on the distribution of purchasing power. The rather surprising answer is that changes in relative prices appear to have been uncorrelated with distributional characteristics. This is consistent with the view that the original set of subsidies and taxes were poorly targeted on distributional grounds, combined with the observation ... that there is little variation in distributional characteristics that would allow indirect taxes and subsidies much purchase on distribution' (1994: 7–8). There is some evidence to suggest that, as the subsidies were removed, they were partially replaced by tax-exempt social benefits in enterprises. Enterprise benefits may have offset the decline in the subsidies and this might account for part of the reason that Newbery does not detect distributional effects.

Conclusion

One of the major developments accompanying the economic transition in Hungary has been a sharp drop in the real wage bill amounting to 23 per cent between 1989 and 1992. Much of this reduction was accomplished by shedding workers during this period – 13 per cent of the workforce. For those workers who remained employed, the decline in the real wage per worker was 12 per cent. At the same time, however, real non-wage compensation increased by 36 per cent, or, on a per worker basis, by 56 per cent. The increase in real non-wage compensation per worker has offset much of the decline in wages, resulting in a net decline in real compensation per worker of only 5 per cent. Of course, some of the benefits did go to dismissed workers; thus the decline in compensation per retained worker may have been somewhat greater.

Although non-wage compensation as a whole has increased dramatically, not all benefits have moved in tandem. There have been large increases in some benefits – mainly those more cash-like – and large reductions in others – mainly those given in kind. However, the classification of benefits is inconsistent, with different benefits included in different data sources. Because there are such divergent trends across benefits, very different pictures can emerge concerning trends, depending on how benefits are measured. To understand better what these trends mean, we asked first what factors have determined the changes in benefits, and second what social functions enterprise benefits might have served.

Our case-studies suggest that enterprise benefits have responded both to the cost of benefits relative to wages and to the preferences of workers concerning benefits and wages. On the cost side, government has been active in reducing the costs of benefits for commodities such as food and clothing by exempting a basic cash subsidy from taxes. Enterprises have responded in varying ways, designing benefit packages to attract and retain the kinds of workers that seem most suitable to them. There has also been a clear tendency for enterprises to cut back on benefits requiring substantial infrastructure investment, which could reflect cost concerns – an attempt by enterprises to find less expensive ways to deliver benefits. However, the infrastructure cutbacks could also result from changes in worker needs and preferences, and cost considerations are likely to interact with the needs and preferences in affecting benefits. This study gives only a preliminary indication of the determinants of change because it is based on the qualitative evidence from our case-studies. More definitive results depend on collecting quantitative data across firms and performing more rigorous tests.

Our other major question concerns the social functions of enterprise benefits. During the period of transition, a realignment of social responsibilities has begun between enterprises and other sectors. Social protection, for example, had previously been provided primarily by government. But, as enterprises began shedding workers, government raised the cost of doing so by requiring the payment of severance pay. It also gave enterprises an incentive to use early retirement, but again enterprises would have to share some of the cost. Whereas enterprise social protection benefits have so far grown mainly in relation to the shedding of workers, new legislation is aimed at increasing enterprise involvement in supplementary pensions and health insurance. The aim apparently is an eventual shift in responsibilities away from government and to enterprises. There has already been a shift in costs from government to enterprises in the case of sick leave.

In contrast, enterprise involvement in social services has been diminishing. Enterprises have cut back on child care and health clinics. While enterprises have cut their services, other sectors such as local governments and an emerging non-profit sector have played an increasing role. Outside of social services, there have been similar enterprise cuts in cultural and recreation activities.

One large and growing area for enterprise benefits has been commodity subsidies such as for food and clothing. Although enterprises decide on these based on their business policy, the government has been actively involved through the tax incentives it offers. The rationale for considering these as social benefits may not be clear, but the involvement of government makes them a part of social policy.

Our study suggests that the period of transition has brought substantial change to the area of enterprise benefits, and has also initiated a realignment of social responsibilities between enterprises and other sectors of the economy. However, our results are preliminary and need quantitative verification. Our results also suggest guidelines for further investigation. Data on benefits should be disaggregated as finely as possible. This is necessary because different kinds of benefits move in different directions. It is also essential in order to detect the variations across enterprises in benefit policy. Clear standards are needed for classifying benefits. The current designation of 'social' is applied inconsistently. Narrower categories indicating social functions can give interesting insights, as we have shown. The costs of benefits need to be measured carefully and worker needs or preferences somehow identified. Finally, the behaviour of government needs to be carefully traced and, to the extent that it is endogenous, to be modelled. Future research along these lines should improve our understanding of the Hungarian benefit system during the period of transition.

NOTES

The authors would like to acknowledge the immense assistance provided by Andre Gacs, Ministry of Finance of Hungary; Judit Lakatos, Central Statistical Office of Hungary; and Agnes Simonyi, Elte University, Budapest. Any errors, of course, are the responsibility of the authors.

1 Three of the case-studies were carried out by Martin Rein and three by Dr Iren Stuber, PhD in economics, retired associate professor of the Semmelweiss Medical University, and author of several articles on enterprise-level social policy in Hungary.
2 The data for 1992 were compiled by Gáspár Fajth and Gyula Fekete from unpublished sources. The estimates are preliminary, but nevertheless interesting.

REFERENCES

Kameniczky, I. (1984), 'The improvement of the organization and incentives for cooperative labor: The case of the USSR and Hungarian industry', unpublished PhD dissertation, Moscow.

Kollo, J. (1993), 'The report of the Hungarian Household Panel, First Wave: Living in Budapest', Tarki, mimeo.

Newbery, D. M. (1994), 'The distributional impact of tax and price changes in Hungary', mimeo, 9 February.

UNICEF (1993), *Public Policy and Social Conditions*, Regional Monitoring Report No. 1, Florence: UNICEF, 19 November.

II Institutional analyses

8 Fringe benefits in transition in Hungary

GÁSPÁR FAJTH and JUDIT LAKATOS

Introduction

Fringe benefits have increased as a proportion of overall labour costs in Hungary, a formerly planned economy currently undergoing transition to the market economy. This is in direct contrast to the generally held perception that, as the communist system collapsed, so too would the important role fringe benefits once played in providing social wages. Nevertheless, the role of fringe benefits has shifted from social protection to incentives, affecting the various social groups unequally. Families with children have been the losers, whereas elite, highly skilled workers have benefited from the changes.

Using Hungary as a case-study, the paper will explore the role played by fringe benefits under central planning and why and how that role has shifted. Drawing on data from the first Hungarian Labour Cost Survey conducted in 1992, from the 1988 compulsory 'balance sheet reports' formerly filled in by all enterprises and institutions, and from a 1994 pilot survey of social wages conducted by the Hungarian Statistical Office, this paper will attempt to document the changing composition of social protection expenditures and fringe benefits in overall labour costs.

In this paper, a wide definition of fringe (or employee) benefits is used. Following the most broadly used concept, fringe benefits include all remunerations other than wages paid to employees as compensation for their labour, including those determined by taxation policies (OECD, 1998; Owens, 1988) – a broader concept than is usually employed in Hungary (Miszori, 1988; Mészáros, 1988; Stuber, 1993a). In addition, we include hidden wages and bonuses resulting in more unequal income distribution. Besides statutory and non-statutory social benefits or contributions, benefits in kind, and turnover costs, we tend to include items of labour costs accounted as 'mission expenditures' associated with business trips, and even 'payments to non-members of the staff', although

167

we could not always be exhaustive. Payments for time not worked (e.g. holidays seen as part of general working conditions in Hungary) are excluded from our numerical estimates, although in many countries they are regarded as core elements of fringe benefits (US Congress, 1988). For the most part, the focus is on fringe benefits paid by enterprises.

The role of fringe benefits during the planned system in Hungary

Under the planned system, enterprises provided fringe benefits for several reasons. First, employers were required to pay some of these benefits by government regulations, which also reflected political considerations. Second, enterprises provided fringe benefits for some 'special' advantage that wages could not grant – providing goods in short supply that were otherwise not (or not easily) accessible – and, after the 1968 reforms, that involved incentives of ownership or 'membership'. As in market economies there were prestige and public relations gains, and, quite importantly, efforts to avoid taxes. Moreover, because decision-makers are not simply neutral actors, but have their own personal interests, they themselves stood to gain from such benefits.

Under the old system, fringe benefits were rarely seen as part of firm-specific contracts because a clear separation between firms, party, and state was never established. Social and welfare services were provided in a collaboration among the main agents of the state: central and local governments and employers (state enterprises). Following this approach, fringe benefits provided by enterprises were extensions of government policy, not a replacement for effective government services. This argument – which was the official one – stressed the role of state (central) intentions. The issue of why some public benefits were allocated via state enterprises and not by the state administration itself received little explanation.

The provision of certain benefits and their linking to employment relations were certainly a precondition of the postwar economic development, which was based on the transfer of household and agricultural labour to industrial labour. This is true mainly of benefits providing social and public goods (such as kindergartens, training, health care, and housing). Yet fringe benefits had other functions as well. They were clearly an important tool of central political control in the communist regimes. Only (Communist Party dominated) trade union members were formally eligible for most of the benefits, and allocation was by a 'triangle' of management, party, and trade union leaders. On the other hand, even in 'classical' command economies there was some room for the many particular interests of regions, branches, and enterprises. This was even more so the case in 'reformer' countries.

In Hungary, central planners determined enterprise fringe benefits in great detail before 1968. After the 1968 reforms, planners manipulated enterprises in a less direct way by prescribing the compulsory minimum size of 'welfare funds' to be created from profits. The greater independence of enterprises in their labour decisions (however limited) and the drying up of both actual and potential labour reserves resulted in a new relevance for fringe benefits. Whereas wage rises were kept under strict control by taxes on wages and regulations on wage brackets, 'welfare funds' providing mainly in-kind services were tax free and less rigidly regulated. Fringe benefits therefore became an important incentive tool in the (re)allocation of labour, especially as wage competition remained limited owing to incomes policy and macroeconomic considerations.

As part of the 1968 'reform package' employees could receive extra cash payments ('bonuses') payable from profits. In the 1970s, party hardliners' criticism of the reforms led to the elimination of such profit-sharing. A new wave of industrial agglomeration launched at the same time, however, helped the spread of other benefits of a more welfare type. Moreover, political considerations gave preference in incomes policies to the 'working class' employed in large enterprises, in contrast to other social groups (especially cooperative peasantry, who were thought to be profiting too much from the reforms). Employee benefits again proved to be handy instruments for biased incomes policies.

Large enterprises were well able to use their social provisions (e.g. support for sports or cultural facilities, such as swimming pools or theatres) as a means of influencing local community decisions (e.g. on local infrastructure or on human resources) or, even more importantly, to gain local political support for central subsidies on which they always tended to rely.

The well-known privileges of high-ranking communist cadres (including, in most Central and East European countries, a second 'closed' network of shops and services) reduced the importance of employee benefits, because they were attached more to party or state administration rank than to a particular workplace. These privileges prevailed in Hungary too, but to a smaller degree than in other socialist countries. Also, because the market was more developed in Hungary than in other command economies, the provision of 'shortage goods' was less important, although still not negligible.[1]

Finally, it has to be stressed that, as well as employee benefits, wide-scale public welfare benefits were provided by central regulation, partly within the framework of social security, partly as universal rights.

Although holiday provisions, maternity and sick leave, sick child leave and parental leave, free health services, health and safety regulations, etc. affected production costs and labour markets, they were regulated centrally and hence were outside the control of enterprises. In Hungary these welfare provisions became more significant than in most industrialized countries, including many 'sister' communist states (Fajth, 1994) and the emergence of the socialist 'welfare state' made 'welfare society' (an expression borrowed from Martin Rein) less needed.

From the late 1960s, highly successful new programmes of social security such as 'parental leave' (extended leave available for either of the parents of a child up to the age of 3) started to empty formerly crowded nurseries. Improvements in public health services and a broader network of municipal kindergartens made employers' facilities less important during the pre-transition reform years. In 1986, 26 per cent of kindergarten and 14 per cent of nursery places belonged to employers, which was still a sizeable proportion but much less so than earlier. At the same time, two-thirds of organized holidays were to employers' recreation resorts, whose development has been accelerated. Almost all new houses built with preferential (fixed at 3 per cent) rate loans from the National Savings Bank received additional loans from employers at zero interest rates. Managers, industrial and trade leaders, party officials, and white-collar workers tended to capture an above-average share of such benefits.

Nevertheless, at this time 'welfare' employee benefits served the less skilled or lower-ranked broad mass of employees too. Enlarged workers' hostels and reimbursement of the expenses of commuting to and from work made it possible for large state enterprises to attract labour from less industrialized or nearby regions despite a frozen housing market. (People could own only one house or apartment per household and no rented apartments were readily available for ordinary workers.) Thousands of employees of large firms or important institutions had access to rented housing through informal ties between employers and municipalities.

Changes in the political and economic conditions of fringe benefits between 1988 and 1994

The radical political and economic transformation that gripped the region drastically altered the conditions of employee benefits in Hungary from the end of the 1980s. Several factors were at work.

First, government efforts to maintain the 'welfare state' (apart from employee benefits) entailed high new taxes (personal income tax, unemployment tax) or led to an increase in former wage taxes (e.g. the social security tax), which had an indirect effect on fringe benefits by creating stronger incentives for non-taxed forms of remuneration. Moreover, the provision of some benefits was passed directly to employers, enlarging the scope of statutory employee benefits (prescribed by law). At the same time, earlier central prescriptions concerning enterprises' 'welfare funds' ceased to exist, which gave employers a free hand as regards traditional employee benefits. In addition, revolutionary changes manifested in the ownership structure and the labour market led to shifts in fringe benefit policies.

Economic reforms accelerated from 1988, and the establishment of basic market institutions and tax reforms entailed massive deregulation. As part of the reforms, the obligations on enterprises to maintain 'welfare funds' were lifted. At the same time, labour costs increased as wages were 'grossed-up' with reference to the new personal income tax. Complete tax exemption for all welfare fund type fringe benefits was, however, maintained until 1990, when with the first free elections the former political system was fully terminated.

Since then the former party-state pressure on employers to provide in-kind services has been replaced by complete neglect of the issue. The end of the Communist Party state removed the ideological and political background for state support for social elements of wages provided at the enterprise level. Currently, the Ministry of Labour has neither a policy nor any staff working on this issue. The new Labour Code of 1992 deals with the issue in a single paragraph (No. 165) prescribing some very vague rules as follows:

> (1) Employers can support the improvement of cultural, welfare, health and living conditions of their employees. Such benefits are determined in the collective agreements, but the employer can offer further benefits as well. (2) If the work involves strong pollution of clothing the employer must provide uniforms for the employees.

The Law on the Civil Service accepted by parliament at the same time prescribed a wider range of social benefits for public servants. Even so, the most important changes reflected fiscal considerations and were to be found scattered in tax rules without any central policy coordination. The lack of a harmonized government policy was a handicap to the maintenance of the role once played by fringe benefits in providing social income. Concurrently changing tax laws became the prime determinant of recent developments in fringe benefits.

The general economic climate has not been favourable to improvements in employee remuneration: economic performance has considerably declined since 1988. Nevertheless, because output declined faster than public expenditures, the relative levels of taxation were maintained or even increased, and the motivation to avoid taxes became stronger. Faced with shrinking revenues, the government attempted to transfer some of the social security provisions directly to enterprises.

The new social security responsibilities have considerably increased employers' social burdens. Unemployment compensation has become widely available on a social insurance basis. The expenditures of the centrally administered Solidarity Fund were financed by contributions from employers (and to a lesser degree from employees) in addition to compulsory social security contributions. Redundancy payments, introduced in 1991, imposed direct burdens on enterprises laying off employees. Via other labour market measures, such as early retirement schemes, employers took on further responsibilities. In other cases former social security entitlements were enlarged: paid parental leave was extended and family allowances became universal from 1990 (only to be curtailed in 1996). Employers were also compelled to take on an increasing share of the administration of benefits and taxes.

Some of the cash benefits formerly financed through social security have been transferred to employers – which is clearly an indirect form of taxation as former government functions become 'decentralized'. The best example of this is sick pay. Prior to 1991, employers had been responsible for providing only three days of sick leave, whereas after this they had to provide ten days. In most cases, this would mean that employers now fully support employees on short-term sick leave.

The state also endeavoured to transfer the provision of public benefits in kind (mostly health and education) to local governments. Although local resources to cover these services are usually weak, the new law on local governments increased their fiscal independence by allocating some powers of taxation to them. New fiscal conditions as well as changes in the ownership and management of enterprises reduced the scope for using enterprise-provided fringe benefits as tools of local political pressure.

Within enterprise-initiated employee benefits the new economic context has clearly resulted in a shift from social protection functions to incentive functions. Non-statutory social security contributions (such as supplementary pension schemes) appeared, but did not gain much importance because the state had not radically altered its basic social security provisions.

The industrial restructuring and changes in ownership and size distribution of firms did not affect fringe benefits unequivocally. While fringe benefits typically provided by large enterprises, often with a social context, lost ground, others, mainly led by tax considerations and preferred by smaller enterprises, gained in importance.

Trade unions were preoccupied with their own transition and rivalries in the period investigated. The argument that selling welfare facilities can save jobs silenced those who spoke out against divestiture. (What has happened at Bajatex, a firm downsized by new owners, is quite untypical. Workers there have been able to win back from the State Property Agency their two weekend houses by claiming in court that they had been built through 'communist work at weekends' by the workers.) It was only recently, near to the end of the privatization process, that the largest trade union started to demand that trade unions should be able to veto decisions on the ownership of social services facilities when a firm is privatized. Many new proprietors wish to spend as little as possible on social transfers. A human resources manager at a newly established 100 per cent foreign-owned firm cited guidance from overseas directors as follows: 'employees must receive what is prescribed by the law here and what is truly necessary for production – and nothing more.' Well, the issue of what is 'truly necessary for production' is presumably interpreted differently for different groups of employees.

Changes in employees' bargaining positions have been substantial. Blue-collar workers or employees with primary or secondary education have been in over-supply since the transition started: by 1994 the unemployment rate had reached 12–13 per cent of the labour force, affecting almost exclusively blue-collar workers. In other segments of the labour market short supply has appeared: demand has increased considerably for highly skilled staff and managers, especially for those with experience in market conditions and with Western language skills.

At the same time, employees in higher positions have lost important fringe benefits that were previously provided not directly by the enterprises but by the party-state system itself. As a result of the transition, low-rent apartments, often in villas or city centres, allocated by the municipalities, private apartments sold at subsidized prices through the National Savings Bank, systematic training and monitoring, job move opportunities, subsidized leisure in party and trade union facilities, free hunting, and other political and economic benefits derived from their positions have been lost. This has increased the importance of employee benefits for highly placed persons. On the other hand, new opportunities for fringe benefits from enterprises have opened up. Since 1990, membership of the board of directors of semi-private enterprises has become a main instrument for providing fringe benefits to politicians or their staff, who are often in public service. New enterprises typically have executive boards to reconcile different owners' interests. By 1994, around half of former state-owned enterprises had been privatized. Privatization, however, resulted in only a partial sale of shares in most cases; the state kept some stocks and maintained positions on company boards.

The changing composition of social protection expenditures and fringe benefits in total labour costs of enterprises

The above developments suggest that conditions for fringe benefits have changed considerably in Hungary with the transition to a market economy. Data from the 1992 Labour Cost Survey allow us to draw some quantitative conclusions on the net effect of the changes. From the perspective of labour costs the outcome has been a modest increase in the welfare-related expenditures of enterprises and a large expansion in other types of employee benefits or fringes paid.

A large part of the growth in labour costs other than wages occurred with the increase in tax burdens or with enterprises' increasing their direct expenditures on social security type benefits and similar labour market services. The increase in such costs of 'welfare services' has been substantial mainly among bigger firms. Even larger than the growth of social wages, however, has been the increase in status-related benefits and in hidden wage elements, particularly among smaller enterprises trying to maintain a competitive edge in the labour market.

The main traditional source of information on enterprises was the annual compulsory 'balance sheet reports' that all economic units were obliged to submit to the planners and fiscal supervisors. Since these reports have been considerably simplified they became too aggregated to allow any conclusions on items of labour costs, so the Hungarian Central Statistical Office introduced a Labour Cost Survey in 1992. This survey covered enterprises with more than 20 employees outside agriculture (also excluding government) and allows only a partial comparison with earlier years.

According to the survey the average monthly per employee labour cost was Ft 39,600 (around US$500), while gross earnings amounted to Ft 22,500, or 57 per cent of the total labour cost on average in 1992. Statutory contributions paid by employers amounted to Ft 11,500, or 29 per cent of labour costs. They embraced

- social security contributions, which are imposed at a rate of 44 per cent on gross wages and some other items at varying rates;
- unemployment (Solidarity Fund) contributions, which were introduced in 1991 at 2 per cent of gross wages, but which had already reached 5

per cent in 1992 (and 7 per cent in 1993, but which were reduced from 1994);
- compulsory contributions to vocational training (1 per cent in 1992).

Finally, the per employee fringe benefits (expenditures other than direct remuneration and statutory contributions) amounted to Ft 5,600, or 14.1 per cent of all labour costs.

Wages certainly declined as a proportion of labour costs. This was due partly to an increase in fringe payments (discussed below), and partly to a considerable increase in the tax burdens on employment. In 1988, before the introduction of the personal income tax, enterprises paid 43 per cent social security contributions on (the considerably smaller) gross wages and the unemployment contribution from the above list was missing.

It is certainly not easy to draw a clear distinction between the different kinds of benefits as fringe or non-fringe payments. We use a very broad concept that includes all labour cost elements other than wages and statutory contributions. We do this partly for simplicity, partly because almost all such items may have a 'benefit' nature (even items such as 'payments to non-members of the staff').

If just 'traditional' or 'welfare fund' type fringe benefits are considered between 1988 and 1992, the data would suggest a growth or a stabilization in per employee expenditures. The so-called 'cost of welfare services' amounted to Ft 1,100 per employee on average, or 2.8 per cent of all labour costs. This group can be seen as comprising social benefits as officially declared. The Labour Cost Survey adopted the official (fiscal) classification of 'welfare and cultural activities'. In 1992 this group consisted of the following items:

canteen vouchers
housing support for employees
costs of childcare facilities
leisure and cultural expenditures including sporting activities
youth policy expenditures
social assistance, other cash benefits.

In order to estimate changes in expenditure on welfare services (welfare fund type employee benefits), we compared data from the 1992 survey with those from the 1988 compulsory balance sheet reports. Because reporting was different in different sectors in 1988, we chose the 'all industries' branch, from which detailed data were collected (this branch is broader than manufacturing industry because it includes mining and electricity supply). The ratio of expenditures from social welfare funds to wages was 3.9 in 1988 as opposed to 4.9 in 1992. The one-point increase seems substantial, especially if it is considered that several items paid under this category in 1988 have since ceased (state and party ceremonies, bonuses paid for voluntary work in the community, etc.). In net terms, however, the 1988 and 1992 levels were almost the same, because some taxes were already imposed on the above fringe benefits by 1992.

Table 8.1 compares the importance of different labour cost items other than wages and statutory contributions. We categorized the various elements into seven main groups according to their 'social' or 'incentive' nature.

In our view, besides the costs of welfare services, social security type benefits paid directly by the enterprise as well as some non-statutory payments have a social insurance nature. These items are grouped here as 'social wages'.

Social security type benefits provided by employers, often compulsorily replacing public provision, have become almost as important as the welfare services discussed above (see table 8.1). These items are almost all new. In 1988, only disability insurance (important only in the mining branch) and a small proportion of sick pay (paid by employers for the first three days of illness) were the responsibility of employers. As previously mentioned, since 1992 employers have had to cover longer periods of sick pay. (A recent increase to the 30th day of illness means that practically all the responsibility for short-term illnesses falls on employers at present.)

Rather generous severance pay regulation, introduced in late 1991, aimed to lessen the rate of dismissals and ease the burden of public payments on unemployment benefit (which is paid out of the Solidarity Fund). In 1992 enterprises had to pay 50 per cent of the costs of early retirement schemes in monthly instalments; now they have to pay part of it in advance in a lump sum, because many of them disappeared or stopped paying their monthly shares.

In the case of the proliferating private (health, life, accident, and pensions) insurance schemes, the state provides strong incentives in the form of tax allowances. The underlying consideration is similar to that in the case of statutory benefits: to lessen the pressures on public expenditure.

Social wages (groups (a)–(c) in table 8.1) are of growing importance in relation to wages or total labour costs. In 1992 they reached about two-fifths of all fringe benefits (and similar payments) or 9–10 per cent of gross wages and about 5 per cent of all labour costs. Even if the relative importance of the cost of welfare services appears to be just slightly higher than in 1988, new items added to this group confirm an

Table 8.1. Hungary: fringe benefits or labour costs other than gross wages and statutory contributions, 1992

	Fringe benefits		
	% share	As % of gross wages	As % of total labour costs
Social wages:			
(a) Cost of welfare services	19.7	4.9	2.8
(b) Benefits replacing public social security benefits	17.9	4.5	2.0
Sick pay	4.6	1.2	0.7
Disability insurance	0.4	0.1	0.1
Early retirement	4.9	1.2	0.1
Severance pay	8.0	2.0	1.1
(c) Private insurance schemes	0.8	0.2	0.1
Total	38.3	9.6	4.9
Other fringe benefits:			
(d) Wage-like elements	4.8	1.2	0.7
Benefits in kind	3.6	0.9	0.5
Jubilee gratuities	1.2	0.3	0.2
(e) Employment-promotion benefits	10.8	2.5	1.5
Vocational training	3.8	0.8	0.5
Reimbursement of expenses of commuting to work	6.2	1.5	0.9
Grants to trade unions	0.8	0.2	0.1
(f) Other staff fringes	35.2	8.8	5.0
Honorariums	3.0	0.8	0.4
Status-related payments	12.4	3.1	1.8
Business trip expenses	16.5	4.1	2.3
Other payments not elsewhere classified	3.3	0.8	0.5
(g) Payments to non-members of the staff	10.9	–	1.5
Total	61.7	13.3	8.7
Total fringe benefits	100.0	22.9	13.6

Source: Authors' calculations on unpublished data from the 1992 Hungarian Labour Cost Survey.

unequivocal increase in total social wages (between 1988 and 1992 their weight as compared with wages approximately doubled!). We shall shortly investigate the explanation for this increase. It should be stressed, however, that the share of social wages (here interpreted as the sum of traditional 'welfare services' and employee benefits replacing social

Table 8.2. Labour costs and fringe benefits by size of enterprise, 1992 (%)

	No. of employees					
	21–50	51–100	101–200	201–300	301–500	501 +
Earnings	54.6	55.9	56.6	56.7	56.6	57.4
Statutory expenditures	28.2	28.8	29.0	29.0	29.0	29.0
Fringe benefits and other labour costs of which:	17.2	15.3	14.4	14.3	14.4	13.6
(a) Cost of welfare services	1.9	2.0	2.4	2.5	2.6	3.2
(b) Benefits replacing public social security benefits	1.1	1.8	2.5	2.8	3.2	2.8
Sick pay	0.4	0.6	0.6	0.7	0.7	0.7
Disability insurance	0.0	0.0	0.0	0.1	0.0	0.1
Early retirement	0.2	0.4	0.5	0.5	0.8	0.8
Severance pay	0.5	0.8	1.4	1.5	1.7	1.2
(c) Private insurance schemes	0.2	0.2	0.2	0.2	0.1	0.1
(d) Wage-like elements	0.4	0.6	0.6	0.8	0.5	0.8
Benefits in kind	0.3	0.5	0.4	0.6	0.3	0.6
Jubilee gratuities	0.1	0.1	0.2	0.2	0.2	0.2
(e) Employment-promotion benefits	1.3	1.4	1.5	1.5	1.5	1.5
Vocational training	0.6	0.5	0.6	0.7	0.4	0.5
Reimbursement of commuting expenses	0.5	0.7	0.8	0.7	1.0	0.9
Grants to trade unions	0.2	0.2	0.1	0.1	0.1	0.1
(f) Other staff fringes	9.7	7.1	5.1	4.8	4.7	4.0
Honorariums	1.2	0.9	0.7	0.7	0.6	0.2
Status-related payments	4.1	2.9	2.0	1.8	2.1	2.1
Business trip expenses	4.0	2.9	2.0	1.8	1.6	1.2
Other payments not elsewhere classified	0.4	0.4	0.4	0.5	0.4	0.5
(g) Payments to non-members of the staff	2.6	2.2	2.1	1.7	1.8	1.2
Total	100.0	100.0	100.0	100.0	100.0	100.0

Source: Authors' calculations using unpublished data from the 1992 Hungarian Labour Cost Survey.

security benefits) must have declined within all fringe benefits, because other types of fringe benefits (especially items in groups (f) and (g) in table 8.1) demonstrated a rapid increase as the downsizing of enterprises, privatization, and deregulation gained momentum.[2]

'Other staff fringes' and 'payments to non-members of the staff' explained 46 per cent of total wage costs other than wages and statutory contributions. Items in group (f) were especially important: payments accounted as 'business trip expenses' alone reached 16 per cent of total benefits and 4 per cent of gross wages in 1992 (and in the construction, trade, transport, and real estate branches these figures were about double the average); status-related benefits (cars, clothing vouchers, and the like) were almost as important. These two items explained a larger share of labour costs than did welfare services and were almost as important as all social wages. Of course, they represent actual cost reimbursements in part, but this part was presumably quite small in 1992. Too often, these expenses are explained simply by income tax or social security and other tax evasion considerations. (This is also reflected in the frequent changes by which the tax authorities attempt to cover new 'fashionable' forms of tax evasion.)

These items, as well as honorariums (e.g. payments to members of boards), are benefits of the 'elite': owners, managers, directors, high-ranking cadres, and the like. 'Payments to non-members of the staff' often do not go very far if family members or friends of the owners of small enterprises are the recipients. Expert fees and the like typically still go to highly skilled employees.

The correlation between firm size and the importance of different types of fringe benefits is clearly affirmed by the data in table 8.2. Whereas the costs of welfare services or benefits replacing public social security benefits are more important in larger enterprises than in smaller firms, the items that we call 'wage-like elements' and 'employment-promotion benefits' reveal no differences by size of firms. Finally, status-related payments, business trip expenses, and payments to non-members of the staff are far more important in smaller than in larger firms.

Recent trends in the welfare policies of enterprises

The majority of enterprises still see the provision of welfare services as an important part of their human resource policies, according to a 1994 pilot survey of the traditional welfare services of enterprises implemented by the Labour Division of the Hungarian Statistical Office. A small majority (somewhat more than 50 per cent) of employers reported that they give as much importance to welfare services as they did five years previously. Many of them, however, noted that present government policies are not favourable for such provisions. On the other hand, around 30 per cent of employers agreed with the strongly worded statement that employers should pay wages instead of such benefits. Around 75 per cent of employers interviewed still draw up 'plans' on social issues, although this is no longer compulsory. Trade unions can influence these plans, according to 62 per cent of the respondent firms (although in most cases this may be a formality). In 8 per cent of enterprises, trade unions have no control over firm-specific welfare policies.

Several firms interviewed expressed a desire to receive data on the outcomes of the survey, which, together with the relatively high response rate, shows their interest in the issue of fringe benefits.

The results of the survey of actual provisions affirm the increasing role that welfare benefits have recently been playing in labour costs. Total expenditures, in real terms, slightly declined in the responding firms between 1988 and 1993. However, on a per capita basis, expenditures on the traditional group of 'social services' increased by 17–18 per cent in constant prices while wages were falling rapidly. Employment declined by 25 per cent, which is above the national average, among respondent firms, and expenditure on 'social services' rose by 170 per cent in nominal terms between 1988 and 1993 (the CPI grew by 193 per cent during the same period). The growth in nominal per capita expenditures was over 500 per cent in around one-third of enterprises, was 300–500 per cent in another third, and decreased in real terms in the remaining enterprises (at 5 per cent, decreased even in current terms).

The results of the 1992 Labour Cost Survey, which grouped all 'traditional' elements of welfare benefits as one single item, are too aggregated to allow a deeper insight into the question of how enterprises reformulated their policies on specific social or welfare items such as childcare facilities, recreation, housing support, workers' hostels, meal subsidies, school-start aid, and similar occasional aids (included in group (a) in tables 8.1 and 8.2).

The 1994 pilot survey mentioned above included explicit questions on enterprises' policy approach to these fringe benefits and on the performance of different welfare benefits.[3] This survey revealed that the growth in real per capita social wages is mainly attributable to a considerable increase in recreational facilities and meal subsidies (in the form of meal coupons, which have become a common fringe benefit in the period investigated) and to the introduction of taxes on most traditional fringe benefits. On the other hand, benefits in the form of several formerly important items, such as childcare and cultural facilities and kitchens or workplace cafeterias, have been declining.

Crèches

About a quarter of all surveyed enterprises possessed crèches in 1988. This proportion had decreased by 7 per cent by the end of 1993. The reason for closures was partly the decline in demand as a consequence of the low birth rate and the increased use of parental leave. (About 70 per cent of eligible women apply for this parental leave at present, and at least 70 per cent of children under the age of 3 are cared for by their mother or father.)

Kindergartens

More than one-third of surveyed enterprises had kindergartens at the end of 1988. Over the next five years half of them were closed and one-quarter considerably decreased their capacity. The main reason for closure was again the decrease in demand, according to employers, although the majority of respondents also mentioned economic reasons. Some of the units have been transferred to local governments, but many, especially those in more populous locations, have been sold and now serve other functions.

Holiday homes

In 1988 86 per cent of enterprises possessed holiday homes. This facility traditionally played an important role in large state-owned firms. By the end of 1993 only 10 per cent of them had liquidated their holiday homes despite economic difficulties (and in a further 10 per cent capacity had been reduced). However, this decrease was smaller than the decrease in employment and in 30 per cent of enterprises capacity grew considerably. These services are used more frequently by higher-paid employees; because fees have risen as well, those with higher incomes have easier access. The majority of employers cover only a part of the cost – in most cases the extent is determined by the threshold under which it is free from social security contributions. It is a general experience that enterprises sell their holiday homes only when they are in extreme difficulties. Here again, a possible explanation is that it is the decision-makers who use this kind of welfare service more than the average.

Holiday homes for children

Child recreational facilities have traditionally been rare if related to other recreational services. The majority of them were closed between 1988 and 1993. Not only are children's holiday homes more costly in relative terms owing to the salaries of trained tutors, but also the responsibility is greater. With the transition, the majority of traditional forms of child recreational activities – pioneer camps, summer school camps, etc. – ceased too, and many parents are unable to pay for the new type of camps and holiday courses at the market price.

Cultural centres, libraries, and clubs
Such types of facilities (mostly libraries) were owned by 75 per cent of enterprises in 1988. This proportion fell below 60 per cent in 1993. Although the actual demand for the use of such facilities decreased in connection with changes in the leisure-time activities of employees, enterprises sell such facilities only where they are situated in a separate building and can be sold for a good price.

Sports facilities
Half the enterprises owned some kind of sports institution in 1988. Since then one-quarter of them have ceased to exist. Because enterprises usually supported mainly competitive sports, the decrease doesn't imply a similar decrease in the actual level of benefits for employees.

Workers' hostels
The number of workers' hostels and their capacity decreased rapidly between 1988 and 1993. About one-third of those existing in 1988 were closed, and in a further third the number of beds decreased. Only a few new hostels have been opened. Employers again cited a drop in demand as the main reason for the closures. The number of employees living a long way from their workplace in fact fell considerably. They were too expensive for employers and supply exceeded demand in this segment of the labour market. The quality of services has increased as a result of the fall in demand (e.g. six-bed dormitories were converted into smaller bedrooms). Firms in Budapest were able to sell their units at a profitable price (they often became cheap, low-star hotels).

Medical units
The majority of large industrial enterprises owned and still own medical units. The operating cost of these units is low, hence there are no economic arguments for their closure. On the other hand, their importance in health security is high, because quick and professional medical care can save lives. The importance of this facility is increased by changes in the general health insurance system. (The latter uses 'family doctors' as filters to lessen the burdens on the health service and this bottleneck can be avoided by using the services of doctors in factories.)

The survey also included other cash or cash-like items such as: meal subsidies (including food coupons), subsidized credit for home-building, contributions towards rental costs, recreational support, contributions to the cost of child care outside firm institutions, and social aid.

Meal subsidies

Meal subsidies show the largest increase although they also played an important role earlier. About 30 per cent of employees of large enterprises received such benefits in 1988 while in 20 per cent of firms this kind of benefit did not exist. By 1993 75 per cent of employees were covered and, even more striking, in two-thirds of enterprises everybody was covered. However, this does not entail a larger number of employees receiving a warm mid-day meal. In more than 80 per cent of cases, employees were given meal subsidies in the form of cashable food coupons (and in smaller firms there is no cafeteria at all).

The total amount of meal subsidies represented one-fifth of the welfare and social costs of surveyed enterprises. Enterprises provided Ft 800–3,000 as monthly meal subsidies, the value depending on their fiscal position in 1993. The most typical amount was Ft 1,000 per employee per month, because above this threshold employers were forced to pay social security contributions and employees were liable for personal income tax as well. This part of welfare expenditure tends to supplement wages and not to serve real social purposes – it is simply cheaper for employers to pay food contributions than to increase wages.

Housing credit and rental contributions

The number of persons receiving subsidized loans for housing decreased remarkably after 1988. In about 20 per cent of the surveyed enterprises, such loans were terminated, and in another 50 per cent the decline in the number of affected persons was greater than the decline in employment. Per capita loans were usually under Ft 100,000. This amount has not increased since 1988, whereas building costs have grown by 180 per cent. Employers are now granting loans almost exclusively on labour market grounds and not because of social considerations. (This also means that managers or other important employees are advantaged and may receive extremely large housing loans.) Contributions towards rental costs were never as widespread as loans for home-building and here no change is perceived by 1993 (as rental costs were not taxed until the beginning of 1994 this benefit was a partial substitute for workers' hostels).

Recreational support

The majority of employers contributed to recreation in cash as well, including for those employees using the firm's or the trade unions' holiday home.

Social aid
'Social aid' included the so-called school-start aid and special aids for
pensioners and was an important part of enterprise social activity in
1993. The number of persons involved did not change and the per capita
amounts did not keep pace with inflation.

Conclusions

The empirical evidence from different surveys and reports on labour-
related expenditures clearly shows the increased importance of fringe
benefits. Employee welfare benefits ('social wages') have declined in real
terms, but their relative importance to wages increased between 1988 and
1994 in Hungary. Fringe benefits as channels of employee reimbursement
are, however, now increasingly used for incentive purposes and less for
social purposes; and in any case they tend to amplify wage inequalities
even more than before. Moreover, the apparent increase in different
types of welfare-related expenditure is largely due to more taxes or to
shifts in providers (as happened with sick pay) and not to greater
provision. In addition, a large part of the increase in per employee
benefits is due to the drop in employment and the poor economies of
scale of many welfare services. The above findings on costs are not
therefore in contradiction with the findings that, from the welfare output
aspect, services from enterprises declined considerably.

Although this process has contributed to some new welfare problems
(e.g. the closing of workers' hostels has exacerbated the homeless
problem), so far it has not led to major dislocations in public welfare
(Fajth and Lakatos, 1995). This outcome has everything to do with
heroic public efforts to maintain the welfare state in Hungary – at least
until mid-1995. Most recently, however, this public policy seems to be
collapsing.[4] If the withdrawal of public programmes turns out to be as
radical as it seems now, this may have consequences for the need for and
appeal of some fringe benefits from employers. This seems to be an
appropriate time to rethink how public policies should address or orient
such developments: with the loss of the 'premature' welfare state, the
'welfare society' might well be more in demand.

NOTES

We are grateful to MaryAnne Burke, Fabrizio Coricelli, Peter Rosner, and
Viktor Steiner for useful comments on an earlier version of this paper. All
remaining errors, however, are ours.

1 It is worth mentioning that 'fringe benefits' played an important role in the

emergence of the private sector in Hungary. Reflecting the partial admission of the failure of the basic economic system, some changes in the social positions of employees have been allowed since the 1960s. Access to ownership-driven marketable production resulted in the widely analysed famous 'second economy'. The most successful initiative of Hungarian socialism, the collaboration between small private plots and large cooperatives in agriculture, started as fringe benefits received from cooperatives. Private entrepreneurship in the service sector and in industry gradually gained ground in a similar way in the 1980s in Hungary, giving employees a limited and regulated opportunity to make private use of the assets of public companies. With the transition to a market economy, such 'economic partnerships' were terminated or transferred into independent entrepreneurship (e.g. limited liability companies).

2 The items in groups (d) and (e) are presumably exempt from this trend. They are in fact special wage components rather than fringe benefits. Benefits in kind are mainly traditional extras, accounting for a large share of benefits in mining enterprises (free fuel) and in enterprises such as hotels and restaurants (free catering). They are significant in only a few other special industries (free beer at brewers, etc.). Jubilee gratuities, in contrast, were compulsory payments received by all employees after 30 years of employment; these payments were removed after 1992.

Some items in group (e), here called 'employment-promotion benefits', provide 'merit goods', and as such could be considered to be social wages. We prefer to leave these turnover costs out from such accounting. These items were traditionally important, but are now losing ground (perhaps with the exception of the costs of vocational training in some newly developing areas such as financial intermediation) as a result of overall excess supply in the labour market.

3 The questionnaire included three sets of questions on fringe benefits. The first asked about the size of employment and social service expenditures (in the same the official/fiscal terms as the 'Cost of welfare services' item in tables 8.1 and 8.2 did), as well as about explicit welfare policies. The second set inquired about changes in various facilities and provisions between December 1988 and 1993. And the third set of questions examined cash benefits. The sample was a non-representative but large panel of 185 large firms in industry (where social benefits are traditionally important). The survey was not compulsory, but the response rate was still above 50 per cent.

4 In March 1995 the government announced a set of stabilization measures entailing a shift away from universal welfare entitlement to targeted social policies.

REFERENCES

Fajth, G. (1994), *Family Support Policies: Challenges and Constraints*, Innocenti Occasional Papers EPS 43, Florence: UNICEF ICDC.

Fajth, G. and J. Lakatos (1995), 'The transformation of employee benefits in Hungary', *Economics of Transition*, 3(2).

Lakatos, J. (1994), 'Vállalati szociális tevékenység az átalakulás időszakában', *Statisztikai Szemle*, 72(8), Budapest.

Mészáros, J. (1988), 'A vállalati szociálpolitika változásai 1987-rol 1988-ra', *Munkaügyi Szemle*, 1988/1–2, Budapest.

Miszori, I. (1988), 'Az iparvállatok szociálpolitikai tevékenysége', *Munkaügyi Szemle*, 1988/10, Budapest.

OECD (1988), *The Taxation of Fringe Benefits*, Paris: OECD.

Owens, J. P. (1988), 'The taxation of fringe benefits', *Intertax*, 3.

Stuber, E. (1993a), 'A munkáltatói szociálpolitika', *Valóság*, 7.

(1993b), 'Van-e jövöje? -Eszrevételek a munkáltatói szociálpolitika és a költségalakuláshoz', *Munkaügyi Szemle*, 1993/7–8, Budapest.

US Congress (1988), *Congressional Hearings on Fringe Benefit Policies*, Washington DC.

9   Social security in companies

The case of the Republic of Slovenia

SONJA GAVEZ and MARINA LETONJA

Introduction

Under the Slovenian constitution, the government is obliged to provide and regulate social security for its inhabitants. In the past, the Republic of Slovenia provided a wide range of social security measures in comparison with other socialist countries. During the transition period from a socialist system to a market economy, the high level of social protection has been reduced and some changes in the social protection system have already occurred. However, the adjustment to these changes will take a number of years – some experts think about 20. Adjustment will also require changes in 30-year-old habits of thinking. In a new social security system the government will take on a different role: it will not only create the legal framework for the social security system in general, but also link elements provided by different (state) institutions into an integrated system. The system is based on the principle that each individual is responsible for securing social security for him/herself and family, while the government is responsible for creating the necessary conditions for making this possible.

Since 1991 a few laws regarding social policy have been passed in the parliament. They have been directly or indirectly influenced by the changes in social protection. The social protection system in Slovenia allows for a wide range of social benefits. The share of social protection in GDP is about 25 per cent, or half of public consumption.

This paper offers an overview of the social security system in the Republic of Slovenia and in selected companies in various forms of ownership.

The legal and institutional framework

The social security policy in the Republic of Slovenia was created in 1991 and was implemented by new legislation that regulates the social security of residents at the governmental and the employers' levels:

The Law on Pension and Disability Insurance
The Law on Contributions to Pension and Disability Insurance
The Law on Health Care and Health Insurance
The Law on Social Security
The Law on Employment and Insurance for Unemployment
The Law on Household Income

Mandatory payments by employers and employees

It is mandatory for every employer to pay several kinds of insurance for their employees. These payments are accumulated in two funds and in the government's budget, as follows:

- The system of compulsory insurance for pension and disability is regulated by the Law on Pension and Disability Insurance. The benefits (regular pension, payments for disability, family pension, early retirement payments, partial pension, etc.) are funded by contributions based on gross wages by employers and employees (15.5 per cent each), which are paid straight into the Pension Fund.
- Compulsory and voluntary health insurance is regulated by the Law on Health Care and Health Insurance. Compulsory health insurance contributions are paid by both employers and employees direct into the governmental budget (6.10 per cent of gross wages each). Employees and other residents can secure voluntary health insurance for themselves by paying contributions to the Health Insurance Company. Voluntary insurance includes contributions towards a higher standard of health care that are not defined by this law.
- Compulsory unemployment insurance is regulated by the Law on Employment and Insurance for Unemployment. Both employers and employees pay compulsory contributions (0.70 per cent each) direct to the governmental budget. In this way they provide the resources for the following benefits: cash benefits for those temporarily laid off, cash benefits for the unemployed, and cash benefits for socially endangered people (those on low incomes).

The Law on Social Security has restored and united the system of social security at a national level, made the system of social benefits uniform, tightened the conditions for benefits, and achieved pluralism in the provision of social protection benefits.

Table 9.1. Slovenia: the structure of social security contribution rates in companies, 1991 and 1994

Insurance	Payer	Contribution rate (%)	
		January 1991	April 1994
Pension and disability insurance	Employer	14.40	15.50
	Employee	14.40	15.50
	Total	28.80	31.00
Employment insurance	Employer	1.70	0.70
	Employee	1.70	0.70
	Total	3.40	1.40
Health insurance	Employer	6.60	6.10
	Employee	7.09	6.10
	Total	13.69	12.20
Accident at work insurance	Employer	0.00	0.50
	Employee	0.00	0.00
	Total	0.00	0.50
Maternity leave insurance	Employer	0.00	0.10
	Employee	0.00	0.10
	Total	0.00	0.20
Contribution based on net wages	Employer	12.00	0.00
	Employee	0.00	0.00
	Total	12.00	0.00
Total insurance	Employer	34.70	22.90
	Employee	23.19	22.40
	Total	57.89	45.30

*The structure of social security contributions and
of public sector income*

The public sector income structure in the Republic of Slovenia differs significantly from that in other European countries, particularly as regards contributions by employees, which are much higher than in other countries and almost equal the employer's contribution.

The total burden of the social security of employees is very high for employers and is reflected in the lower competitiveness of Slovene companies. After the introduction of the new Law on Social Security in November 1992, the total contribution rate towards social security paid by employers and employees was reduced by 12.59 percentage points, from 57.89 per cent in January 1991 to 43.40 per cent. In 1992, the contribution rate increased to 50.35 per cent and was then gradually reduced until December 1993, when it was 45.40 per cent. An additional reduction was made in May 1994 to 45.30 per cent (table 9.1). In spite of these reductions, the total contribution rate is still one of the highest in Europe.

In the three years 1991–1993 retirements accelerated owing to the increase in unemployment. Under the Law on Pension and Disability Insurance people can retire earlier. This resulted in an increasing number of pensioners and required an increase in the contribution rate. Funds for pensions are being provided by the economically active population, but because of the rapid increase in the number of people taking retirement, the relationship between the active population and pensioners has worsened. In view of this situation, some adjustments to the pension system may be required to achieve a lower burden on the active population.

Today, there are about 430,000 receiving pensions, compared with a total of 845,000 in the active population. Although the contribution rate has been reduced, it is still high and can probably not be reduced if funds for pensions are to be secured.

The sources of finance for social security

The main sources of finance for social security are still wages and other household incomes, with property gaining importance lately.

Public funds for social security come from two main sources: insurance and the state budget. Two public insurance funds have been established to administer compulsory social insurance: the Pension Fund and the Health Insurance Company. The insurance funds are totally independent and are not part of the state budget. They operate within the balance of state revenue.

In 1993, there were 61 different social benefits in the Republic of Slovenia. The majority were financed by the governmental budget (40), followed by the Pension Fund (16), the Health Insurance Company (3), and local budgets (2).

Total public sector income represents about 48 per cent of GDP. Contributions for pension and disability insurance (30 per cent) make up the biggest share, followed by contributions for health (13 per cent) and by contributions for employment (3 per cent).

Social security cash benefits

Under existing legislation, Slovenian residents can receive seven types of social benefits, classified into three groups:

(1) *Basic income*: pensions, cash benefits (e.g. for illness), and disability payments. The material and social protection of pensioners is

Table 9.2. The structure of cash benefits and their share in GDP, 1986–92 (%)

Benefit	Share in total cash benefits (%)		
	1986	1990	1992
Pensions	54.6	58.2	54.6
Unemployment benefits	0.2	4.3	5.0
Family care	7.4	7.3	6.8
Health care and maternity leave benefits	37.7	30.1	33.6
Share of cash benefits in GDP (%)	8.8	13.0	14.7

provided by pensions; the unemployed have the right to various cash benefits; and disabled people receive disability payments.

(2) *Payments based on special merit* (e.g. for those who served their country well during World War II).

(3) *Supplementary benefits*: scholarships, subsidies, and supplementary cash benefits.

The structure of cash benefits and their share in GDP are shown in table 9.2.

In the early 1980s, contributions to social security funds amounted to a relatively low share of GDP. In the period from 1986 to 1992 this share grew as a result of the increasing cost of providing pensions and, in the early 1990s, owing to the increase in unemployment. In spite of the increasing share of pensions and unemployment provision, the costs of unemployment insurance are still not high in relation to the number of the unemployed. In other countries with lower unemployment rates the share of unemployment costs is much higher. In addition, the costs of family care in Slovenia are the lowest in comparison with the other ex-socialist countries and with other European countries.

Trade unions' role in social security

The role of trade unions in the social security of employees in companies has changed along with the political and economic changes in the Republic of Slovenia. Trade unions have become a legal partner in negotiations with the government as they represent the interests of their members.

The main achievement of trade unions as regards the social security of employees is the Collective Agreement that was signed by trade unions, representing employees (Confederation of Trade Unions '90 of Slovenia,

Independent Trade Unions of Slovenia, Independence-Confederation of the New Trade Unions of Slovenia, Trade Unions of Commercial Banks, and Association of Free Trade Unions of Slovenia), and by employers' representatives (the Chamber of Commerce of the Republic of Slovenia and the Handicraft Chamber).

Trade unions represent employees and are an equal negotiating partner with employers. In the Collective Agreement some basic concepts of social security are prescribed:

- equal pay for equal work,
- the rights and obligations of employers and employees,
- overtime bonuses, anniversary gratuities, food and transport allowances, paid vacations, severance payments, payments of trade union's representative, etc.,
- conditions of trade union's activities in companies.

Each employer has to provide conditions for a trade union representative's work inside the company. Employees are members of different trade unions, but the majority of them belong to the Independent Trade Unions of the Republic of Slovenia. The position of unions is quite strong in socially owned companies and rather weak in private companies. As a rule, private companies are small and do not have union representatives among their employees. For this reason and so as to strengthen trade unions, the unions want to organize themselves in branches.

Trade union members pay a membership fee. Funds collected by fees are partly used for the social security of socially endangered employees (money for food, clothing, rent, interest-free loans, etc.). However, needs are usually much greater than the funds available. In addition, unions provide legal assistance, when needed, free of charge. They offer additional training for employees, retraining, and intermediate job search.

An important trade union role is the protection of employees in companies that have undergone bankruptcy. Before the bankruptcy is declared, employees have the right to obtain their salaries. If the salaries are not paid, after the bankruptcy has been declared the employees become creditors of the company in the bankruptcy process.

Social security in selected enterprises

The minimum social security of employees is regulated by several laws at the state level and by the Collective Agreement. In addition, a company can provide better social security for its employees by giving them

Table 9.3. Some basic data on the selected companies

Basic data	SOC	PC	POC
Number of employees (1993)	1,502	206	50
Year of establishment	1947	1963	1990
Industry	Production of buses and lorries	Medicine	Software

bonuses. The range of bonuses and their amount depend on the company's economic situation.

In order to highlight the functioning of the social security system it was decided to survey companies under various forms of ownership. Three companies were interviewed: a socially owned company, a publicly owned company, and a privately owned company that are active in different industries.

The socially owned company (SOC) was established in the early 1950s and was one of the biggest companies in the Republic of Slovenia. Before the restructuring process, it had more than 8,000 employees. In 1991, the company was reorganized into a holding company. Several divisions were established as independent legal and business entities, and the number of employees was reduced to 5,000. One of the nine subsidiary companies, the largest one, is the selected company, employing 1,502 people. Under the Law on Privatization, the company started to prepare a privatization plan and intended to finish the privatization process by the end of 1994.

The second company was established in 1963 as a company of special public interest and it became a public company (PC) in 1992. The number employed in this company is 206.

The third company interviewed was a privately owned one (POC) right from the beginning of its activities. It is a small company and employs only 50 people.

In all three companies the level of social security was analysed. In terms of the law there is no doubt that the companies provide an adequate level of social security for employees. Companies also respect and consider trade union requests on the basis of the Collective Agreement. The study attempts to find out what companies do to provide a higher level of social security. A questionnaire was prepared and interviews were conducted in the selected companies.

In table 9.3 some basic data on the companies are shown.

Social security in a socially owned company (SOC)

It was found that the SOC provides an adequate level of social security for its employees, as prescribed by laws and the Collective Agreement. In the past, the company offered a wider range of social security compared with today. The company used to be a part of a larger company and had its own canteen, in-house health service, and holiday facilities. The company created a Social Security Fund and a Housing Fund. In 1994, with the introduction of new accounting standards, the Social Security Fund and Housing Fund were abolished. Along with these advantages, the company provided interest-free loans or loans at a low rate of interest for employees buying or building a house. Today, companies are operating under market conditions and are reducing this expense. Therefore, the SOC avoids almost all costs that might affect production.

According to the results of the questionnaire, the company's monthly average gross wage (in 1993) was SIT 60,551 (compared with a monthly average gross wage of SIT 61,991 in this industrial sector). Overtime bonuses accounted for 15–50 per cent on top of gross wages for work within normal working hours. Four employees received additional average payments of a total of SIT 91,000 for overtime work.

However, as a result of a programme to reduce production, some employees did not have enough work. They stayed at home as temporarily laid-off employees. They received substitute payments of 70 per cent of their regular wages for the time they were at home. In 1993, 106 employees were laid off and earned a total average of SIT 34,000 during a period of six months.

Every employee received monthly food allowances of an average SIT 7,040. Transport allowances of SIT 3,818 were also paid to employees every month.

Once a year, employees receive payments for holidays (paid vacations) in the range of 60–100 per cent of the average Slovene gross wage. In 1993, employees each received an average payment of SIT 60,000.

For employees who have worked for 10, 20, or 30 years the SOC pays anniversary gratuities. In 1993, 17 employees received an average SIT 45,518.

The SOC also paid benefits for education. In 1993, 444 employees received benefits of an average SIT 3,474 per employee. The company also paid scholarships to students. In 1993, seven students received scholarships of an average SIT 11,897 per month.

Under the Law on Pension and Disability Insurance women can retire after 35 years at work and men after 40. Employees when retiring received severance payments of their average net wage of the previous three months. In November 1993, only one employee retired, receiving a severance payment of SIT 209,984.

In December 1993, two employees left the SOC and became self-employed. They received cash compensation for self-employment of SIT 315,924 per employee.

In order to reduce the number of unemployed a company can 'buy off' working years for its redundant employees. In January 1994, one employee received a prepaid retirement contribution.

A total of SIT 675,000 was paid to employees in allowances for work clothing (225 employees received an average amount of SIT 3,000 each per year).

Besides benefits and allowances regulated by the law and by the Collective Agreement, the SOC provided bonuses that offered a higher level of social security to its employees:

- It paid key personnel life insurance of an average monthly amount of SIT 7,200 per person for eight key people.
- It paid additional health insurance for all employees at an average monthly rate of SIT 887.
- It paid collective accident insurance for all employees at an average monthly rate of SIT 431.
- Before starting a job, each person has to pass a medical examination. The SOC paid an average monthly amount of SIT 19 for this purpose.

Social security in a public company (PC)

The public company in this survey is middle sized. As regards the law and the Collective Agreement it provides all due benefits and allowances to employees. In addition, it provides a higher level of social security for its employees.

The average monthly gross wage in the PC exceeds the Slovene average of SIT 75,362. In 1993, the average gross wage in the PC was SIT 135,019. In 1993, 21 employees received overtime bonuses of an average SIT 6,809.

The company also paid food allowances of an average SIT 8,840 per employee per month and transport allowances of an average SIT 2,288 per employee per month.

Once a year, the company makes payments for vacations to employees. In 1993, each employee received vacation pay of an average SIT 118,984. In 1993 the company also paid anniversary gratuities for 20 employees at an average SIT 29,150 per employee.

Know-how is a very important factor in this company. In 1993, 53 employees received benefits for education of an average SIT 4,500 per month, and two students received scholarships of an average SIT 8,375 per month.

In 1993, five employees retired and received severance payments of an average SIT 289,400 per employee. Cash compensation for self-employment was paid in 1993 to one employee only, who received SIT 687,000 (12 average gross wages).

Along with benefits and allowances the company also provided bonuses for a higher social security level, paying:

- additional health insurance for all employees of an average SIT 887 per employee per month, and
- collective accident insurance for all employees of an average SIT 430 per month.

Social security in a privately owned company (POC)

The privately owned surveyed company is a small company employing only 50 employees. It provides all benefits and allowances required by law and the Collective Agreement and in addition a higher level of social security for its employees.

The average monthly gross wage of SIT 99,623 in the POC in 1993 was above the Slovene average. The company paid no overtime bonuses but did pay food allowances of an average SIT 6,637 per employee per month and transport allowances of an average SIT 18,927 per employee per month.

Once a year the company makes payments for vacations to employees. In 1993, each employee received vacation pay of an average SIT 74,868. The company did not pay anniversary gratuities in 1993.

Know-how is an even more important factor in the POC. In 1993 all employees were trained and received benefits for education of an average SIT 10,286 per month. One student received a scholarship of an average monthly amount of SIT 4,050.

As well as benefits and allowances, the company provided bonuses for greater social security:

- The company paid key personnel insurance of an average SIT 186,000 for 21 key personnel.
- It paid additional health insurance of an average SIT 887 per employee per month for all employees.
- Collective accident insurance of an average SIT 430 per month was paid for all employees.

Table 9.4. The components of monthly earnings in the surveyed companies, 1993 (SIT per person)

Components of earnings	SOC	PC	POC	SOC %	PC %	POC %
Wages & salaries	60,551	135,019	99,623	95.6	99.9	100.0
Overtime bonuses	230	58	0	0.4	0.1	0.0
Cash benefits for temporarily laid-off workers	2,392	0	0	3.8	0.0	0.0
Substitute payments for redundant employees	156	0	0	0.2	0.0	0.0
Total	63,329	135,077	99,623	100.0	100.0	100.0

Table 9.5. Statutory payments by employers, 1993 (SIT per month)

	SOC	PC	POC	Contribution rate on gross wages (%)		
				SOC	PC	POC
Pension & disability insurance	9,816	20,929	15,442	15.5	15.5	15.5
Health insurance	3,863	8,236	6,077	6.1	6.1	6.1
Employment insurance	443	945	697	0.7	0.7	0.7
Accident at work insurance	317	675	498	0.5	0.5	0.5
Maternity leave insurance	63	135	100	0.1	0.1	0.1
Total	14,502	30,920	22,814	22.9	22.9	22.9

Comparison of results

In this section the questionnaire results from the three observed companies are summarized and the labour cost elements are compared. Tables 9.4–9.6 offer an overview of the components of earnings, employers' statutory payments and social benefits and bonuses. The absolute numbers (in SIT) represent average monthly values per person.

Table 9.4 shows that the socially owned company and the public company provided wages, salaries, and overtime bonuses to their employees, whereas the privately owned company provided only wages and salaries (there was no overtime work). The highest average wage was paid in the PC. It was 35 per cent higher than that in the POC and

Table 9.6. Social benefits and bonuses, 1993 (SIT per person per month)

Payments	SOC	PC	POC	SOC %	PC %	POC %
Benefits and allowances	17,182	23,646	42,170	92.6	93.6	84.6
Food allowances	7,040	8,840	6,637	37.9	35.0	13.3
Transport allowances	3,818	2,288	18,927	20.6	9.1	38.0
Paid vacations	5,000	9,915	6,239	26.9	39.2	12.5
Anniversary gratuities	43	236	0	0.2	0.9	0.0
Benefits for education	1,028	1,156	10,286	5.5	4.6	20.6
Scholarships	55	81	81	0.3	0.3	0.2
Solidarity contributions	105	0	0	0.6	0.0	0.0
Prepaid retirement contributions	9	0	0	0.0	0.0	0.0
Cash compensation for self-employment	35	278	0	0.1	1.1	0.0
Severance payments	12	585	0	0.2	2.3	0.0
Allowances for work clothing	37	267	0	0.2	1.1	0.0
Bonuses	1,375	1,619	7,699	7.4	6.4	15.4
Key personnel insurance	38	296	6,382	0.2	1.2	12.8
Additional health insurance	887	887	887	4.8	3.5	1.8
Collective accident insurance	431	430	430	2.3	1.7	0.9
Medical examination	19	6	0	0.1	0.0	0.0
Total	18,557	25,265	49,869	100.0	100.0	100.0

even 122 per cent higher than that in the SOC. Cash benefits for temporarily laid-off workers (owing to the lack of orders) were paid only in the SOC.

On the basis of the results of table 9.5 we can conclude that the employers' statutory payments for social security insurance were at the same level in all three observed companies (the total contribution rate was 22.9 per cent). The actual payments differed only because of the different bases (monthly gross wages).

The crucial part of the analysis is presented in table 9.6. The importance of the specific benefits and bonuses varies from company to company. Whereas the shares of some benefits (food allowances, benefits for education) are almost at the same level in the SOC and the PC, they are completely different in the POC. In the SOC and the PC, the share of food allowances is about 35–37 per cent, compared with less than half this share in the POC. Paid vacations have an important role in the PC (first place) and in the SOC (second place), whereas this kind of benefit is of only marginal importance in the POC. In the POC, on the other hand, the benefits for education are much higher than in the other two observed

Table 9.7 The components of monthly labour costs, 1993 (SIT per person)

Components	SOC	PC	POC	SOC %	PC %	POC %
Wages & salaries	60,551	135,019	99,623	62.5	70.6	57.8
Overtime bonuses	230	58	0	0.2	0.0	0.0
Cash benefits for temporarily laid-off workers	2,392	0	0	2.5	0.0	0.0
Substitute payments for redundant employees	156	0	0	0.2	0.0	0.0
Pension and disability insurance	9,816	20,929	15,442	10.1	10.9	9.0
Health insurance	3,863	8,236	6,077	4.0	4.3	3.5
Employment insurance	443	945	697	0.5	0.5	0.4
Accident at work insurance	317	675	498	0.3	0.4	0.3
Maternity leave insurance	63	135	100	0.1	0.1	0.1
Food allowances	7,040	8,840	6,637	7.3	4.6	3.9
Transport allowances	3,818	2,288	18,927	3.9	1.2	11.0
Paid vacations	5,000	9,915	6,239	5.2	5.2	3.6
Anniversary gratuities	43	236	0	0.0	0.1	0.0
Benefits for education	1,028	1,156	10,286	1.1	0.6	6.0
Scholarships	55	81	81	0.1	0.0	0.0
Solidarity contributions	105	0	0	0.1	0.0	0.0
Prepaid retirement contributions	9	0	0	0.0	0.0	0.0
Cash compensation for self-employment	35	278	0	0.0	0.1	0.0
Severance payments	12	585	0	0.0	0.3	0.0
Allowances for work clothing	449	267	0	0.5	0.1	0.0
Key personnel insurance	65	296	6,382	0.1	0.2	3.7
Additional health insurance	887	887	887	0.9	0.5	0.5
Collective accident insurance	431	430	430	0.4	0.2	0.2
Medical examination	19	6	0	0.0	0.0	0.0
Total labour costs	96,827	191,262	172,306	100.0	100.0	100.0

companies. In fact, the POC is development oriented and has high costs of research and development, too.

The bonuses provided by companies are for health insurance only. Key personnel insurance is the highest expense in the POC, while other types of health insurance are the same in all three companies.

To derive more surveyable results we put all labour force expenditures into one table (table 9.7), from which it can be concluded that all three companies provide an adequate level of social security for their employees, as required by law and the Collective Agreement. The biggest social benefit and bonuses expenditures are in the POC, which provides a higher level of social security for its employees, followed by the PC and the SOC. The component of labour costs with the highest share is wages and salaries (58–71 per cent).

The final conclusions that can be drawn on total labour costs are the following: job costs (price of employment) are the highest in the PC, particularly regarding the higher average of wages and salaries. In the PC company the proportion of well-educated persons is quite high, which is reasonable regarding its activities. In the POC, the share of highly educated people is also high, but the company remunerates its employees by giving them bonuses rather than high wages.

Conclusions

In companies, social security is regulated by state law, by government decrees, and by the Collective Agreement. Contributions for social security are paid every month, by both employers and employees, into the budget or into insurance funds.

The main elements of the social security system are:

- Employees' wages are regulated by the Collective Agreement.
- The salaries of key personnel (managers) are regulated by an agreement signed by the Chamber of Commerce of the Republic of Slovenia and the Association of Managers. The salaries depend on the size of the company and the company's average gross wage for employees; they vary from 3.75 times an average gross wage in a small company to 7 times an average gross wage in a large company. The minimum gross wage is also defined (SIT 27,560 per month in June 1994).
- Overtime bonuses for work done on state holidays or at weekends or for overtime: 15–50 per cent on top of the gross wage.
- Six-month payments for redundant workers. After six months, redundant workers go to the Agency of Employment and receive cash compensation for unemployment: 3–24 months, depending on the number of years in work.
- Cash compensation to redundant workers: companies can pay this straight away if they start their own business or become self-employed.
- Prepaid retirement for employees who are less than five years from retirement: a company can 'buy off working years' for them.
- Paid vacations once a year: 60 per cent of the average state-level gross wage in companies that have losses, 80 per cent of the average gross wage of the Republic of Slovenia in companies that are profitable, and 100 per cent of the average gross wage of the Republic of Slovenia if

companies' basic wages are below the Republic's average, e.g. SIT 40,000–83,000.

- State holidays (payments for days not at work).
- Food allowances: 10 per cent of the Republic's average gross wage of the previous month, e.g. SIT 8,000. Amounts above this are taxed.
- Transport allowances: the price of public transport up to 2 km (about SIT 1,800) and above 2 km SIT 10.30 per km.
- Payments for business trips: SIT 20.60 for each kilometre driven; SIT 2,600–7,500 for accommodation and food.
- Anniversary gratuities (payments for 10–30 working years): for 10 years at work the employee receives 50 per cent of the previous three months' average net wage in the Republic of Slovenia, for 20 years 75 per cent, and for 30 years 100 per cent of this average.
- Severance payments (in the case of retirement): the amount of the average net wage in the Republic of Slovenia during the previous three months, or the previous three months' average net wage of the employee if this is more favourable for the worker.
- Solidarity contribution: payment of the employee's average net wage in the case of illness lasting more than three months, natural disaster, married partner's death, etc.
- Benefits for education and training: the amounts of these benefits are not prescribed.
- Scholarships: companies' payments for students and pupils of SIT 5,500–11,400.
- Substitute payments for working in other cities, far away from home: about SIT 31,500.

In addition to prescribed benefits and allowances regulated by the Collective Agreement, a company may pay bonuses to its employees:

- A company car for key personnel (managers); the company pays all expenses relating to the car.
- Life insurance for key personnel (managers).
- Additional health insurance for all employees.
- Collective accident insurance for all employees.
- Allowances for work clothing.
- Preventive medical examinations.

Conclusions for the social owned company

During the transition to a market economy many socially owned companies had to reduce their workforces owing to the restructuring and reorganization of production, leading to a lot of redundant workers. In line with legislation, the SOC company prepared a programme for resolving the problem of redundant workers and paid them six months' wages at 70 per cent of their regular monthly wages. For redundant workers who started their own business and became self-employed, the company paid cash compensation. The workforce was further reduced by means of early retirement (prepaid retirement for employees who were less than five years from retirement).

Owing to the restructuring programme and a poor economic situation in the company, several social benefits were abolished. Some of the firm's holiday houses were kept and operated on a non-profit basis. The company's unprofitable canteen was abolished and spun-off.

In 1991, the Law on Dwellings was introduced. Under this law, people could buy company flats at very low prices (only 40 per cent of the market price), which almost completely exhausted the company's flats fund. Interest-free loans for flats and houses were also abolished.

The position of the trade union is quite strong, with more than 90 per cent of employees in the company being unionized.

Nevertheless, the company still provides an adequate level of social protection for its employees. Although its employees' wages are the lowest compared with the other two observed companies, all kinds of social benefits and allowances as well as bonuses are assured at a satisfactory level.

Conclusions for the public company

The observed company is of special public interest and was not influenced by market changes.

The PC provides all kinds of social protection for its employees. In comparison with the other two observed companies, its wages and salaries are the highest, which is understandable given the high educational level of the company's employees.

Some holiday houses have been kept, but the company flats have almost all been sold.

Some of the employees' social benefits are high in comparison with the other two observed companies (food allowances, paid vacations, anniversary gratuities, and severance payments). We can conclude that the company assures a level of social protection for its employees that is above the prescribed minimum.

Conclusions for the privately owned company

The POC was established at the beginning of 1990, after the Companies Law was introduced. It is very development oriented and employs highly educated persons (more than 80 per cent of its employees are graduates).

The salaries and wages of the company's management and employees are not very high and the company prefers to reward its employees through several kinds of bonuses (for example, key personnel insurance is at a very high level, the company provides company cars and covers all expenses relating to cars). It also provides a higher level of some social benefits and allowances than the other two observed companies (very high benefits for education and extremely high transport allowances). But, compared with the other two companies, the remaining social benefits and allowances are the lowest. Moreover, all kinds of social benefits from the former socialist system are missing (no holiday houses, no company flats, no solidarity contributions, etc.).

Final remarks

Until 1991, before Slovenia declared its independence, the social security system was similar to the one applied under the socialist system. It was financed by contributions and by taxes. The goals of the social policy were to create a universal programme that would provide an approximately equal standard for all employees. Changes in the social security system in Slovenia resulted in the new Social Programme, accepted by the government in 1991. The main principle of the new programme is that every individual who has an income has to provide social security for him/herself and his/her family according to their ability and capability, while the government provides a minimal standard for the unemployed and other vulnerable groups. The role of the state is to ensure adequate conditions for this change (the principle of solidarity).

Residents with adequate sources of income are obliged to insure themselves against risk. Social security is provided by the government only for those who are unable to obtain it by themselves. This principle is to be implemented step by step. These changes will bring the Slovenian social security system closer to the conservative corporate model.

By introducing the solidarity principle, the role of the family in social protection will increase and stimulate the withdrawal of public institutions. At the same time, a policy to stimulate civil social initiatives in the private sphere (e.g. private health services, education, kindergartens, etc.) has been announced by the government.

An active employment policy is becoming more and more important to re-employ the unemployed who are able to work. In this connection some flexible forms of employment have been introduced (part-time employment, temporary employment, job-sharing, working at home).

The main goal of the new social policy is to maintain and to improve the minimum social security network for those residents who have no other sources of income. The adjustments to the new social security system require changes in some laws relating to pensions and disability insurance, war veterans' care, child and family care (the introduction of a universal cash benefit for children), social security (the introduction of cash benefits where there are no alternatives), employment, and tax legislation.

BIBLIOGRAPHY

Kondža, J. (1994), *Pregled prihodkov javnega sektorja v letu 1993*, Zavod Republike Slovenije za makroekonomske analize in razvoj, št.3/III/1994 [*An Overview of Public Sector Income in 1993*, Institute of Macroeconomic Analysis and Development, No. 3/III/1994].

Vmesno poročilo o stanju na področju denarnih prejemkov prebivalstva in javnih sredstev s predlogi strategije za oblikovanje socialne politike, Republike Slovenije, Poročevalec DZ RS, št. 30/93, avgust 1993, Ljubljana [*Intermediate Report on Household Income and Public Sources with Suggestions for a Strategy for Creating Social Policy*, A Report Gazette of the State Assembly of the Republic of Slovenia, No. 30/93, August 1993, Ljubljana].

10 Social protection in enterprises
The case-study of Albania

ERMIRA BRAHJA, EDMOND LEKA, and
RUBIN LUNIKU

Introduction

The purpose of this study is to analyse the social benefits provided by
Albanian firms during the early stage of the economic reform process in
Albania. First, we must clarify the types of benefits that we are
considering: we have considered as benefits (direct and indirect) all types
of expenditures by firms, excluding wages and excluding benefits
reimbursed by the state. The cost of these benefits is considered to be the
social wage.

In the study, the firm is the unit that intervenes to reduce particular
risks or meet certain needs of the recipients – i.e. a firm's employees. We
examine all forms in which this intervention takes place, including non-
wage benefits or advantages that improve the recipient's welfare and that
are transferred from the firm to employees. The important point here is
that the costs of these so-called 'fringe benefits' are strictly borne by the
firm. We excluded from consideration benefits such as maternity leave,
industrial accident allowance, payment for the birth of a child, and
funeral allowance because these benefits are reimbursed by the state.

The social functions of enterprises in Albania are closely related to the
recent historical development of the state. Before the early 1990s, when
the political and economic transformation began, the social functions of
state enterprises were more or less the same across the whole economy,
and the proportion of social benefits supplied by them was quite generous
given the current state of some restructured or newly created firms. Since
then, the social functions of enterprises have gradually changed and the
extent of these changes is closely related to the economic performance of
enterprises.

In this study we attempt to give a general picture of these social benefits
provided by Albanian enterprises, addressing both their structure and
their value. Our methodology involved surveying a sample of 25

randomly chosen enterprises, of which 19 are state owned, 4 are joint ventures, and 2 are privately owned; these are representative of the structure of the economy as a whole. We must also take into account that the social protection system is being reformed and the final system will be different from that described here.

In addition, the study attempts to compare the social benefits in enterprises during two different periods, 1989 and 1993 (unfortunately, however, we were able to obtain data for only one enterprise), in an attempt to determine changes in the structure and value of enterprises' provision of social benefits over time.

To meet the objectives of this study we give a detailed picture of the direct and indirect benefits provided by Albanian firms, with particular emphasis on the structure of the total cost of labour. For this purpose we designed a questionnaire based on Eurostat's methodology of labour cost evaluation. These labour costs consist of the regular components of earnings, mandatory payments by employers, payments for days not worked, and other social benefits.

This work might contribute to a more general discussion of total labour costs in the Albanian economy and of the social protection system established in an economy in transition.

The structure and description of statutory social contributions from employees

In this section, we provide a description of the social protection system in Albania, including the institutions involved, how the system is organized, and the role of trade unions.

Mandatory social contributions by employers

Employers are obliged by law to pay several kinds of social insurance for their employees. All of these payments are collected by the Social Insurance Institute (SII), which is an independent public institution. The SII administers the Social Insurance Fund, which is fully independent from the state budget. Moreover, the Social Insurance Institute is prohibited by law from using the Social Insurance Fund for profitable purposes, and the state guarantees SII payments in the event of the SII's inability to meet its financial obligations.

The Social Insurance Fund comprises five independent components:

(1) The Health Insurance Fund, from which preventive and primary healthcare services are financed.

(2) The Maternity Insurance Fund, which covers maternity leave payments.

(3) The Retirement Pension Insurance Fund, which covers all kinds of pension payments (old age pension, disability pension, orphans and widows pension, partial pensions, etc.).

All three of these funds are financed by the employers' mandatory contribution of up to 26 per cent of basic wages and salaries and by the employees' mandatory contribution of 10 per cent of their basic wage and salaries. As a result of low workers' wages, the 10 per cent employee contribution to this fund is being financed partially by the state for the period 1993–1996, and thereafter the budget subsidy will gradually be removed. The contribution schedule between employees and the state for the 1993–1996 period is as follows:

Year	Employees	State Budget	Total
1993	0%	10%	10%
1994	3%	7%	10%
1995	6%	4%	10%
1996	10%	0%	10%

(4) The Industrial Accidents Insurance Fund, which covers payments in the event of industrial accidents and illness. This fund is financed entirely by employers and it amounts to 0.5 per cent of basic wages and salaries.

(5) The Unemployment Insurance Fund is financed by the employers' contribution of 6 per cent of basic wages and salaries, and it serves to finance unemployment benefits.

The sum of these five independent insurance funds gives the total mandatory insurance payment of 42.5 per cent of workers' basic wages and salaries, of which employers pay 32.5 per cent and employees contribute 10 per cent.

Table 10.1 summarizes the components of the Social Insurance Fund by income source.

The Social Insurance Institute collects and administers these funds through its five branches, with funds prohibited from being transferred between branches. Usually, firms make several payments to workers entitled to benefits for the above-mentioned types of social insurance allowances, and this amount is then deducted from the firms' contribution to the Social Insurance Fund. For some types of benefit, the enterprise is reimbursed directly from the Social Insurance Fund. These include:

Table 10.1. Albania: income of the Social Insurance Fund

Income source	Paid by	Rate (% of gross wages)
1. Health insurance	Employer	26.0
2. Maternity insurance	Employee	10.0
3. Pension insurance	Total	36.0
4. Industrial accidents insurance	Employer	0.5
	Employee	0.0
	Total	0.5
5. Unemployment insurance	Employer	6.0
	Employee	0.0
	Total	6.0
Total insurance	Employer + employee	42.5

Sickness payment
Payment at the birth of a child
Funeral allowance
Care allowance for a disabled family member

All of these allowances are paid by firms, but they are mandatory by law and are thus excluded from our consideration of voluntary social benefits supplied by firms.

The new social insurance policy

We can distinguish two main features of the new policy on social insurance.

First, the newly introduced employees' contribution of 10 per cent of their basic wage and salary is a new income component of the Social Insurance Income scheme.

Second, the change in the present general social insurance system based on the current Law on Social Insurance (No. 7703, 11 May 1993) allows four forms of social insurance:

(1) Statutory basic insurance
(2) Voluntary insurance
(3) Supplementary insurance
(4) Special state pensions

Any economically active individual,[1] in addition to the obligatory insurance defined and guaranteed by the state and which is the same for all citizens, is permitted to obtain insurance in each of the other types of social insurance mentioned above. In this way, the social insurance system allows higher-income groups to be distinguished from the lower-income groups through paying higher insurance contributions and receiving higher pensions and other social benefits. For the purposes of our study we will consider payments transferred from the enterprises' funds to the voluntary or supplementary forms of the insurance system to be social contributions from enterprises to workers.

The role of the trade unions

Albanian enterprises have inherited the system of so-called 'craft unions', which were strictly linked to the former Communist Party and did not play any role at all in negotiations over wages and working conditions. The 'unions' were defined as 'tools of the party' in the implementation of its policy within enterprises.

The changes in the economic structure of the country were accompanied by an increase in the role of the newly created trade unions. Their rapid expansion and the large number of employees involved were the main factors in determining the trade unions' influence. During this period their social role was very high.

During the transition, the difficult economic situation of state enterprises limited the scope of trade union action, obliging them to make concessions to the managers at the expense of workers. The subsequent economic reforms led to a large number of job cuts and thus a high unemployment rate. Hence, the trade unions' role was limited to social rather than economic activity. In joint venture companies involving state and foreign partners, the trade unions play an important role, particularly in determining the average wage and working hours. The development of the private sector appears to be accompanied by a reduction in the trade unions' role within enterprises.

The sample and the organization of the survey

As the aim of this study is to analyse the social benefits provided by enterprises in the Albanian economy, we organized and carried out a survey of a sample of Albanian enterprises.

We prepared a questionnaire in Albanian, which conformed to the Eurostat classification of labour costs (Eurostat, 1978, vol. 2), in which the enterprises were asked to provide some data on the problem we were addressing. The questionnaire consisted of five parts:

(1) General data, such as the value of the enterprise's assets, the rate of

return on these assets for 1992 and 1993, profits before tax, the year in which the enterprise had begun its activity, the form of ownership.
(2) Information on the components of earnings.
(3) Data on payments for days not worked (national holidays, payments for sickness covered by the enterprise, etc.).
(4) Mandatory payments by employers.
(5) Figures on social benefits provided to the enterprise's workers.

We attempted to separate the benefits provided by Albanian enterprises in a way that was as similar as possible to the classification used by Eurostat. This turned out to be a difficult task, owing to the different accounting system used in Albanian enterprises and to the fact that the sources of funding were different – in some cases, funding was excluded from labour costs and transferred directly to the so-called 'director's fund',[2] while in others different sources of funding were used by different enterprises. Therefore, we found it necessary to go direct to the enterprise ourselves and fill out the questionnaires in conjunction with a representative of the financial department at each enterprise.

In a small number of cases, in treating some particular benefits it was difficult to divide up the payments given by the enterprise to a third party for services rendered, because this third party had provided several services to the enterprise and the payment covered all of them.

The survey covered 25 enterprises based in three areas of Albania, namely Tirana (the capital), Durres (the second-largest city), and Korca. The Central Western region, which comprises the towns of Tirana (400,000 inhabitants) and Durres (110,000), is considered to be the main industrial region in Albania in which more than 40 per cent of the national industry is located. The district of Korca (90,000 inhabitants) is located in the South-Eastern region and is also considered to be an important industrial centre.

The enterprises included in the sample were chosen to include different ownership structures, reflecting the way that changes have occurred during the economic reforms in Albania. Of the 25 enterprises in the sample, 19 are state owned, 4 are joint ventures, and 2 are privately owned. Only the state-owned enterprises have been operating over a long period.

Although in state-owned enterprises the capital is owned by the state, they no longer receive any subsidies from the state budget, nor do they receive any tax advantages, and they must operate in a commercial environment.

Of the four companies classified as joint ventures, three are joint ventures between the state and foreign partners. The fourth is a joint venture between an Albanian private partner and an Italian one, and could thus also be considered to be a private enterprise.

Two privately owned enterprises were selected to represent the two types of private enterprise currently operating in the Albanian economy. One is a private company with 100 per cent foreign capital registered and operating in Albania. The other is a previously state-owned enterprise that has gone through the privatization process and is now operating as a private enterprise.

Table 10.2 gives a summary of the enterprises included in the survey. As shown in the table, the enterprises operate in various sectors of the economy. The sample includes companies of varying sizes, ranging from 16 employees in one of the publishing companies to around 2,000 at the textile factory. The majority of Albanian enterprises fall within this range. Many of the former big conglomerates have been broken up into several small enterprises or have stopped production.

Voluntary social benefits provided by enterprises

Analysis and a detailed explanation

In our sample of 25 enterprises, 14 types of social benefits for workers are offered. These include 6 indirect social benefits and 8 direct social benefits. In our description of the kinds of social benefits provided by the enterprises, we have taken into consideration all the benefits provided, even those provided by only a single enterprise.

The indirect and direct benefits are considered separately in order to give a better understanding of both types of benefits. We begin with a discussion of indirect social benefits.

Indirect social benefits

Table 10.3 illustrates the distribution of the various kinds of indirect social benefits among the enterprises. The six benefits represent 41.8 per cent of total social benefits, and their contribution to total labour costs is 1.5 per cent.

Subsidized canteen. This is offered by six of the enterprises in the form of a price subsidy, i.e. the firm subsidizes the difference between the actual cost of a meal and the price paid by the workers for it. All of a firm's employees are entitled to use the subsidized canteen.

Medical care centre (policlinic). Offered by seven enterprises, this benefit usually involves primary health services to workers. In some cases the

Table 10.2. The enterprises surveyed

Name of enterprise	Location	Ownership	No. of employees	Kind of activity	Branch of economy
INSIG (Social Insurance Institute)	Tirana	State owned	270	Services	Insurance
BKT (National Commercial Bank)	Tirana	State owned	166	Services	Banking
KARTOGRAFIKE (cartographic enterprise)	Tirana	State owned	78	Production	Publishing & printing
BUKA (bread factory)	Tirana	State owned	855	Production	Food processing
POLIGRAFIK (Tirana printing house)	Tirana	State owned	353	Production	Publishing & printing
DAJTI	Tirana	State owned	100	Production	Metal products
NPV (clothes production)	Tirana	State owned	800	Production	Cloth manufacturing
TEX-LESH (wool textile plant)	Tirana	State owned	340	Production	Textiles
MIN-Mush (coal mine of Mushqeta)	Tirana	State owned	468	Production	Mining
KARBURANT (petrol import and export)	Tirana	State owned	85	Services	Retail sales
N.R.Sh. (poultry)	Korca	State owned	42	Production	Poultry
KARTONI (board factory)	Tirana	State owned	144	Production	Paper processing
NPKL (leather factory)	Tirana	State owned	30	Production	Leather processing
NPSH (textile factory)	Tirana	State owned	350	Production	Textiles
KOMBINATI TEXTIL (textile combine)	Tirana	State owned	1,957	Production	Textiles
NPP (porcelain factory)	Tirana	State owned	207	Production	Ceramics products
BDPH (banking document printing)	Tirana	State owned	16	Production	Publishing & printing
PORTI DURRES (port)	Durres	State owned	1,580	Services	Transport services
N.P.Sh. (sweetmeat production)	Tirana	State owned	83	Production	Food processing
ALB-BETON 5	Tirana	Joint venture	130	Production	Building materials
INTERCONSTRUZIONI (construction)	Tirana	Joint venture	22	Production	Construction
KANTJERI DETAR (Durres-Gdansk shipyard co.)	Durres	Joint venture	512	Production	Ship building
FK (shoe production factory)	Tirana	Joint venture	1,200	Production	Footwear factory
NPP (private beverage factory)	Tirana	Private	40	Production	Food processing
MAK-ALBANIA	Tirana	Private	233	Production	Construction

Table 10.3. Indirect social benefits offered by the surveyed enterprises

Type of benefit	No. of enterprises offering the benefit	State owned $N=19$	Joint venture $N=4$	Private $N=2$
Temporary housing	1	0	0	1
Subsidized canteen	6	5	1	0
Medical care centre	7	5	2	0
Shop with subsidized prices	1	1	0	0
Subsidized holiday travel expenses	2	2	0	0
Transport allowance	3	2	1	0

firm pays all personnel and material expenses and in other cases only part of them. The rest of the costs are financed by public health institutions.

Transport allowance. This is offered by three enterprises. In one of the three enterprises, the physical means of transportation is provided; in the other two enterprises, where only a small proportion of workers require transport, the firm reimburses the cost of the employees' fares.

Subsidized holiday travel expenses. This is offered in only two enterprises. The firm partially or totally subsidizes employees' travelling expenses, at the discretion of the managers.

Shop with subsidized prices. Provided in only one enterprise (the coal mine), this consists of a grocery shop, which may be used only by the miners and their families. The enterprise partially subsidizes the retail price of products in the shop.

Temporary housing. This is offered by only one enterprise, which operates in the construction industry. The company is a privately owned company with foreign capital and its management staff is composed of foreigners with a need for temporary housing. The enterprise offers temporary housing to its own managers and to those workers who do not live in the area. It may also be considered as a firm-specific social benefit.

Direct social benefits
The direct form of social protection seems to be the more usual type of benefit provided by enterprises. We observed this form of contribution in 24 out of the 25 enterprises examined. It comprises 2.08 per cent of the

Table 10.4. Direct social benefits offered by the surveyed enterprises

Type of benefit	No. of enterprises offering the benefit	State owned $N = 19$	Joint venture $N = 4$	Private $N = 2$
Childcare allowance	7	6	1	0
Jubilee gratuities	9	6	2	1
Professional training	3	3	0	0
Work clothes allowance	18	15	2	1
Life insurance allowance	1	1	0	0
Early retirement	1	0	1	0
Assistance for families in economic difficulties	10	8	1	1
Assistance for exceptional events	15	14	1	0

total labour cost and 58.3 per cent of the total benefits distributed by the enterprises. In table 10.4, we list the direct benefits and the number of enterprises providing them.

Work clothes allowance. This allowance is covered completely by the enterprises. We encountered this allowance in 18 out of the 25 enterprises. Usually it is given in the form of goods and consists of one work outfit per worker per year. Its distribution among employees of the same enterprise is not necessarily the same. Also the amount of the benefit provided to workers in different enterprises is related to the existing conditions on the workplace.

Assistance for families in economic difficulties. This benefit was also found frequently, being offered by 10 of the enterprises. It is a benefit that has been used only in recent years. It is related to the economic crisis and the high cost of living relative to wages. It is usually provided in the form of cash, but goods or food may also be provided. It is distributed to workers who are facing economic hardship within their families (e.g. have large families, or have members of their family who are unemployed). It is not given regularly, but is at the discretion of the employer.

Assistance for exceptional events. This benefit is provided in the case of the birth of a child, a wedding, or a death in the employee's family. In our sample, this benefit is given by 15 enterprises. It usually consists of cash payments.

Jubilee gratuities. The benefit is found in nine of the enterprises and usually though not always consists of cash payments made in special cases to some or all employees. The occasion for this could be a national holiday jubilee or a special worker jubilee. Sometimes it is used to give gratuities to employees with a long service record in the enterprise or who have shown special devotion to their work.

Childcare allowance. This is found in seven of the enterprises. The benefit is given in the form of allowances to mothers with small children, usually upon their return from maternity leave. It could also consist in some special cases of special food for children financed totally by the enterprise.

Professional training. There are two types of professional training payments: payments for the days not worked when the worker has been attending training (we have included this type of payment in the payments for days not worked – see table 10.6 below); payments from the enterprise to third parties for the organization of courses (charges for the room, fees for the lecturers, etc.). This kind of benefit is offered by three of the firms.

The amounts per employee spent for this purpose by INSIG (an insurance company) and the National Commercial Bank (the biggest bank in the country) are so large as to be affordable only by companies making huge profits and not by ordinary enterprises. We must also mention that in 1993 these companies were undergoing restructuring, including the retraining of personnel, the introduction of computers, and the upgrading of working practices. All of these processes have training costs attached to them. In this sense 1993 could be considered to be an unusual case, with a much smaller incidence of these kinds of costs likely in these enterprises in coming years.

Early retirement allowance. This benefit is offered by only one enterprise (a joint venture shipyard company). It is a cash payment of part of the retirement pension to those undertaking early retirement. In this firm it was negotiated by the labour unions and was seen as a relatively painless way of reducing jobs. The other portion of the retirement pension is paid by the Social Insurance Institute.

Life insurance allowance. Only one company offers this benefit (the insurance company INSIG). It is a new kind of social benefit for Albanian enterprise. The amount dedicated to this allowance (more than 30 per cent of the wage) is so large that it could be provided only by companies making huge profits, such as INSIG.

Some special benefits
In addition to the above direct and indirect social benefits, workers received three other types of benefits from the enterprises. Two of them, compensation for food price increases and remuneration for dangerous working environment, differ from voluntary social benefits in that they are mandatory. The third, interest-free loans, is not considered to be typical of Albanian enterprises.

Compensation for food price increases. Price liberalization brought a sharp increase in the cost of living. The increase in prices of some basic food products highlighted the problem of protecting the population's standard of living. This led to a decree by the Council of Ministers (No. 310, 24 July 1992) which stated that all individuals, whether retired or employed, in the state or the private sector, were entitled to monthly compensation for food price increases of up to 280 lek per person plus up to 200 lek per month for their dependants. The state budget covers the financial costs of this compensation for retired people and employees of government budgetary institutions. For employees in the state and private sectors these expenditures are financed completely by firms and are included in their costs of production.

The government decree leaves it up to enterprises to determine the actual amount of this compensation, although it should not exceed the above limits. Most of the enterprises gave the maximum compensation allowed by the government decree, because of the significant difference between nominal wage and price increases.

We treated food price compensation as a special benefit for two reasons. First, although it was mandated by the Council of Ministers' decree, and so was not a voluntary social benefit, the amount paid was decided by the enterprise itself based on its financial circumstances. Second, we deemed that it would be more accurate to consider food price compensation as a component of earnings and not as a social benefit. In fact, from January 1994 food price compensation was included as a component of the new wages and salaries system, and is no longer counted as a separate payment.

Remuneration for dangerous working environment. Under the Labour Code, enterprises are obliged to give special treatment to all workers exposed to dangerous or polluted working conditions. This benefit is given in the form of an extra meal or a quantity of food (milk, sugar, etc.). The figures in the sample regarding the amount of this benefit vary because they depend on the proportion of workers receiving this benefit in the total workforce.

Interest-free loans. This is a new kind of benefit provided by Albanian enterprises. Its aim is to contribute to the solution of the permanent housing problem, which is acute in Albania, with prices for flats ranging from US$200/m^2 to US$400/m^2 whereas wages are barely US$50 per month. Usually this benefit is given in the form of a long-term interest-free loan to employees to buy a flat.

Only one company examined in the sample was offering this benefit (the National Commercial Bank). Another company planned to introduce the benefit in 1994 (INSIG, the insurance company). What is common to both of these companies is the huge profits they earn and their monopoly position in their respective markets.

The monthly amount given per person in the case of the National Commercial Bank is approximately US$95 (in unpaid interest),[3] which is more than twice the average wage the Bank is paying to its employees.

We must underline here that the number of employees receiving this benefit is very limited. We have omitted this benefit from the sample average because, if included in the sample average, it would substantially distort the results and give misleading conclusions.

Social benefits in state-owned enterprises

Of the 25 enterprises included in our sample, 19 were state owned. We could consider this randomly chosen sample of 19 enterprises as broad enough to allow us to generalize the results to all state-owned enterprises.

As a result of the economic reforms taking place in Albania the state-owned enterprises are under commercial pressure. Many of them are in transition and are engaged in organizational restructuring, staff retrenchment, etc. By maintaining a particular internal organizational structure, state enterprises are continuing to provide many of the direct and indirect social benefits previously given to workers, although during this transition period workers' interest is shifting towards the preservation of the workplace.

In our sample of 19 state-owned enterprises, all provided voluntary social benefits. The average contribution of total voluntary social benefits to total labour costs in state-owned enterprises is 5.16 per cent, varying from 0.12 per cent for a small company (a printing house) to 25.5 per cent for an insurance company (INSIG).

The separation of direct and indirect benefits allows us to analyse their

Table 10.5. The structure of voluntary social benefits in state-owned
enterprises

Benefit	As % of total benefits
Indirect benefits	
Temporary housing	0.00
Subsidized canteen	20.15
Medical care centre (policlinic access)	2.00
Shop with subsidized prices	1.00
Subsidized holiday travel expenses	3.00
Transport allowance	1.16
Total	27.31
Direct benefits	
Childcare allowance	4.80
Jubilee gratuities	3.10
Professional training	7.34
Work clothes allowance	24.15
Early retirement	9.50
Assistance for families in economic difficulties	17.20
Subsidy for exceptional events	6.60
Total	72.69

distribution across enterprises. It can be pointed out, as shown in table
10.5, that enterprises prefer direct methods of social protection to indirect
ones. Of total social benefits, 72.7 per cent are of the direct type and 27.3
per cent are of the indirect type.

One of the most frequent forms of indirect benefit is the subsidized
canteen, which constitutes 20.2 per cent of total social benefits.
Previously this service was provided by state-owned catering companies,
but now that the services sector is mostly private, companies are
organizing their own canteens. In some cases, this is more expensive than
paying a third party for the service. This could be one of the reasons
firms are now shifting towards direct forms of social benefits. In fact only
8 out of the 19 firms are using indirect methods of social benefits,
whereas direct methods are used by all of them.

Other widely used indirect benefits are the medical care centre and the
subsidized holiday travel expenses, accounting for 2 per cent and 3 per
cent of total social benefits, respectively.

As we said before, the direct methods of social benefits outweigh, in
kind and amount, indirect ones. Their contribution to total labour
costs is 3.76 per cent, but within the sample we observed a wide
variation, ranging from 0.05 per cent (NPSh, a food processing

company) to 25.5 per cent (at INSIG, the insurance company) of enterprises' total labour costs.

Some direct social contributions are widely used by state-owned enterprises, such as the work clothes allowance, accounting for 24.2 per cent of total social benefits, the subsidy for exceptional events (6.6 per cent of the total), the childcare allowance (4.8 per cent of the total), and jubilee gratuities (3.1 per cent of the total).

We also observed some new kinds of direct benefits, such as professional training and assistance for families in economic difficulties, accounting for 7.4 per cent and 17.2 per cent of total social benefits, respectively. Such benefits are related to the special situation faced by enterprises during the transition period, including the need to retrain employees and economic difficulties faced by workers as a result of high living costs.

Other kinds of benefits, such as interest-free loans or the life insurance allowance, appear to be associated with companies that enjoy a special status and make huge profits.

Social benefits provided by joint ventures and private enterprises

In our sample we analysed just six enterprises with different ownership structures, two of them privately owned and four joint venture companies. The sample was too small to generalize the results to all companies with similar structures, but we can discuss general trends.

The main trends are as follows:

- a lower level of social benefits provided by these firms compared with state-owned enterprises: 4.43 per cent against 5.16 per cent of total labour costs, respectively;
- a lower number of social benefits offered by the joint venture and private firms in comparison with state-owned ones;
- an even stronger preference for direct rather than indirect benefits.

We must stress here that there are some differences within the group of joint venture and private companies chosen in the sample. The main reason for these differences lies in the capital structure of these enterprises and in the background to their creation.

For joint venture companies, the presence of the state as one of the partners often means that they inherit more or less the same structure of social benefits as those previously guaranteed by the state-owned enterprise.

Regarding private companies there are differences between newly founded ones and those that were created as a result of the privatization of once state-owned enterprises. New private enterprises offer a very reduced range of benefits as compared with the former state-owned ones, which retain their former structure of social benefits.

From our analysis we observe that social benefits are more developed in state-owned enterprises than in privately owned and joint venture companies, but we should stress here the relative differences in wages paid by these companies and those paid by state-owned ones. We found that the average wage paid by the private and joint venture enterprises was 1.46 times higher than the average wage paid in the state-owned companies. This indicates a tradeoff between the wage and social benefits distributed by the enterprises (see table 10.6).

Comparative analysis of the social benefits provided by enterprises before and after the transition period

It is interesting to see how the social benefits distributed by the enterprises changed during the transition period. This problem could be studied only in the case of state-owned enterprises because they are the only kind of enterprise that was in existence both before and after this period.

Unfortunately, it was not possible to conduct a parallel survey on the same sample on the situation in the enterprises before the transition period. This was because many enterprises going through the transition process have been restructured, split into smaller ones, or in the extreme ceased operations completely.

Despite these difficulties, we undertook a comparison in one enterprise that had preserved its structure intact from 1989. The company is called POLIGRAFIK and is a printing house located in Tirana. The company has undergone reform but has retained its shape and structure. It cut its workforce by 47.4 per cent, falling from 670 employees in 1989 to just 353 in 1993, while retaining the same scope of operations.

In 1992 and 1993 the company showed increased profits, the rates of return on its assets being 18.9 per cent and 30.3 per cent, respectively (after-tax profits). This could be the result of the reduction in the wage bill, the increase in productivity, and to a certain extent the market power that the company enjoys (it is at least three times bigger than its nearest competitor).

However, we now return to our discussion and consider in more detail the benefits the company distributed in 1989 and 1993 (see table 10.7). Because of the high inflation faced by the Albanian economy in this period, it is necessary to deflate the nominal 1993 values to real 1989

Table 10.6. The structure of labour costs in the surveyed enterprises (%)

	All enterprises	State-owned enterprises	Joint venture and private enterprises
Number of employees	10,226	8,089	2,137
Monthly basic wages and salaries	53.63	51.98	59.88
Bonuses and allowances paid regularly	2.48	2.74	1.47
Remuneration for overtime	0.40	0.14	1.35
Remuneration for dangerous environment	0.85	0.85	0.84
Bonuses for shiftwork (e.g. night work)	0.11	0.13	0.01
Profit-sharing bonus	5.87	7.42	0.00
Other income	0.00	0.00	0.00
Earnings	63.33	63.27	63.54
Compensation for food price increases	9.22	9.87	6.78
Total earnings	72.55	73.14	70.32
Holidays	1.16	0.90	2.14
Sick payment (working disability)	2.64	2.19	4.35
Maternity leave	0.01	0.02	0.01
Health care for a family member	0.01	0.01	0.00
Training courses	0.72	0.91	0.00
Total payments for days not worked	4.54	4.02	6.50
Total of mandatory payments	17.05	16.60	18.75
Temporary housing	0.20	0.00	0.97
Subsidized canteen	0.87	1.04	0.26
Policlinic access	0.19	0.10	0.52
Shop with subsidized prices	0.04	0.05	0.00
Subsidized holiday travel expenses	0.11	0.15	0.00
Transport allowance	0.05	0.06	0.02
Total of indirect benefits	1.48	1.40	1.77
Childcare allowance	0.20	0.25	0.00
Jubilee gratuities	0.24	0.16	0.53
Professional training	0.30	0.38	0.00
Work clothes allowance	1.30	1.25	1.50
Life insurance allowance	0.39	0.49	0.00
Early retirement	0.01	0.00	0.07
Assistance for families in difficulties	0.82	0.89	0.55
Subsidy for exceptional events	0.27	0.34	0.01
Total of direct benefits	3.53	3.76	2.66
Total of voluntary social benefits	5.01	5.16	4.43
Interest-free loans	0.85	1.07	0.00
Total labour cost	100.00	100.00	100.00

Table 10.7. The structure of earnings, benefits, and labour costs in POLIGRAFIK, 1989 and 1993

	1989		1993		
	Lek	%	Lek	%	Adjusted to 1989 prices[1]
Monthly average wage	550.00	72.65	2,713.80	50.32	301.87
Bonuses paid regularly	22.90	3.03	152.20	2.82	16.93
Overtime payments	0	0	106.40	1.97	11.84
Remuneration for dangerous working environment	10.10	1.33	399.00	7.40	44.38
Payments for scientific research	3.80	0.50	0	0	0
Compensation for food price increases	0	0	467.40	8.67	51.99
Profit-sharing bonus	2.02	0.27	453.00	8.40	50.39
Total earnings	588.82	77.78	4,291.8	79.58	477.40
Holiday payments	8.50	1.12	5.90	0.11	0.66
Sickness payments	24.70	3.26	92.10	1.71	10.24
Vocational training	11.60	1.53	0	0	0
Payments for days not worked	44.80	5.92	98.00	1.82	10.90
Contribution to social insurance	101.00	13.34	897.50	16.64	99.83
Subsidized canteen	14.90	1.97	83.10	1.54	9.24
Medical care centre	0.60	0.08	12.00	0.22	1.33
Fitness equipment	0.50	0.07	0	0	0
Subsidy for cultural activities	0.23	0.03	0	0	0
Subsidized holiday travel expenses	1.14	0.15	0	0	0
Total indirect benefits	17.37	2.29	95.10	1.76	10.58
Jubilee gratuities	0	0	4.00	0.07	0.44
Work clothes	4.50	0.59	0	0	0

Allowance for exceptional events	0.53	0.07	6.50	0.12	0.72
Total direct benefits	5.03	0.66	10.50	0.19	1.17
Total benefits	22.40	2.96	105.60	1.96	11.75
Total labour costs	757.05	100.00%	5,392.90	100.00%	599.88
No. of employees	670		353		
Rate of return (%)			30.3		

1 The value of the labour cost component adjusted by the CPI for 1993 with 1989 as the base year.

prices. The increase in the CPI from December 1989 to 1993 was 899 per cent.

By comparing the figures for the two years we note the following changes:

- There was a reduction in the real wage of nearly 45 per cent. The remuneration of the workers appears to be more related to the company's economic results. In 1993 a large component of earnings was the profit share, which contributed 8.4 per cent to total labour costs or about 11 per cent of the cash payments to workers.
- There was a significant reduction in the total social benefits distributed by the company, from 2.96 per cent to 1.96 per cent of labour costs.
- The range of social benefits provided by the enterprise in 1989 was considerably wider than that provided in 1993 (seven forms of benefits in 1989 and only four in 1993). This is more evident for indirect benefits.
- Indirect social benefits were bigger in 1989 compared with 1993, as regards both the number of benefits provided (six in 1989 and two in 1993) and their share of total labour costs (2.29 per cent and 1.76 per cent, respectively). Another signal in this direction is the expressed intention of the management of the company to eliminate the medical care unit. Once this happens, the only indirect benefit offered by the enterprise will be the subsidized canteen.

  As regards the provision of permanent housing, we should clarify that the enterprise was contributing to this kind of social benefit in both periods. Funds for the construction of flats came from the state budget, but the company incurred the costs of organizing and monitoring the whole process. Unfortunately it is not possible to separate out these costs because they are included in the administration costs of the whole enterprise.
- The decrease in direct benefits is even more dramatic. They contribute just 0.19 per cent to total labour costs, compared with 0.66 per cent in 1989 (a reduction of 71 per cent).

Analysis of just one company is not sufficient to permit us to draw conclusions for the whole economy, but we can identify some of the reasons for the present situation.

The deep restructuring that the company has gone through and the very radical reduction in the labour force has meant that workers are interested more in preserving the enterprise than in preserving the social benefits they were getting from the company. The same is true of the labour unions operating within the enterprise.

The government's commitment to a very rigid policy in cutting subsidies to loss-making companies has significantly affected the wage bill and also cut the social benefits provided by the company. In a more stable financial situation for the company and in a more stable economic environment, it may be that the company would decide to extend social benefits.

Another reason for the reduction in social benefits is that, after the privatization of the services sector, some services became so expensive that many companies simply eliminated them.

Summary

In this section, we offer some conclusions about labour costs in Albania, taking into account the limited number of enterprises in the survey (25) and the early stage of the privatization process. We recall here that the aim of the study was to focus on the actual state of the social benefits system in Albanian enterprises. According to the figures, benefits represented 5.01 per cent of labour costs and 7.17 per cent of total earnings. The important fact to be stressed here is that there has been a decrease in the level of social benefits provided by firms, indicating that firms are seeking greater efficiency and are tending to eliminate those activities that involve them in economic losses.

Over time, real wages have declined, as have social benefits, and employment has fallen as a result of the privatization process and economic reforms (table 10.7).

Insurance contributions are calculated as 42.5 per cent on the wages and salaries component of labour costs, of which 32.5 per cent is covered by the employer and the remaining 10 per cent by the employee. This is considered to be a relatively high rate, but we should note that 15 per cent of the sum collected goes on unemployment insurance contributions, which are related to the present difficult economic situation and may be reduced in the future.

If we compare the structure of total earnings, we observe that a larger part of remuneration is related to the economic performance of the company. A relatively important type of remuneration is bonuses and profit-sharing schemes.

Social protection in state enterprises is more developed than in the privately owned and joint venture companies but there is a tradeoff between higher wages supplied by private firms and social benefits supplied by state ones. Within the private and joint venture companies there are differences related to their history of formation and to the presence of the state in the ownership structure.

The social protection system as a means of increasing employees' welfare is in the process of transformation. Direct forms of social benefit appear to be preferred over indirect ones, with the range of indirect benefits offered by enterprises being considerably reduced. The economic reforms have been accompanied by moves towards new kinds of direct social benefits. For example, life insurance, interest-free loans, and assistance for families in economic difficulties are all ways of increasing the economic welfare of employees in this early phase of economic reform.

The role of the trade unions is diminished both in general but particularly in private enterprises, largely because of the high unemployment rate and the privatization process under way.

We conclude that, at this early stage of economic reforms towards a market economy, the ownership structure is significant in shaping the relative balance between the monetary wage and the social wage.

NOTES

We would like to thank all those who helped us in the preparation of this paper. We are particularly grateful to Univ.Doc. Dr Andreas Wörgötter for his very helpful comments and remarks. In addition, we would like to thank all those who contributed to the completion of the survey, particularly the heads of each of the financial departments at the enterprises included in the sample.

We extend our gratitude to the Institute for Advanced Studies for the financial support that made it possible to complete the paper.

We would gladly welcome any comments on the paper.

1 'Economically active individual' is a term used in the law in order to include all individuals regardless of whether they are employers, employees, or self-employed.
2 The 'director's fund' is inherited from the old system of management in Albanian enterprises. This fund provided various benefits for employees, in some special cases in order to help them financially.
3 It is calculated on the basis of the average interest rate on loans and the average of the principal (the cost of the flat).

BIBLIOGRAPHY

Eurostat (1978), *Labour Costs in Industry, 1975*, vol. 1: *Detailed results by industry*, vol. 2: *Structure of labour costs*, Luxembourg: Eurostat.
Rein, M. and L. Rainwater (1986), *Public/Private Interplay in Social Protection. A Comparative Study*, Armonk, NY: M. E. Sharpe.

11 Social protection in the enterprise
The case of Slovakia

JÁN PLÁNOVSKÝ and
ANDREAS WÖRGÖTTER

Introduction

To speak about social protection in the enterprise, we must first clarify how we use the term 'social protection'. We follow the approach of Eurostat when defining 'social protection expenditure' (Rein and Rainwater, 1986): 'Any expenditure involved in meeting costs incurred by individuals or households as a result of the materialisation or the existence of certain risks, contingencies, or needs insofar as this expenditure gives rise to the intervention of a third party, without there being any simultaneous counterpart by the beneficiary.'

In our study 'the intervention of a third party' means the firm, which intervenes to reduce particular risks or to meet some needs of recipients – the firm's employees. Loosely speaking, we look at all forms of non-wage benefits, advantages, and allowances[1] that improve the recipient's welfare and that are supplied by a firm to workers. The costs of these so-called 'fringe benefits' are strictly borne by the firm. We do not distinguish between benefits mandated by collective agreement as a result of bargaining between management and trade unions, and benefits supplied by firms 'voluntarily'. On the other hand, several kinds of allowances (e.g. child allowances) are supplied by the state through the firms. These benefits are excluded from our consideration because the state reimburses the firm for its expenditure on such benefits. Similarly, some benefits are applicable only to union members and are financed exclusively from union funds. We do not treat them as social benefits supplied by the enterprise. Another important issue relates to whether particular expenditures are still a 'social benefit' or are now a component of worker's earnings. We will discuss this problem later in a more concrete context.

The social function of the enterprise in Slovakia is very closely connected with the recent historical development of the state. Slovakia (as part of Czechoslovakia until 1 January 1993) started the process of massive

227

economic transformation after the 'Velvet Revolution' in November 1989. However, the transformation of a social system is a long-lasting process and the general framework of this transformation is still in the stage of creation. A similar situation prevails at the firm level. Some particular measures regulating social protection have been adopted recently, but no general legislative framework regulating social protection has been set up yet.[2] The development of private insurance and pension funds, occupational insurance companies, etc. is currently not possible owing to the lack of necessary legislation in this area. Government concepts of the transformation of the social sphere will be discussed.

Looking at the historical development of social protection, we must be aware of the fact that the 'socialist' state assigned an important social function to the firm. The firm was an agent of the state in providing social protection. These functions were uniform throughout the whole economy because all enterprises had been nationalized in the recent past. The proportion of social protection supplied by socialist firms was quite generous in comparison with the current situation in some transformed or newly created firms. On the other hand, the rules regulating social protection were very rigid. If a firm wanted to provide some additional benefit to workers, it had to operate at the margins of the law.

When we attempt to compare the proportion of social protection supplied by firms in the different stages of privatization, we must consider that most of the currently private firms have their roots in the socialist 'national enterprises'.[3] They carried out the same or very similar social functions (subsidized housing, non-returnable loans, subsidized canteens, recreation, etc.). So the main difference among privatized enterprises depends on the speed with which new managers shed their responsibilities for particular social services. On the other hand, there has been some room for establishing new kinds of social protection, although each activity leading to an increase in non-mandatory social protection is dependent on a particular firm's characteristics (e.g. firm size, economic performance, the power of trade unions, etc.).

We will seek to present a compound picture of social protection provided by 19 Slovak firms at different stages of the privatization process. In particular, we investigate the structure of total labour costs. For these purposes we have developed a special questionnaire (see the Appendix) designed according to Eurostat's methodology of labour cost evaluation. We divided these labour costs into the three main groups:

- *Direct labour costs* consist of wage costs (including payments for days not worked, various bonuses, etc.) and employers' mandatory payments (see table 11.1 below).

- *Social protection equipment* comprises the resources designed for social purposes (for instance, kindergartens, vacation homes, medical facilities, etc.). The firm's expenditures on operating this equipment are here called *indirect social protection*.
- *Direct social protection* includes those social benefits that can be directly paid in cash (e.g. financial loans, recreation contributions, meal subsidies, etc.).

We must also point out that this study does not aspire to generalize its findings to the economy as a whole, not least because our sample of 19 firms is not a representative one.[4] The average number of employees is 924, and it varies from 10 to almost 6,000 workers. The wage level also has a wide spread, from Sk 3,122/month[5] to Sk 11,000/month. The least representative variable is so-called privateness, which ranges from 0 per cent to 100 per cent, with a mean of 80 per cent privatized (for more details, see table 11.5 below). If we look at the regional distribution, seven firms are located in two eastern-Slovakian towns. There is also some bias as regards economic branches: five firms operate in the building industry, and another four produce foodstuffs.

Moreover, the social protection system is in transformation, hence current observations do not represent the final expected state. Nevertheless, we attempt to test our initial hypothesis that the proportion of social functions is dependent on the ownership structure. We also look at the impact of the firm's size (measured by the number of workers) and of the average wage on the level of social protection provided. Finally, this work might help to determine the extent to which social protection should be decreed by law.

The legal and institutional framework

The main purpose of this section is to provide the basic background concerning which institutions are involved in the system of social protection and how this system is currently organized in Slovakia. The government view of the future development of the social sphere and the role of trade unions are examined as well. Our findings here are based on material from the Ministry of Labour, Social Affairs and Family (1993) and the Confederation of Trade Unions (1993), and on interviews with union and state[6] representatives.

Mandatory payments by employers

Every employer is obliged by law to make several kinds of insurance payments for their employees. All these payments are accumulated in the National Insurance Company (NIC), which was established on 1 January 1993. There are four independent funds within this company:

(1) The Health Insurance Fund, from which preventive, primary, and secondary health care is financed: the mandatory contribution from employers is 10 per cent of gross wages (more precisely, the worker's taxable income basis); employees contribute 3.7 per cent of their gross wages.

(2) The Disability Insurance Fund, which funds sickness pay, maternity leave, sick family member leave, etc.: the mandatory payment from employers is 4.4 per cent of gross wages, while workers pay 1.4 per cent of their gross wages.

(3) The Pension Insurance Fund, which covers all kinds of pensions expenditures (old age pension, disability pension, widows and orphans pension, etc.): the mandatory employer's contribution is 20.6 per cent of gross wages and the employee's contribution is 5.9 per cent of gross wages.

(4) The Employment Fund, which is designed to finance an active employment policy: the employer's contribution is 3 per cent and the worker's contribution is 1 per cent of gross basic wages.

Thus the total mandatory insurance payment is 50 per cent of gross wages, of which the employer pays 38 per cent and the employee contributes 12 per cent.

Table 11.1 summarizes all sources of income of the NIC. In practice the NIC makes the administration of their funds easier in that the firm deducts all state contributions (which are expenditures for the NIC) for entitled workers from its payments to the NIC. So the firm actually pays to the NIC only the difference between the total amount of contributions collected and the total expenditure on particular cases of insurance payments. NIC expenditures that are deducted from payment to the NIC are paid to recipients through regional insurance companies.

The following allowances are excluded from our consideration of social protection supplied by the enterprise, because these payments are guaranteed and mandated by the state:

Sickness payment
Care allowance for a disabled family member
Financial support during maternity
Adjustment contribution in maternity
Contribution at birth of child
Funeral allowance

Table 11.1 Slovakia: income of the National Insurance Company

NIC fund	Paid by	Rate (% of gross wages)
Health Insurance	Employer	10.0
	Employee	3.7
	Total	13.7
Disability Insurance	Employer	4.4
	Employee	1.4
	Total	5.8
Pension Insurance	Employer	20.6
	Employee	5.9
	Total	26.5
Employment Fund	Employer	3.0
	Employee	1.0
	Total	4.0
Total contribution by employer		38.0
Total contribution by employee		12.0
Total insurance payment		50.0

Allowances for children
Substitution for health spa care supplement
Parental contribution

The reform of social security

In this section we will discuss government proposals for the future development of social policy in Slovakia, as set forth by the Ministry of Labour, Social Affairs, and Family of the Slovak Republic.

The current state of the social sphere is characterized as a 'strongly bureaucratic, centralist, and administrative system, based on a centrally planned economy and uniformity' (Ministry of Labour, Social Affairs and Family, 1993). This situation does not respect the needs and interests of citizens and is no longer sustainable. 'The Slovak social net is one of the most expensive nets in Europe, whereas the outputs (pensions, social contributions and services) are low and insufficient' (Ministry of Labour, Social Affairs and Family, 1993).

At the beginning of the 1950s, the socialist social security system abolished the insurance funds of previous generations; moreover it did not accumulate any financial capital and reserves during its existence. The present social system does not allow any individual additional insurance activities and does not single out higher-income groups to which higher pensions should correspond.

Transformation of the social net as a result of pluralization, democratization, and privatization is inevitable. The main principles of the resulting system will be personal participation, social solidarity, and state guarantees. This transformation of the social sphere must simultaneously ensure the maintenance of economic changes.

The reform of the social security system is based on a transition from state social security to social insurance.[7] The systems of social and labour relations are schematically presented in table 11.2. The social function of the enterprise is expressed here in individual labour relations guaranteed by labour law and in collective labour relations, which are closely linked to the position of trade unions within the firm.

The enterprise is engaged only marginally in the category of social relations. The firm is not an executor of these functions, although the main resources for financing these expenditures (namely for social insurance) are created in firms. Nevertheless, there is still some scope for firm activity in the field of the supplementary retirement system.

We shall now describe the expected foundation of individual social relations. Social insurance will be formed by the following three pillars:

(1) a mandatory basic system, which is defined and guaranteed by the state;
(2) a supplementary pension insurance system;
(3) an individual private insurance and security system.

The basic system will be designed to finance short-run disability insurance and long-run retirement insurance. The value of these endowments will be based on the recipient's salary. This basic system has a public and legal character because it is uniform and obligatory for all citizens. Its independence from the state budget is achieved by the creation of an autonomous Fund for Social Insurance[8] and by its self-managing organs. The establishment of this basic system must inevitably be accompanied by the development of supplementary retirement insurance systems. They would encourage firms to take responsibility for their workers, as well as citizens taking responsibility for their own future beyond the framework of the basic system. Individual private insurance is mainly designed as another supplementary source of income in the event of long-term illness and old age.

Another subsystem of social security is represented by 'state social support' – contributions by means of which a state addresses defined life situations (e.g. contributions for housing, or for a chronically sick child in a family). This support will be based on a minimum living

Table 11.2. Social and labour relations

Labour relations		Social relations	
Individual	Collective	Individual	Collective

(1) Contractual relations:
  – Labour Code
  – Legal working rules
  – Unemployment
    insurance
(2) Civil service:
  – Civil Service Act
	(1) Tripartite, general
	    agreements, regional and
	    local tripartite
	(2) Association and coalition
	    rights, social partnership
	(3) Collective bargaining
	(4) Employees' participation
		(1) Social insurance:
		  – retirement and disability
		    insurance
		  – supplementary insurance
		  – individual insurance
		(2) State social support
		(3) Social assistance
		(4) Health insurance, curative
		    and preventive care
		(5) Special endowments and
		    services
			(1) Accident insurance
			(2) Participation in social
			    security
			(3) Supplementary insurance
			(4) Public legal institutions
			(5) Social security
			    administration
			(6) Non-state subjects
			(7) State subjects

standard. The general economic situation of the state remains the decisive factor determining the extent of benefits. Social support has to deal with those life situations that are not covered by insurance.

The system of social assistance completes the set of supplementary resources, being aimed at social need in the lowest income groups.

The trade unions' point of view

Trade unions play a very important role in determining the level of social protection provided by enterprises. The reason is not only that the position of unions is relatively strong and stable in state enterprises and in recently privatized large firms (participation rates of around 90 per cent are not exceptional), but also that the unions are a legal partner in negotiations with the government.

Trade unions are governed by the Confederation of Trade Unions of the Slovak Republic (KOZ). Although union membership has been decreasing in Slovakia, this organization (which covers 47 professional trade unions) still has 1.8 million members, which represents about 80 per cent of the Slovak labour force.[9]

The supreme organ of tripartite negotiation is the Council of Economic and Social Agreement of the Slovak Republic, which consists of an equal number of government, trade union, and employer representatives. All initiatives concerning employees and their living expenses are subject to discussion in this institution. The potential legislative initiative of unions is mediated through political parties, which are entitled to submit these legislative proposals to parliament.

The power of unions is quite weak in private firms and in small firms recently privatized. Some private firms even require job applicants to cancel their union membership as a condition of employment. As the KOZ representative claims, 'many private firms (and firms with foreign capital participation) violate employees' rights (e.g. no written working contract). Some private employers promise to pay higher salaries than competitors, but they do not pay mandated social and disability insurance for their employees, or they do not pay salaries on time. Another problem is the legal enforcement of violated rights due to the lack of labour legislation.' Nevertheless, the rights of workers are defined and guaranteed by commercial law. For example, one-third of the supervisory board of joint stock companies should consist of employee representatives. If there is a trade union within a firm, these 'employee representatives' are usually union activists, but not necessarily. A related problem is caused by the problem of distinguishing between managers and employees. There is no general definition of a manager, so in fact managers in some firms are considered as employee representatives. Concerning the future development of the social protection system, KOZ representatives embrace the idea that 'it is not appropriate to copy mechanically any concrete foreign (e.g. French or German) social insurance system, even if it operates efficiently in a particular country. This assertion is fully in accord with foreign experts' opinion. It is important to create our own system, which takes into account particular foreign experience. Our experts are working on our concept of social policy transformation.'

We will not comment on the statements of trade union representatives here, but we must add a note concerning the distribution of so-called 'enterprise collective consumption' under socialism. This was certainly an important component of total consumption and part of it was equally accessible to all workers (such as canteens or health services). Part of it, however, was distributed unequally and trade unions (in enterprises and especially at higher levels) acted as 'power centres' where apartments and attractive holiday vouchers were distributed. Sometimes tickets for cultural events or places in crèches were also allocated in a preferential way. In other words, unions controlled the distribution of scarce goods and used their power in accord with the goals of the communist regime. As a result, not only 'captains of the market economy' but also people themselves prefer to have equal access to the advantages offered by unions.

Social protection and taxation

In this section we describe how concrete labour cost components (numbered and labelled in accordance with our questionnaire; see Appendix) are treated from the tax point of view.

Direct labour costs (II)[10]

- *Basic wages and salaries* are subject to income tax[11] on the full amount.
- *Mandatory payments to the NIC* are already a form of tax; the amount paid to the NIC increases labour costs for a firm and so eventually decreases a firm's pre-tax profits; other voluntary insurance payments are not allowed to be deducted from taxable income.
- *Other labour costs*[12] (*not included in parts III and IV*) – according to income tax law, only 'expenses for working and social conditions and health care'[13] can reduce taxable income.

Social protection equipment (III)

- *Kindergartens, vacation homes for employees, vacation homes for children of employees, workers' housing, sports facilities,* and *cultural centres* – in accounting terms (and according to a decree of the Federal Ministry of Finance[14]) expenditures on these facilities are operational costs and can reduce taxable income by a limited amount.
- *Medical facilities* and *canteens* are treated in the same way as 'other labour costs' (*II*).

Direct social benefits (IV)

- *Firm's contribution to social fund* is expressed as a share of the firm's wage costs, usually ranking from 1 to 2 per cent (the Social Fund Bill was adopted in 1994).
- *Interest-free loans, recreation contributions, food subsidies, private insurance contributions, social assistance,* and *other benefits in kind* are basically financed from the social fund (if a firm creates one). All these benefits are subject to employee income tax, with the exception of tax-exempt receipts (e.g. food allowances in non-cash form or social assistance[15]). From a firm's point of view these expenditures cannot be deducted from taxable income.

Social protection in selected enterprises

This part of the paper focuses on the detailed structure of social protection provided in three selected enterprises. We present an analysis of our observations collected in questionnaires and interviews from one state enterprise (SSE), one partially privatized joint stock company (JSC), and one almost completely privatized firm (PRV).[16]

To give a more complex picture of social protection we picked three firms at different stages of the privatization process. The firms are located in different parts of Slovakia and they operate in different industries. All of them are relatively large in terms of the number of workers. It is important to note that all three firms operated as 'national enterprises' for many years. The current form of ownership is the decisive distinguishing feature of the firms (see table 11.3).

The first firm (SSE) is still a state enterprise, so one can say it has been privatized by 0 per cent. This firm is a branch of a huge state concern and was founded in 1957. There are currently 2,980 employees in the firm. Privatization of the company is uncertain at the moment.

The second firm (JSC) was founded in 1953 as a state enterprise. It was transformed from a state enterprise into a joint stock company on 1 May

Table 11.3. The basic characteristics of the three firms

	SSE	JSC	PRV
Number of employees (1993)	2,980	5,993	5,146
Shares in FNM (%)	0	80	10
Shares in IPF & DIK (%)[1]	0	20	90
Date of establishment	1 May 1957	1953	1 April 1951
Date of privatization	?	1 May 1992	1 May 1992

FNM = National Property Fund
IPF = investment privatization fund
DIK = individual shareholder
1 This figure determines the level of a firm's 'privateness'.

1992. At that time the number of employees was 6,943 workers, while most recently it has totalled 5,993 workers. This firm was included in the first wave of voucher privatization in 1992/93, which resulted in a shift of 20 per cent of property to the investment privatization funds (IPFs) and individual shareholders (DIKs). The remaining shares are held by the National Property Fund (FNM). So the firm has been privatized by 20 per cent, because 20 per cent of its property is owned by private individuals.

The organizational history of the third firm (PRV) is similar to that of the JSC. The company was established in 1951 and transformed into a joint stock company (with 100 per cent shares in the FNM) on 1 May 1992. After five rounds of voucher privatization (in 1992/93) the majority of shares (90 per cent) is held by private investors, so we call this firm a private firm.

Methodology of investigation
We extensively investigated the level of social protection in these firms. We distributed a special questionnaire, in which we asked five basic questions:[17]

(1) Could you provide essential information about your company? (When was the company established? What is the type of ownership? etc.)

(2) How has the total number of workers changed in recent months (years)?

(3) What are monthly earnings of employees? (Components of earnings including basic wages and salaries, bonuses paid regularly, remuneration for overtime, payment for days not worked, etc.)

(4)   Could you evaluate the employers' mandatory payments for workers (health insurance, disability insurance, etc.)?

(5)   What social functions does your enterprise carry out?

The last question of the questionnaire was crucial. We asked about many possible kinds of benefits here[18] and asked for an evaluation of their monetary value.

In the next stage we interviewed the firms' personnel managers and trade union representatives. We were interested in the main objectives of social policy in the enterprises, in the changes over time in the provision of social functions, in relations between management and trade unions, in the system of entitlement selection for particular benefits, in the firm's initiatives towards the creation of a supplementary social insurance system, etc.

Summary of questionnaires

The compound summary reported in table 11.4 provides a detailed evaluation of the components of workers' earnings, employers' mandatory payments, and social benefits. The absolute numbers represent the average monthly values per person in Slovak crowns (Sk). Percentage values for components of earnings and social benefits are calculated as shares in adjusted total labour costs (total costs minus NIC payments), while mandatory payments are computed as shares in total costs.

Looking at the components of earnings in table 11.4, 'personal remuneration' plays a quite important role in the PRV. It is a flexible part of wages reflecting workers' individual performance and the location of the workplace. 'Bonuses paid regularly' comprise supplements for shiftwork, dangerous environment, weekend work, etc. 'Payments for days not worked' denote payments for regular annual holidays and for public (state) holidays.[19] The firm's 'profit-sharing bonus' is relatively low in comparison with other components of wages. This figure is lowest in the JSC owing to the very restricted entitlement of employees to this payment.[20] The situation is different in the SSE and the PRV, where all employees are entitled to profit-sharing. The 'holiday contribution' is a firm-specific payment introduced recently in both the SSE and the PRV. To understand the whole story behind recreation benefits, we must compare this figure with the recreation subsidy under 'social benefits'. We can then conclude that managers in the SSE and the PRV decided to restrict formerly quite generous subsidies for recreation and instead substituted a direct holiday contribution as a component of earnings. The JSC has maintained a wide range of subsidized recreation. But looking at the concrete absolute values of recreation subsidies in the

Table 11.4. Compound summary for the three establishments

Components of labour costs	Monthly values per person			Share in total labour costs (minus NIC payment)		
	SSE (Sk)	JSC (Sk)	PRV (Sk)	SSE (%)	JSC (%)	PRV (%)
Workers' earnings						
Basic wages and salaries	5,880	4,683	3,304	55.30	56.59	49.71
Personal remuneration	506	0	595	4.76	–	8.95
Bonuses paid regularly	573	1,094	1,158	5.39	13.23	17.42
Payments for days not worked	1,327	478	620	12.48	5.77	9.33
Profit-sharing bonus	386	137	162	3.63	1.66	2.44
Holiday contribution	781	0	65	7.35	–	0.98
Other	760	1,315	287	7.15	15.89	4.32
Vocational training	28	20	2	0.27	0.24	0.03
Employers' mandatory payments (NIC payment)						
Health insurance (10%)	1,127	468	675	7.50	4.66	7.32
Disability insurance (4.4%)	496	206	297	3.30	2.05	3.22
Pension insurance (20.6%)	2,322	965	1,390	15.46	9.59	15.08
Employment fund (3%)	447	140	208	2.98	1.40	2.26
Social benefits						
Housing (permanent)	0	56	32	–	0.67	0.48
Housing (temporary)	7	47	22	0.07	0.56	0.33
Kindergarten	15	3	32	0.15	0.04	0.48
Subsidized canteen	292	294	237	2.75	3.55	3.56
Policlinic access	34	49	15	0.32	0.59	0.23
Fitness facilities	11	0	1	0.11	–	0.01
Cultural events subsidy	0	0	1	–	–	0.01
Sanatorium treatment	1	0	0	0.01	–	–
Transport allowance	0	2	20	–	0.02	0.30
Jubilee bonuses[1]	0	26	2	–	–	–
Recreation subsidy	4	19	11	0.03	0.24	0.17
Non-returnable loans	0	0	0	–	–	0.01
Interest-free loans	0	78	1	–	0.94	0.02
Work clothes allowance	26	0	33	0.24	–	0.49
Severance & early retirement[1]	0	21	40	–	–	–
Other	1	0	49	0.01	–	0.73
Total costs (TC)	15,026	10,055	9,216	100.00	100.00	100.00
Total social benefits ⇔ result 1	391	548	453	2.60	5.45	4.92
TC adjust = TC – NIC payments	10,633	8,275	6,647	100.00	100.00	100.00
Total social benefits ⇔ result 2	391	548	453	3.68	6.62	6.82

1 The value of these items is excluded from the total costs because these payments are included as a component of wages (in accordance with firm statistics) and are subject to taxes like other income.

JSC and the PRV, they are not comparable with the generous holiday contribution in the SSE. From this point of view, the workers in the SSE are better off. The last component, 'other', includes various payments such as the indexation of wages in the SSE, severance and early retirement payments and jubilee bonuses in the JSC and the PRV,[21] benefits paid irregularly, etc. So this item is introduced to correct for the differences in local firms' statistics.[22]

'Vocational training' expenditure is treated separately in accordance with Eurostat labour cost methodology, but the importance of this item is very marginal in all three firms.

The crucial findings of our study are presented in the 'social benefits' group. All three firms spend about the same (in absolute terms) on a subsidized cafeteria. This is the most important benefit from the expenditure point of view. Subsidized housing (both permanent and temporary) plays an important role in the JSC and in the PRV, whereas this kind of benefit is only marginal in the SSE. Free access to the firm's policlinic, subsidized kindergarten, and recreation subsidy are the remaining benefits that are common to all three firms.

Several other benefits are specific to only one or two of our firms. For the JSC one such important benefit is interest-free loans. Such social help was typical of many socialist firms. Now the firms are trying to get rid of these loans, because they pose quite systematic problems of repayment. In the JSC a significant sum is spent on a recuperation subsidy (included under 'other'). The most questionable provision seems the work clothes allowance, because the obligatory internal rules for providing workers with clothing and other protective equipment vary from firm to firm.

It is clear from the 'total social benefits' row that the highest social benefit expenditures occur in the JSC, followed by the PRV, and the lowest are in the SSE. Looking at social expenditures as a share of total labour costs (result 1) suggests that the JSC provides the highest level of social benefits for its workers from the expenditure point of view. The private company has the second highest level, while the lowest proportion of social benefit expenditure is in the state enterprise. This ordering of firms also corresponds to a ranking by absolute figures.

However, looking at employers' mandatory payments (NIC payments), the values for the JSC on all the insurance items are relatively less than in the other two firms. It is possible that this is the result of an input data error, or perhaps the total wage basis determining mandatory payments is substantially lower in the JSC. Considering that these statutory payments affect neither workers' earnings nor social protection expenditures, we decided to deduct these four items from total costs (the item marked 'TC adjust'). After this correction we obtained result 2, which changes the ranking of the firms according to relative expenditures. The SSE remains lowest, but the PRV is now slightly better than the JSC. These relative differences are so small (6.62 per cent in the JSC vs. 6.82 per cent in the PRV) that we can conclude that the relative social benefit expenditures are equal in the JSC and the PRV.

Social protection in a state enterprise (SSE)

As the SSE is a state firm, its social functions are regulated by state law and government decrees. The principal act that currently governs social security in the SSE dates from 1988. It has been updated by several supplements. There were changes not only in social security legislation, but also in the important Act on State Enterprise of 1988, whose paragraphs controlling financial activities were modified. As of 1 January 1993 the SSE's Fund for Cultural and Social Needs (FKSP) was cancelled.[23] Until 1993 this fund was financed by a contribution of 2.5 per cent of the firm's total wage bill. After the latest legislative changes, a state enterprise can create a 'social fund' (SF) from net profits (i.e. profits after tax and mandatory contributions). The state budget Act (No. 14/93) for 1993 approved a contribution to the personal needs of workers totalling Sk 1,500 per person per annum deductible from the firm's profits.[24] At the same time it is possible to draw on the remaining resources of the old FKSP. The size of these resources determined the level of social benefits provided by a firm in 1993. The concrete economic rules are defined in the decree on the FKSP and in collective agreements. The main objectives of social protection covered by the FKSP and social funds include:

- a contribution towards the price of food in a firm's facilities;
- recreation subsidies;
- physical training and sporting subsidies;
- supplementary health care;
- interest-free loans and social assistance.[25]

Health protection equipment, the operating costs of health and educational centres, vocational training and retraining expenses, and the operating costs of catering facilities (i.e. practically all staff and material expenses) belong in the category of 'expenses for working and social conditions and health care'.[26] These expenditures might be included in production costs, which means that they are deductible from taxable income.

The housing policy in the past allowed a firm to allot an apartment to a worker, which in practice meant that an employee was provided with a flat free of charge. Now it is possible to allocate only vacant flats in this way. The SSE manages 856 apartments (compare this with the number of employees – 2,980), but not all of them are occupied by the firm's workers. The letting of flats is regulated by the state. If the costs of accommodation exceed the rent, the difference is fully covered by the firm. So the enterprise does not contribute to housing in a regular way. The state subsidy for heating is applied here as well, which decreases the final amount of the rent. The firm also offers temporary housing until an applicant has solved their housing problem. The rent of such apartments is subject to a price reduction specified in the collective agreement.

The enterprise owns and operates two kindergartens, which are also utilized by non-employees. Of the total capacity of 240 places, only 71 are used by workers' children. The expenses of Sk 31 per child a day are covered by the firm.

Catering is supplied by the firm's own kitchen. Staff and materials expenditures of Sk 16 for one portion are fully covered by firm. The FKSP makes an additional contribution of Sk 8.60 per portion. Given that the actual cost of one portion is Sk 32, workers pay only 25 per cent of the total cost of the food. This food allowance is defined in the collective agreement. During the first half of 1993, 64 per cent of workers, on average, availed themselves of subsidized food.

The operating costs of a health centre are financed by the firm, while the medical personnel and material expenses are covered through the NIC. Supplementary medical care is available as a firm-specific service in a special convalescent centre.

Sports facilities are rented by the firm. Workers can choose activities in accordance with their preferences. The range of services is defined in the collective agreement and depends on the available financial resources.

Sanatorium treatment is financed from disability insurance. The firm provides supplementary support for treatment by special request.

Under a new collective agreement, jubilee bonuses (financial bonuses on the 50th birthday and on important work anniversaries) are not provided from the FKSP. The financial grants (provided on the occasion of a 50-year jubilee and upon retirement) are treated as a part of labour costs, so they are included as components of workers' earnings.

The recreation contribution was set at a uniform value of Sk 1,000 per person in 1993, and is financed from the recreation fund (a component of the FKSP or social fund). For the purposes of recuperation and recreation the firm runs its own vacation centre. The costs of this are financed from the FKSP. The selection procedure for recuperation is determined in the collective agreement.

No non-returnable loans were granted at all in 1993. Interest-free loans are provided for housing purposes, and occasionally for social purposes. The entitlement conditions are defined in the collective agreement.

Benefits for education are restricted to vocational training costs, including regular courses, training programmes, and psychological tests.[27] The firm ensures a full range of safety equipment and work clothes for employees. These expenses are included in production costs.

The state budget provides a 'state adjustment contribution' of Sk 220 per child per month to all employees as well as 'family allowances' according to the number of children. Both allowances depend on the level of the employee's salary. These contributions are distributed through the firm, but the state reimburses this compensation. Therefore we do not include these payments as a childcare allowance.

Conclusions

Now we briefly summarize the overall situation in the SSE. The development of social protection over time is characterized by increasing salaries and decreasing non-wage benefits. Employment is being maintained at a stable level during the period of economic transformation, despite decreasing demand for the firm's production. If we look at employment itself as a kind of social function, then the probability of being laid off from the SSE seems relatively low in comparison with many recently privatized enterprises. The explanation is quite straightforward. Because the firm's privatization is expected in the near future, managers prefer to postpone unpopular decisions such as layoffs for a new owner. The logical result of this decision is decreasing productivity over time.[28]

Several benefits were recently abolished (transport subsidy) or reduced (interest-free loans) in the SSE. One interesting issue was the recreation subsidy. Managers argued that only a limited number of workers were helped by subsidized recreation each year, and they replaced this kind of social support with the direct payment of a uniform holiday contribution to every worker. Nevertheless, the firm's holiday houses are still kept, and they are operated on a non-profit basis. This policy makes all workers better off.

Although there are no exact data on the distribution of wages in the firm, we can argue that there are significant differences in remuneration among occupational categories. Our findings based on interviews indicate that blue-collar workers are better paid than employees in middle management positions. This is probably a hangover from the old socialist system of compensation, which strongly favoured manual over non-manual workers.[29] Of course, top management is not affected by any wage restrictions, which might increase average wages in the firm.

Managers in the SSE solve the problem of encouraging retirement[30] in a much less diplomatic way than in the JSC (discussed below). If a person of retirement age does not leave the firm voluntarily, then a personnel manager tries to persuade the worker in a discussion. If the worker still stays on, then one extreme procedure is the elimination of the worker's position. Then the worker has to leave (he/she is actually dismissed and so is entitled to a severance payment), and the firm must deal with the problem of how to rename and re-establish the cancelled position.

Social protection in a partly privatized enterprise (JSC)

As the JSC was recently a state enterprise, its social system is very similar to the system in the state enterprise. The new social functions are developing slowly, and this process tends to restrict some previous 'socialist' benefits (subsidized housing, non-returnable loans) that incurred losses for the firm. The improvement in worker welfare is focused on direct additional payments (e.g. the profit-sharing bonus, which is sometimes called the 'thirteenth salary'). This trend results from the underdeveloped legislation of social protection, which is in the process of transformation.

The JSC social fund amounts to Sk 29 million per year (in 1993). These funds are strongly targeted. Subsidies for permanent housing cost the firm Sk 4 million in 1993, so the firm is attempting to get rid of the houses. The problem is that, although the firm owns these houses, it is not allowed to dispose of them at will. 'Temporary housing' refers to the difference between the real rent and the price paid by the worker, the difference being borne by firm. The same principles as in the SSE apply to the subsidizing of the kindergarten, health centre, and catering.[31]

Sports facilities (swimming pool, gymnasium, pitches) are available to workers free of charge. Unfortunately, the firm does not record any data for these social benefits.

The firm introduced a new health programme in accordance with WHO recommendations in 1990. This includes recuperation stays of 2–3 weeks for strictly selected categories of workers (basically for those working in a dangerous environment). These stays are fully financed by the JSC and the worker is entitled to full average salary during that period.

Quite significant sums for jubilee bonuses (on average: Sk 26 per month per worker) and for severance payments (Sk 21 per month per person) are already included as components of workers' earnings. Both are financed from the firm's labour costs.

A limited number of shift workers are entitled to a transport subsidy, which is included in the firm's production costs.

The recreation contribution is also an important kind of social benefit provided by the JSC. A worker is entitled to a 60 per cent discount on the price of recreation, which includes all family members. Foreign holidays are excluded from the subsidy. In the case of children's recreation the price discount rises to 70 per cent.

Non-returnable loans were abolished approximately five years ago. Interest-free loans are still a very popular kind of social protection. Loans of Sk 25,000 per person were granted to 300 employees in 1992.

There is no special benefit for education except for vocational training costs in the JSC.

Five hundred workers in the highest-risk working category are covered by collective life insurance, which is mandatory under the collective agreement.

Conclusions

Several new benefits have recently been introduced in the JSC. It is difficult to decide whether to consider severance payments and benefits for induced retirement as a kind of social protection. One can argue that they both involve quite significant sums (equivalent to five average monthly salaries) that improve workers' welfare for a certain period. From this point of view they reduce workers' insecurity about losing a job and about retirement, respectively. However, the firm's main incentive in establishing such a benefit is to persuade the workers to replace their permanent income from the firm by the much lower pension paid by the state. Workers of retirement age now face a dilemma: either they leave a firm within three months and receive a benefit, or they remain in a firm (for an uncertain period) and lose their entitlement to benefit. This situation probably increases workers' insecurity about their future prospects in a firm.

On the other hand, we must recall payments for loyalty (also recently introduced), which are designed to reduce labour force fluctuation and to make a firm more attractive to workers with longer work experience. A comprehensive health programme established in 1990 is also a very firm-specific kind of social protection.

There is thus a clear trend in the JSC to shed those social activities that incur losses for the firm (the subsidized flats and vacation houses, kindergartens).

The position of unions (with a participation rate of about 65 per cent) is weaker than in the PRV. Management–union relations are characterized as 'quite good' (from the management viewpoint), but unions sometimes 'want to influence decisions that are beyond their competence'.

In the field of private insurance systems, the firm initiated the creation of an *enterprise insurance company* as an independent legal entity. Owing to the lack of legislation in this area, this activity is only at a very early stage. However, managers already predict future troubles with pension payments, because the current system will not be able to meet the demands of higher-income groups in full. The independence of NIC insurance funds is also questioned.[32]

Social protection in a private enterprise (PRV)

Several of the social benefits provided by the PRV (temporary accommodation, transport subsidy) are determined by the high dispersion of the firm's construction workers, who work within the whole of the former Czechoslovakia. Financial rules concerning social benefits in the PRV are similar to those in the other firms. The firm funds its social fund by a contribution of 0.8 per cent of its wage bill. In 1992 this share was 2.0 per cent (as is legally allowed), but it was decreased as a result of the bad economic situation of the firm in 1993.

The PRV subsidizes 660 flats for workers to the tune of Sk 2 million per year, and provides a subsidy for temporary housing for construction workers as well.

Funding of kindergarten and catering[33] subsidies is again shared by the social fund (which contributes to the price of a meal) and the firm's production costs (which cover the operating costs of the kindergarten and cafeteria, including the salaries of staff).

The firm's medical facilities are used by workers of several organizations (in addition to the PRV) free of charge, so these organizations share the operational costs of the policlinic building with the PRV. Medical staff and materials are financed by the NIC.

A minimal subsidy for cultural activities from the social fund is spent mainly on supporting the firm's folk music group.

A significant transport allowance is a quite firm-specific benefit. It is determined by the nature of the firm's production. More than 1,000 construction workers are entitled to subsidized transport to construction sites.

Jubilee bonuses and severance and early retirement payments are guaranteed by the collective agreement, but are treated as enterprise labour costs. It means that they are included as components of workers' earnings. The significant sum for work clothing is a component of the firm's production costs.

Only one person was granted a non-returnable loan from the social fund in 1993, and this type of benefit was cancelled by law at the beginning of 1994. Interest-free loans (financed from the social fund) were also provided to a very small extent.

The recreation contribution was restricted to children's recreation in 1993, and this benefit was replaced by the holiday allowance, which is currently included as a component of workers' earnings.

Recuperation treatment is a new firm-specific social benefit. Significant amounts for this purpose were funded primarily from the firm's production costs (as the new tax system allows) and secondarily from the social fund.

Conclusions and results of interviews

The main objectives of social policy in the PRV are characterized by the personnel manager as 'a decrease in labour turnover, stimulation for higher achievement, and preservation of the firm's competitiveness'.

Speaking about developments over time, the firm's representatives are happy that they have succeeded in keeping social benefits from previous years, because they consider these advantages as a privilege, which 'makes the firm relatively more attractive in comparison with many small private enterprises, which do not supply any social services'.

The position of trade unions is quite strong because 95 per cent of employees in the firm are unionized. According to one manager, relations between management and the unions are 'not conflictual'. Although the collective agreement defining social benefits was worked out by the employer, nevertheless the unions accept all social benefits as 'something that must be given to workers automatically'. A trade union representative, on the other hand, evaluated these relations as 'tense and conflictual'. Some 'managers pressed employees (especially those in lower managerial positions) to leave the union'. The main source of conflict between the union organization and management is the composition of the firm's supervisory board (the trade union has no member on the supervisory board).

The level of social benefits has been shrinking recently. We again refer to the words of a trade union representative here:

> 'The level of social protection is closely linked with the problematic economic situation of the firm. The firm closed down two kindergartens and the construction of new flats has been stopped. A large part of the Social Fund goes on subsidized catering. Financial loans were abolished, the contribution for recreation was substantially reduced and it was restricted to employees' children's recreation. Management decided to cancel subsidized catering for former employees/pensioners on November 1, 1993.'

On the other hand, the loyalty bonuses have been increased and jubilee bonuses have also been preserved in order to retain workers. The law on income tax allows the introduction of recuperation breaks, which are partly financed from the social fund.

As far as the selection system for individual benefits is concerned, basically all workers are entitled to privileges defined in the collective agreement. Of course, not all benefits can be provided for all workers. A special 'social committee' consisting of 22 people – both union and employer representatives – decides who is to be granted particular benefits. For example, for interest-free loans the primary entitlement criterion is the social situation of a worker.

The situation as regards the firm's assets (flats, vacation houses) is similar to that in the JSC. The flats owned by the firm are really a burden, because they incur only financial losses. The problem is that, although the firm is the owner, it cannot dispose of them at will. The eventual solution is not clear yet, because the legal framework has not yet been set up. In the case of holiday houses the firm prefers to keep them.

In the area of supplementary insurance activities, the firm has initiated the establishment of an insurance company for its industrial branch, but 'a minimum of 20,000 participating workers was required. Unfortunately, no partner firm was found to support this idea.' And again, 'waiting for new legislation measures' (manager) is the only current outcome.

According to a trade union representative: 'Unions are attempting to create their own insurance company. We are forming a fund for financial support in unemployment. Dismissals from our firm were not high during the transformation period. The recession hit our firm after a time-lag – until the middle of 1993 the situation was stable. Now we face problems of searching for customers.' In this context, additional layoffs will be inevitable. 'We suggest strong measures for improving working discipline.' The union representative summarizes the general situation in the following words:

> 'The mandated social security payments for employees declined from the previous level of 45 per cent to the current share of 38 per cent of the firm's wage bill. Many social benefits have been abolished, e.g. financial support for students who signed a future employment contract with a firm. The level of social security is dependent on the health of the economic branch in which the firm operates. In other words, the economic situation of a firm is decisive for the provision of social benefits. Our bad situation means that the SF is funded by only 0.8 per cent of the firm's wage bill (under the collective agreement), whereas this share is defined at 2 per cent by law. Because of this, the trade union concentrates its activity mainly on primary benefits such as food

subsidies, cultural and sporting activities, and financial loans. As new social benefits we can consider the extended paid holidays (increased from 20 to 25 days per year) and the reduction of the working week from 42.5 hours to 40 hours.'

Empirical results

This section analyses the data on social protection supplied by 19 Slovak firms. Table 11.5 provides a basic set of variables characterizing our sample:

SIZE = the average number of workers in 1993.

WAGES = average monthly wages expressed in Sk/person.

DIR_SP (direct social protection) = firms' expenditures on social benefits, which can be paid in cash (recreation contribution, food or transport allowance, etc.).

INDIR_SP (indirect social protection) = the operating costs of equipment designed for social purposes (vacation homes, canteen, houses for workers).

SP (total social protection) = the sum of indirect and direct social protection.

PRIVAT ('privateness') = the share of a firm's property held by private agents. The majority of our firms (16) are joint stock companies privatized in the first wave of voucher privatization in 1991–2. One firm is still fully owned by the state (PRIVAT = 0 per cent), and two small limited liability companies are completely private firms (PRIVAT = 100 per cent).

SP/WAGES = the percentage share of social protection expenditure in wage costs.

SP/TOTAL = the percentage share of social protection expenditures in total labour costs.

The last four rows of table 11.5 provide the first step of our data analysis. The mean, standard error, minimum, and maximum values are computed separately for each variable. It is interesting to note that direct social protection plays a more important role than indirect protection from the expenditure point of view (this is particularly clear for small firms 120 and 121). There is no firm in our sample without any kind of social protection. Each enterprise spends an average of 5.4 per cent of its wage costs and 3.8 per cent of total labour costs on social protection. This observation corresponds well with our earlier findings from the three enterprises, described as result 1 and result 2 in table 11.4.

Let us now recall our initial hypothesis that the level of social protection

Table 11.5. Empirical results for 19 companies (monthly values in Sk/person)

Firm	SIZE	WAGES	PRIVAT	DR_SP	INDIR_SP	SP	SP/WAGES	SP/Total
19	195	8,408	83%	147	109	256	3.04%	2.18%
35	374	5,083	74%	9	0	9	0.16%	0.12%
46	234	6,260	77%	300	227	527	8.42%	5.88%
49	78	8,718	97%	90	269	359	4.12%	2.95%
50	428	4,970	88%	101	61	162	3.27%	2.43%
61	276	3,122	96%	0	43	43	1.38%	1.00%
63	204	6,567	97%	319	106	425	6.48%	4.46%
64	223	5,022	87%	210	38	248	4.55%	3.29%
65	58	5,422	74%	292	530	822	15.10%	9.62%
69	415	6,501	97%	68	24	92	1.39%	1.09%
72	231	5,251	87%	103	511	614	11.65%	7.89%
75	376	6,097	97%	0	476	476	7.59%	5.42%
84	147	6,816	97%	119	0	119	1.74%	1.26%
100	151	4,802	74%	126	112	238	4.95%	3.50%
111	2,980	10,213	0%	324	67	391	3.83%	2.61%
112	5,993	7,707	20%	393	155	548	7.11%	5.46%
113	5,146	6,191	89%	350	103	453	7.32%	4.92%
120	10	11,000	100%	700	0	700	6.36%	4.41%
121	33	5,850	100%	285	0	285	4.67%	3.31%
Mean	923.79	6,527.47	80.75%	207.13	149.07	356.20	5.43%	3.78%
SE	404.90	447.19	6.13%	39.89	40.20	51.86	0.85%	0.55%
Minimum	10	3,122	0.00%	0.00	0.00	8.71	0.16%	0.12%
Maximum	5,993	11,000	100.00%	700.00	530.00	821.67	15.10%	9.62%

Table 11.6. Correlation matrix of selected variables

	SIZE	WAGE	PRIVAT	DIR_SP	INDIR_SP
SIZE	1.00				
WAGE	.22	1.00			
PRIVAT	−.63	−.33	1.00		
DIR_SP	.34	.62	−.23	1.00	
INDIR_SP	−.08	−.13	.00	−.16	1.00

is related to a firm's ownership structure, to a firm's size, and to the average wage level.

The second step of our analysis is expressed in correlation coefficients between five selected variables, as reported in table 11.6. On this basis there are only two interesting relations between our variables: firm size is negatively correlated with privateness, and direct social protection is positively correlated with wages. Although the first dependence is not our direct objective, figure 11.1 gives a clearer picture of our sample. There is a weak trend showing that the bigger firms are less private. This could lead to the conclusion that the state prefers to privatize smaller firms and keep control over bigger enterprises. The second correlation is much more interesting in terms of our hypothesis testing. Figure 11.2 shows the trend that higher direct social protection expenditure is related to higher wages. There is no significant correlation between wages on the one hand and size and privateness of firms on the other hand. Therefore the relationship between wages and social protection does not derive from the two other variables correlated with wages.

In the next stage we formulated a simple regression model:

$$\text{DIR\_SP}_i = a_0 + a_1^* \text{WAGES}_i + \varepsilon_i. \tag{11.1}$$

Estimating (11.1) by the least-squares method we obtain:

$$\text{DIR\_SP}_i = -152.24 + 0.055^* \text{WAGES}_i + e_i, \quad R^2 = .38$$
$$(-1.32) \ (3.23) \tag{11.2}$$

where e_i denotes LS residuals and the values of t-statistics are in brackets. Looking at the value of the t-statistics in equation 11.2, the estimated value of a_1 is statistically significant. If we accept this hypothesis, a small positive value of a_1 suggests that increasing expenditures on direct social benefits are determined by higher wage levels.

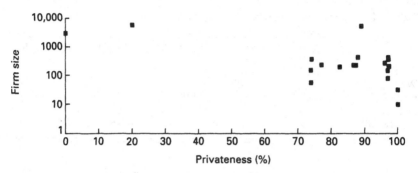

Figure 11.1   Relationship between firm size and privateness

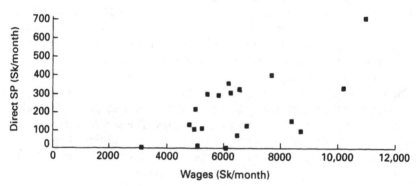

Figure 11.2   Relationship between direct social protection expenditures and firms' average wages

Then we depicted the relationship between WAGES and a new variable DIR_SP/WAGES (fig 11.3). Looking at this chart we can conclude (because there is no visible trend) that the firms' relative expenditures on direct social protection are not dependent on the average wage level in the firm.

Finally, referring to our regression analysis results,[34] *we cannot accept our initial hypothesis* that the level of total social protection is determined by the ownership structure, or the firm size, or the wage level. Only direct social protection was in some cases determined by either wage level (eq. 11.2) or firm size, but the absolute values of the coefficients were close to zero in both cases, and the value of R^2 did not support the appropriateness of the models used. On the other hand, we must stress that all these conclusions refer strictly to our data sample, which is probably not representative (for reasons mentioned earlier).

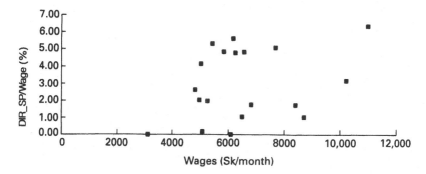

Figure 11.3   **Relationship between relative direct social protection expenditures and firms' average wages**

We have also tested multiple regression specifications. The results revealed unchanged coefficients for wages and insignificant coefficients for size and privateness. This reconfirms the results from our simple correlation analysis. We further carried out tests on the functional form of the relationship between direct social protection and wages. The hypothesis of a log-linear specification was rejected in favour of the presented linear version.

No significant relationship between indirect social protection and wages, size and privateness could be found. The same is true for total social protection.

As regards the distribution of social protection expenditures,[35] figure 11.4 shows that the greater part of indirect social expenditures is directed to firms' canteens and workers' housing, whereas expenditures on sports and cultural facilities are negligible. We present a similar chart for direct social protection (fig. 11.5). Here again the meal subsidy is the most important benefit. Total social expenditures are summarized in figure 11.6. Meal subsidies and coverage of a canteen's operating costs appeared as major objectives of firms' social policy.

Final remarks

To summarize our observations, all firms provide some basic social protection. This includes food subsidies (provided by 15 firms) and recreation subsidies (11 firms). Then there are some additional firm-specific benefits (included under 'other' in figs. 11.5 and 11.6), for instance interest-free loans, transport allowances, recuperation subsidies, which depend on the overall economic situation of enterprise.

If we try to determine the development over time of social protection, it

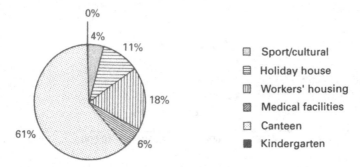

Figure 11.4   The structure of indirect social protection expenditures

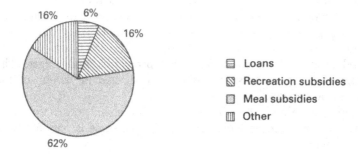

Figure 11.5   The structure of direct social protection expenditures

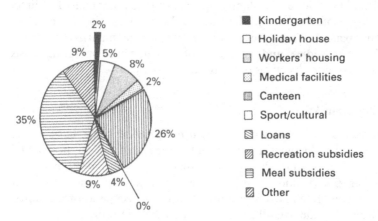

Figure 11.6   The structure of total social protection expenditures

is important to note that several benefits formerly supplied by enterprises have been abolished by law. We mention two of them here. The first is the system of work categories, which affects all former state-owned firms. Officially this system decided entitlement to the old age pension.[36] It distinguished three occupational groups according to the risk and danger to health of the working environment. Group 3 characterized the least dangerous jobs, to which corresponded the lowest pension. Correspondingly group 1 comprised the most dangerous working conditions, to which corresponded the highest pension supplement. This system has not so far been replaced by a new one. The Slovak parliament extended its validity until the end of 1993, and then again for 1994 as well. Another type of social assistance that was uniformly abolished by law was crèches for children.[37]

Finally we attempt to formulate some common features of the social protection supplied by enterprises.

- Every firm provides some minimal level of standard benefits, usually in the form of direct social protection.
- Supplementary firm-specific benefits vary from firm to firm.
- Trade unions play an important role in formulating social policy not only at the firm level (in both state and recently privatized firms) but also at the macro level (in discussions concerning the mandatory creation of social funds); social benefits defined by collective agreements are the most important social functions provided by firms.
- The total level of social protection provided by a particular firm depends on the firm's economic performance and ability to pay higher wages.
- All benefits approved by collective agreements are applicable to all employees, irrespective of whether they are unionized, so this could be one reason that union participation is decreasing over time.
- The government tends to support through preferential tax treatment those benefits that are oriented towards the improvement of health and social conditions.
- The funding of social protection in enterprises is shared by different social funds and by production costs.

These features not only are directly implied from our analytical study but also rely on our findings from interviews and various reports published in Slovak newspapers.[38] Deeper and more sophisticated econometric analysis based on a larger sample of firms offers sufficient scope for further work in this area.

Appendix: Questionnaire on the social function of the enterprise

I. Data on employees:

Date	Number of employees:	Note:

II. Direct labour costs:

	Sk/month (average value)	Note:
Total wage costs		
Mandatory payments to the National Insurance Company		
Other labour costs (not included in parts III and IV)		
II.a. Total direct labour costs		

III. Social protection equipment:

Type of facility	Monthly operational costs in Sk	Note
Kindergarten		
Vacation home for employees		
Vacation home for children of employees		
Workers' housing		
Medical facilities		
Canteen		
Sports facilities		
Cultural centre		
Other		
III.a. Total indirect social protection		

IV. Direct social benefits

	Sk/year	% of wage costs
Firm's contribution to social fund		

Type of benefit	Monthly value of benefit in Sk (per person)	Number of employees exploiting facility
Interest-free loan		
Recreation contribution		
Food subsidy		
Private insurance contribution		
Social assistance		
Other benefits in kind		
IV.a. Total direct social protection		

Total labour costs (II.a + III.a + IV.a)		

NOTES

We are grateful to Jan Mládek (CEU, Prague), Martin Rein (MIT), and Jiri Vecernik (Institute of Sociology, Prague) for many helpful and clarifying comments.

1 Because it is not clear which of these words is the most appropriate term to describe the means by which social protection is provided, we consider these words to be synonyms. However, we have decided primarily to use the term 'benefit' in our paper.

2 There was a big discussion concerning the mandatory creation of social funds in the Slovak parliament in 1993. The most disputed issue was whether to mandate each firm to form such a fund disregarding its economic performance. The Law on the Social Fund was adopted in parliament in September 1994. Each economic unit is mandated to form a social fund for its employees at a level of 0.6 per cent of its gross wage bill. However, this law does not affect our results, because our data were collected before the law was adopted.

3 Actually, these 'national enterprises' existed until 1988. They were replaced by 'state enterprises' in late socialism, and they were later privatized. Nevertheless, it is not necessary to distinguish between 'national' and 'state' enterprises for the purposes of this study.

4 The only criterion imposed on the selection of firms that we asked to collaborate was that the firm was privatized in the first wave of voucher privatization. The final sample was determined by the firms' willingness to reveal internal data. In this context we must express our great thanks to the representatives of the 19 Slovak firms who responded to our questionnaire.

5 Sk = Slovak koruna (US$1 ≈ Sk 30).

6 We refer here to representatives of the Ministry of Labour, Social Affairs and Family of the Slovak Republic.

7 We must admit that the socialist system also recognized 'social insurance', but this form of social security played only a marginal role.

8 This independence is also specified in Act No. 7/1993 of the National Council of the Slovak Republic, which established the National Insurance Company.

9 This figure contradicts the public opinion poll results published by the Slovak Statistical Office in April 1993, which suggest that only 47 per cent of workers are unionized, and 26 per cent of employees surveyed had recently resigned union membership. Another survey (Economic Expectations and Attitudes, November 1993) shows that only 20 per cent of the total active population and 25 per cent of workers in enterprises with unions have a good knowledge of what they are doing.

10 'Direct labour cost' is not a precise accounting term. According to this terminology, labour costs are divided into 'wage costs' and 'other labour costs'. In the estimation and evaluation of these costs we distinguish 'direct costs' and 'indirect costs'. 'Direct costs' are those that we can allocate to each unit of output (product). So only the labour costs of workers who are directly engaged in the production process belong in this category. 'Indirect costs' are those we cannot calculate for one unit of output. We include here the labour costs of employees who are not employed directly in the production process (e.g. workers in delivery, sales, distribution departments, etc.).

11 All kinds of rewards such as profit shares, rewards for invention and

improvement projects, jubilee benefits, and compensation for holidays not taken are taxed as income.

The basic annual income tax and corresponding tax rates are as follows:

Income band (Sk/year)	Basic tax paid (Sk)	Tax rate on income in excess of lower bound of band (%)
< 60,000	0	15
60,000–120,000	9,000	20
120,000–180,000	21,000	25
180,000–540,000	36,000	32
540,000–1,080,000	151,200	40
> 1,080,000	367,200	47

12 According to accounting terminology, 'other labour costs' are part of wage costs, which include rewards for work rendered on a basis other than full-time work (e.g. part-time work).

13 These kinds of expenditures are precisely defined by law. They include: (1) security, health protection, and sanitary arrangements of the workplace, (2) health services for employees in a range determined by special regulations, (3) the services of an educational institution, if the public service organ (local government) is not obliged to pay for this service, or expenditures on the education of apprentices, or the retraining of employees organized by a third party (i.e. vocational training costs are also included here), (4) the services of a firm's own canteen excluding the cost of the food, or subsidies for food up to 55 per cent of the price of a main dish if catering is organized by a third party.

14 Income tax law No. 286/92, §25k (facilities for satisfying the needs of employees or other persons).

15 According to §6 of Act No. 286/92.

16 Only these three firms were included in our earlier version of the paper. They were denoted there as SSE, JSC, and PRV, respectively. We stick to this notation in this chapter, but we also use new numerical abbreviations in later analytical sections (SSE ≡ firm 111; JSC ≡ firm 112; PRV ≡ firm 113).

17 The questionnaire used for these three firms was more extensive than the one used for the remaining firms (see Appendix).

18 The following benefits were listed in the questionnaire: housing (permanent), housing (temporary), other housing rent assistance, kindergarten, subsidized canteen, free policlinic access, fitness facilities, cultural events subsidy, sanatorium treatment, subsidized food store, transport allowance, childcare allowance, jubilee bonuses, food stamps, recreation/holiday subsidy, non-returnable loans, interest-free loans, discount on firm's product prices, benefits for education, work clothes allowance, separation payment for family, life insurance allowance, early retirement and severance payments.

19 In all three firms workers are entitled to a vacation of 20 working days per year (guaranteed by state law), plus 5 additional days according to the collective agreement. In the case of the JSC, public holidays are excluded from this component, which explains the quite low percentage share of this compensation in comparison with the SSE and the PRV.

20 Only 350 employees out of 6,000 workers are entitled to profit sharing totalling Sk 822,500 per month, i.e. Sk 2,350 per entitled person.

21 The value of these items is included under social benefits, but they are excluded from the total costs. These payments are already included as a component of wages (in accordance with firm statistics) and they are subject to taxes like other income.

22 We must emphasize that comparing one firm's individual statistics with those of another is very difficult; in other words there is a high probability that a particular payment is included in one category for one firm and in another category for the other firm. Nevertheless, the resulting total value, which is what is important for our analysis, is correct.

23 We can easily generalize the existence of this fund for all state enterprises, so it was not only specific to the SSE.

24 In the SSE this subsidy is granted to each worker automatically and in a firm's internal statistics it is treated as a component of workers' earnings.

25 Social assistance is a type of interest-free returnable loan.

26 These expenses are described in note 13 above.

27 We treated vocational training costs separately in our questionnaire (in accordance with Eurostat methodology).

28 We assume here a simple definition of productivity such as output divided by number of workers.

29 Corresponding to the ideological tenet that 'workers are the leading class of society'.

30 Workers may not be legally compelled to leave a firm after reaching retirement age.

31 The financing of the catering subsidy is also shared by the social fund and the firm's production costs. A worker pays only Sk 9.50 per meal out of the total price of Sk 33.40 (i.e. 28 per cent of the real price).

32 All employer contributions to the NIC in 1993 went into the government budget, which was running a significant deficit. The NIC had to borrow money from commercial banks (at high interest rates) to finance its activities at the beginning of 1994.

33 The real price of one meal is Sk 32 but workers pay only Sk 12 (i.e. 37.5 per cent of the actual price).

34 We carried out several regression models. Indirect social protection and total social protection expenditures did not appear significantly dependent on either wages, privateness, or firm size. Only the constant term in some regressions appeared important, which can be explained by some fixed (minimal) provision of social protection in each firm. It would be interesting to include other explanatory variables (e.g. firm's profits), but we do not have access to this information.

35 These shares were calculated from the summation of particular benefit expenditures for all firms.

36 However, work categories were also an instrument for privileging some groups not according to risk and danger to health but according to their usefulness to the regime. Typical cases were not only miners and chemical workers, but also high-ranking military officers, policemen, diplomats, etc. So when the federal parliament abolished the system of job categorization in 1992, it was not an 'anti-social' but just an 'anti-privileges' measure.

37 Crèches operated in the same way as kindergartens. The only difference was

that these day-care centres were designed for children below the age of 3 years.
38 We refer to several issues of the *SME* daily and *TREND* weekly of 1993–4.

BIBLIOGRAPHY

Confederation of Trade Unions (1993), *Dokumenty II. zjazdu Konfederácie odborových zväzov Slovenskej republiky* [The Documents of the Second Congress of the Confederation of Trade Unions of the Slovak Republic], Bratislava, June.

Estelle, J. (1993), 'Occupational pension schemes and voluntary savings', preliminary World Bank report.

Eurostat (1978), *Labour Costs in Industry, 1975*, vol. 1: *Detailed Results by Industry*, vol. 2: *Structure of Labour Costs*, Luxembourg: Eurostat.

Ministry of Labour, Social Affairs and Family of the Slovak Republic (1993), 'Koncepcia transformácie sociálnej sféry Slovenskej republiky' [The concept of transformation of the social sphere in the Slovak Republic], preliminary working paper, Bratislava, September.

Rein, M. and L. Rainwater (eds.) (1986), *Public/Private Interplay in Social Protection. A Comparative Study*, Armonk, NY: M. E. Sharpe.

Schmähl, W. and S. Böhm (1993), 'Occupational pension schemes in the private and public sector in the Federal Republic of Germany', *Ageing and Work* 11(3), February.

12 The enterprise social wage in the transitional economy of Ukraine

IRINA TRATCH and ANDREAS WÖRGÖTTER

Introduction

The main purpose of the paper is to explore the social role of enterprises in the transitional economy of Ukraine. First, we explain the factors accounting for social benefits in enterprises in Ukraine during the pre-transition period. Then we analyse the legal and institutional framework of labour costs in enterprises and outline the implications for the composition of workers' compensation packages. This is followed by a presentation of the results of ten case-studies carried out in Ukrainian enterprises. The summary presents the main findings and conclusions.

The role of employee benefits in socialist economies

In contrast to market economies, where firms pursue profits and pay wages accordingly (Ehrenberg and Smith, 1991: 266–77), enterprises in socialist economies pursue both economic and social objectives. One of the major accomplishments of the socialist system was the relatively equal distribution of income, or, in other words, low income inequality, which stemmed primarily from guaranteed employment and low wage differentiation in the state sector. The prime social role of an enterprise was to provide employment to alleviate social problems in its region. In addition, many firms took an active role in providing social services to employees. For example, enterprises operated kindergartens and shops, and provided sporting and recreation facilities, medical care, and so on.

Several studies (for example, Rein and Friedman, 1994, and Fajth and Lakatos, 1994) offer explanations for the social spending of enterprises in socialist economies. Employee benefits stemmed primarily from political and ideological considerations, thus having little to do with economic considerations. Such reasons are summarized below.

First, the provision of certain employee benefits was 'a precondition of extensive way of socialist development based on the transfer of household labor and agricultural labor to "more productive" industrial labor' (Fajth and Lakatos, 1994: 2). Large-scale industrialization in the former USSR, which began in late 1920s, entailed a large-scale transfer of labour from other sectors, in particular from agriculture. In line with the policy of industrialization and with political considerations concerning the improvement of the living conditions of industrial enterprises' employees, in their decisions on allocating public resources central and local authorities gave preference to the proletariat, that is, workers in large enterprises, in contrast to other social groups, that is peasants and the 'intelligentsia'. As a result, a significant social services sector was born, and subsequently attached to large industrial state enterprises. The social infrastructure of enterprises, such as permanent housing, kindergartens, shops, hospitals, sporting facilities, and other social benefits provided by industrial enterprises, was an effective incentive for sectoral migration.

Second, the Communist Party believed in prioritizing the social aspects of work, that is living conditions, the satisfaction of employees' cultural needs, education, recreation, and so on, and strongly advocated the adoption of such prioritization for all government, economic, and public organizations (*Programme of the Communist Party of the Soviet Union*, 1989: 37). In addition, it was officially announced that the enterprise was the main site of people's socialization. As is mentioned in a Ukrainian enterprise-level sociological study (Chornobai, 1992: 94): 'An enterprise is the main link in the satisfaction of people's necessities of life. There they are provided with housing, children's institutions [kindergartens and crèches], and recreation facilities, and also receive a wage in order to obtain all the other necessary goods.' As a result of this policy, social and welfare services were provided by enterprises in cooperation with central and local governments. Moreover, the social services of enterprises were often available not only to their employees but also to local communities.

The provision of these social services was controlled in the following manner. The overwhelming majority of enterprises were state owned and governed by local councils of people's deputies (local authorities in the former Soviet Union). It was obligatory for decisions of local councils of people's deputies to be implemented by all enterprises, institutions, and organizations situated in the councils' territory (*Constitution of the Ukrainian SSR*, 1977, article 127, p. 50). In other words, enterprises were not allowed to provide the benefits only in accordance with profit considerations. On the other hand, large industrial enterprises had an incentive to provide public social services since in that way they could build up the support of central and local governments for further subsidies and other decisions on the distribution of public resources.

Third, employee benefits were an important tool of political control. The allocation of benefits in enterprises was decided by management and the trade unions, which were to a great extent controlled by the Communist Party. In general, managers and heads of trade unions received much larger shares of the total benefits than other employees, despite the fact that it was officially claimed that all employees had access to benefits irrespective of their social status.

Thus, whereas in market economies the provision of employee benefits is consistent with the profit goal of enterprises, in socialist economies enterprises provided benefits mainly for political and ideological reasons, regardless of the profit motive. The provision of social benefits by enterprises in Ukraine during the pre-transition period, as in other socialist economies, was obligatory and determined by the Communist Party's policy of socializing people within enterprises. And, in general, there was no variation in provision across enterprises, except that large enterprises emphasized benefits that required social infrastructure.

The determinants of total compensation

The public social safety net: the role of enterprises and the state

This section considers how the system of social protection has been developing since the beginning of the transition and the role of the state and enterprises in providing employees with social protection benefits. It also focuses on those social benefits of enterprises that are mandated by the state and those that are supplied by them voluntarily, and, in the latter case, on benefits that are a substitute for the benefits provided by the state and benefits that are supplementary.

As is recognized by the IMF (1992: 32), Ukraine has a well-developed system of social protection for the weak and vulnerable groups of society. The main features of the social protection scheme that has been established since 1991 are as follows: first, the roles of the state and enterprises were clearly defined and separated; second, unemployment was officially recognized to be an unavoidable part of the move to a market economy; and, third, heavy payroll taxes to finance the public social safety net were imposed. The social protection scheme consists of the following elements (see table 12.1):

(1) Three extrabudgetary funds, namely the Pension Fund, the Employment Fund, and the Social Insurance Fund, which provide social security benefits.
(2) Family allowances and compensation for price increases, which are financed directly through the budget.

Table 12.1. Ukraine: the social safety net

Element	Revenue sources	Expenditures	Notes
Pension Fund	– enterprises (31.8% of gross wage) – employees (1% of wage) – other	– old-age pensions – invalidity pensions – other	Pensions are issued via local post offices.
Employment Fund	– enterprises (3% of gross wage) – other	– job placement help – unemployment compensation – other	The EF has its own local unemployment agencies.
Social Insurance Fund	– enterprises (5.2% of gross wage) – other	– sick pay (temporary disability benefits) – birth and maternity benefits – sanatoria facilities for children and the temporarily disabled – other	The SIF is operated by trade unions. Benefits are paid by enterprises (deduction mechanism).
The system of family allowances and compensation for price increases	Budget	– uniform family allowances for households with young children and total income equivalent to less than twice the minimum wage – allowances for single mothers – allowances for low-income families – childcare benefits – compensation for price increases – monthly cash benefits for families with children up to age 16 – compensation payments for the increase in the price of children's goods – lump-sum annual clothing allowances for children up to 16 years old	For administrative reasons, the allowances are paid by the Pension Fund, which receives equivalent transfers from the budget. In turn, some of these benefits are paid by enterprises (deduction mechanism).

Source: IMF (1992: 59–61); IMF (1993: 136).

'The level and coverage of the various benefits are comparable to those prevailing in much more affluent OECD countries. About 40% of all Ukrainians are entitled to one or more cash benefits, with one person in four drawing a pension. In total, almost one quarter of GDP is allocated to publicly financed social programs and services' (IMF, 1992: 10–11).

The Pension Fund

The Pension Fund (PF) provides benefits for the elderly and disabled. According to the law on pensions, the compulsory retirement age is 55 for women and 60 for men. In order to be entitled to a full old-age pension, men are required to have worked 25 years and women 20 years. The full old-age pension is based on a proportion of personal previous earnings and is reduced in the case of early retirement. Pensions are issued via local post offices. The main revenue sources of the Pension Fund are payroll taxes, of which 31.8 per cent comes from employers and 1 per cent from employees. The role of enterprises in the provision of employees' pensions is that they can supplement the role of the state. They can pay retirees monthly or one-time additional payments. Such payments are voluntary, are stipulated by collective agreements, and depend on the financial performance of enterprises. In the case of early retirees or of pensioners who are still working, enterprises can also pay supplements. Some enterprises actually do make such additional payments to maintain the incomes of retired people, whose living standards have significantly decreased since the beginning of the transition, but this is not a widespread practice among enterprises, most of which are at present making a loss.

The Employment Fund

The Employment Fund (EF) provides job placement help, training, and benefits to workers who become unemployed. Its activities are decentralized, with offices operating throughout the republic. The law on employment that came into force in March 1991 defines two main categories of unemployed: those made redundant or who become unemployed as a result of bankruptcy; and the voluntary unemployed and new entrants into the labour force. Employers have to give due notice to workers they dismiss and to pay them a full three months' wages. If a worker does not find a new job during this period, he/she can be registered with a local employment agency as unemployed up to ten days before the end of a three-month term. This category of unemployed is paid the full previous wage during the first three months of unemployment, 75 per cent during the next three months, and 50 per cent for another six months (IMF, 1992: 139). In order to receive unemployment insurance benefits, unemployed workers in this category have to follow certain rules of job-seeking. The unemployment benefit cannot be less than the minimum wage or more than the average wage in a given industry. The principal revenue sources of the Employment Fund are 3 per cent payroll taxes levied on employers.

The Social Insurance Fund

The Social Insurance Fund (SIF) provides sick pay, remedial healthcare services, birth and maternity benefits, as well as sanatoria facilities for children and the temporarily disabled. Sanatoria vouchers are distributed by the trade unions in enterprises and enterprises can pay part of the value of such vouchers. Temporary disability benefits are paid to workers for a period of up to four months, and are extendable to one year, after which disabled workers become eligible for invalidity pensions from the Pension Fund (IMF, 1992: 59). The Social Insurance Fund is operated by trade unions. For administrative reasons, sick pay benefits and birth and maternity benefits are paid by enterprises. For example, in order to be eligible for sick pay benefit, temporarily disabled workers must present the medical certificate of their disability to a trade union office in the enterprise. Then the enterprise trade union chief presents the certificate to the accounting office in order to arrange sick pay benefit. The enterprise is reimbursed for the payments by means of a deduction mechanism. It deducts the total social insurance benefits paid to employees from its social contribution to the Social Insurance Fund, which totals 5.2 per cent of gross wages.

The system of family allowances and compensation for price increases

The state budget provides for uniform family allowances for households with young children and total income equivalent to less than twice the minimum wage, allowances for single mothers, allowances for low-income families, and so on. For administrative reasons, these allowances are paid by the Pension Fund, which receives equivalent transfers from the budget. In turn, as in the case of social insurance benefits, some of these benefits are paid by enterprises (deduction mechanism). Thus, the state guarantees the maintenance of some level of living standards for needy categories of employees. Nevertheless, a lot of enterprises pay voluntary additional payments to these and to other categories of employees for whom hardship has increased since the beginning of transition.

Thus, three extrabudgetary funds – the Employment Fund, the Pension Fund, and the Social Insurance Fund – provide social benefits that, together with subsidies and transfers from central and local governments, form a large social safety net. The principal source of finance for the social safety net is payroll taxes of 40 per cent levied on employers and 1 per cent levied on employees. As for the role of the state, it contributes to family allowances and compensation for price increases and mandates enterprises' social security contributions, which total 40 per cent of gross wages. In addition, the state mandates enterprises to provide severance pay to laid-off workers. As for enterprises, they, first, provide three months' severance pay to laid-off workers, second, bear the administrative costs of providing most of the social insurance benefits and family allowances, and, third, supplement a lot of the social benefits provided by the state such as medical care, sanatorium treatment, child care, additional payments to pensioners, the disabled, early retirees, low-income groups of employees, and so on.

Trends in compensation, 1988–93

Our hypothesis is that at the very beginning of the transition the share of monetary wages in the total compensation package increased and that later the share of the social wage increased relative to the monetary wage. Since there are no precise data to support this hypothesis, these tendencies are deduced from wage regulation policies and tax legislation (tables 12.2 and 12.3) and from the analysis of the structure of enterprise funds concerned with labour costs.

Wage regulation

Changes in the system of employees' compensation in state-owned enterprises in Ukraine, in the direction of economic transition, were first introduced by the law on state enterprises by the Soviet Union parliament in 1987. The law removed state control over wages because their liberalization seemed a logical step in the move to a market economy. It became a common practice for enterprises in that period to pay much higher wages than they paid before 1988. Therefore, one may suggest that there was a shift in employee compensation packages away from benefits in kind toward an increase in direct cash remuneration. In late 1991, reflecting the concern to mitigate the effects of price liberalization on incomes, the Ukrainian parliament passed a law on the indexation of wages and social benefits provided by the state. Under this law, many wages were immediately adjusted and in some sectors wage increases were reported to be very high (IMF, 1992: 16). This seems also to support the assertion that cash remuneration relative to social benefits was increasing.

The changes in wage behaviour at the beginning of 1992, caused by the

Table 12.2. Wage and tax policy developments, and possible effects on employee benefits, 1988–93

Date	Legal act	Content	Implication for benefits
1987 (wage)	Law on state enterprises	State-owned enterprises were allowed to free wages.	A shift away from benefits in kind towards an increase in direct cash remuneration.
1991 (tax)	Decree on payroll taxes	Payroll taxes were set at 37% of the wage bill, of which 26% was channelled to the PF and SIF, and 11% to the Economic Stabilization Fund.	The same.
Oct. 1991 (wage)	Law on indexation of wages and social benefits	A sliding scale of index compensation that varied according to the relationship of income to the minimum wage was introduced.	An increase in direct cash remuneration relative to benefits.
Feb. 1992 (tax)	Decree on raising payroll taxes	1% contribution from employees to the PF was introduced and an enterprise contribution of 37% to the PF and SIF, and 3% to the EF was approved.	A shift in compensation packages towards an increase in benefits in kind.
April 1992 (wage)	Decree on wages in the production sphere	Tax-based incomes policy: increases in payments were allowed only proportionally to increases in output. An excess wage tax rate, a multiple of the profit tax rate, was established (thus introducing a tax-based mechanism of wage control).	The same.
1992 (tax)	Decree on enterprise income tax	Substitution of an enterprise income tax for an enterprise profit tax.	The same.
Dec. 1992 (wage)	Decree on the consumption fund of an enterprise	The indexation scheme was abolished; enterprise consumption fund brackets were introduced; a new, tougher excess wage tax was introduced; the minimum wage was increased; the regulation of enterprise managers' payments was introduced.	The same.
June 1993 (wage)	Amendment to the decree on the consumption fund	A new excess wage tax was introduced; the minimum wage was increased.	The same.

Sources: IMF (1992: 9–10); IMF (1993: 25–30).

Table 12.3. An overview of the system of income and profit taxation, as of April 1993

Tax	Main characteristics	Tax rate
Personal income tax	Two parts: (1) Contribution to the Pension Fund (2) Progressive scale based on five income groups. Tax rate is calculated as a function of the minimum wage	1% (1) incomes up to the minimum wage (MW): tax-exempt (2) 1 MW–10 MW: 10% (3) 10 MW–20 MW: 20% + 4,140 UKK (4) 20 MW–30 MW: 35% + 12,140 UKK (5) More than 30 MW: 50% + 30,340 UKK
Enterprise income tax	Income includes wages and profits. Exempt from the tax: – enterprises where more than 50% of employees are disabled – joint ventures – bonuses Partial exemption from the tax: scientific research, environment protection, charity, medicine and medical treatment	18%
Wage fund tax	Wage fund = gross wages and salaries. Payments to employees from the Social Insurance Fund (e.g. sick pay, and birth and maternity benefits) that are paid by enterprises for administrative reasons are not included in the wage fund	52% rate is distributed as follows: – 31.8% Pension Fund – 5.2% Social Insurance Fund – 3.0% Employment Fund – 12.0% Chernobyl Fund

Source: IMF (1993: 135–136).

government's inconsistent financial policy, indicated the necessity of introducing a tighter policy of wage regulation (IMF, 1993: 26) and at the end of April 1992 the government proposed the adoption of a tax-based incomes policy to control wages and prevent a decline in production. Parliament approved the policy in its decree on wages in the production sphere, which became legally binding on enterprises of all ownership types. According to the decree, maximum wage funds, or normative funds, were introduced for 1992. It is suggested that, in addition, the mechanism may have led to an increase in benefits in kind because of enterprises' willingness to support employees' living standards.

At the end of 1992 the government again tried to control wage behaviour. The decree approved on 1 December 1992 introduced an enterprise consumption fund bracket. The consumption fund of an enterprise was defined as the sum of an enterprise's wage fund and various benefits in cash and bonuses. The decree also introduced a new, tougher excess wage tax and provided rules on the regulation of managers' monthly salaries so that they were in line with increases in profits and labour productivity. Nevertheless, we think that it was still possible to direct some profits to the social development funds, which were concerned primarily with the social infrastructure of enterprises. This, in turn, might cause a shift in employees' compensation toward an increase in benefits in kind.

Tax legislation
As for tax legislation, two main changes since the beginning of the transition, namely the substitution of an enterprise income tax for an enterprise profit tax and payroll tax increases, may also have led to an increase in the social wage relative to the monetary wage.

The structure of enterprise labour costs funds
The structure of enterprise labour costs funds and some aggregate data sets provide evidence of a rather high share of the social wage in the total compensation package.

The labour costs of an enterprise are reflected in its different funds: the direct remuneration fund, the additional remuneration fund, the wage fund, the financial incentives fund, the consumption fund, and the social development fund (fig. 12.1).

The *direct remuneration fund*, or *direct wage fund*. This consists of: wages and salaries paid by piece rates, wages and salaries paid by time rates, wages and salaries for overtime work and for high skills, payments for time not worked (vacation payments, vacation allowances, payments for enforced work breaks), payments for working in the evening and at

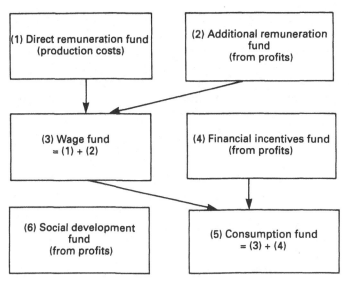

Figure 12.1   Labour costs funds in Ukraine

night, etc. The direct remuneration fund is considered as a production cost of an enterprise.

The *additional remuneration fund*, or *additional wage fund*. This includes various premiums and bonuses, for example premiums for hours worked, premiums for piece-work, premiums for working without accidents, seasonal and annual premiums, payments for increased output, premiums for achieving the production plan, premiums for technical improvements and inventions, premiums for the construction and implementation of new technology, premiums for the rational usage of raw materials and tools, premiums for performing special tasks, jubilee bonuses, and so on. Expenditures of the fund are paid out of enterprise profits.

The *enterprise wage fund*, or *gross wage fund*. This is formed by the direct remuneration fund and the additional remuneration fund. As has already been mentioned, a wage fund tax of 52 per cent was introduced, with 40 per cent earmarked for the social safety net (3 per cent to the Employment Fund, 5.2 per cent to the Social Insurance Fund, and 31.8 per cent to the Pension Fund). Social insurance benefits such as maternity leave, sick leave, and family allowances that are paid by enterprises for administrative reasons are not included in the wage fund. The wage fund tax is paid out of production costs.

The *financial incentives fund*. Payments from this fund are considered to be voluntary payments that are made by enterprises with the purpose of providing employees with incentives to work. Payments from this fund come out of enterprise profits. The following items are included in the fund: various types of financial assistance, sanatorium treatment, temporary housing rent, student scholarships, money transferred to the private ownership of employees for buying shares, transport passes for travel to and from work, subsidized food, discounts on prices, health payments, ecological payments, etc.

The *consumption fund*. This fund was introduced by the government in December 1992 in order to control wages. The consumption fund is made up of the wage fund and the financial incentives fund and is regulated by consumption fund brackets. If the consumption fund exceeds a certain level then an enterprise has to pay a penalty, or an excess wage tax, from its profits.

The *social development fund*. The expenditures of this fund are paid from enterprise profits. There is no explicit norm that determines the percentage of profits directed to the fund. However, the state may use implicit methods of regulation, for example in the form of recommendations to management. This fund is concerned primarily with the maintenance of the social infrastructure that was created in the pre-transition period. The social development fund, like the financial incentives fund, reflects enterprises' voluntary social spending. The items of expenditure and their level are negotiated between trade unions and the management. In general, enterprises spend approximately 14 per cent of their profits on items in this fund (Vasylyk, 1992: 17). The expenditures of the social development fund include: interest-free loans, temporary housing, sanatorium treatment, assistance to gardening cooperatives, the costs of operating kindergartens, policlinics, hospitals, fitness facilities and other social infrastructure, house building, and so on.

Loss-making enterprises are trying to get rid of social infrastructure that incurs losses. Nevertheless, in most cases this is impossible because state-owned enterprises are not allowed to sell social infrastructure facilities owing to a lack of privatization legislation, on the one hand, and there is a lack of buyers, on the other hand. Government policy is not directed toward large-scale privatization and legislation in this sphere is underdeveloped. In addition, enterprises are able to maintain the social infrastructure because, for the most part, they are highly subsidized by the government. According to the Economic Department of the Cabinet of Ministers of Ukraine (*Government Courier*, 1994, No. 62–63, p. 5), 16 per cent of state-owned enterprises made a loss in the first quarter of

Table 12.4. The structure of aggregate consumption funds in some industries in 1993 (%)

Industry	Wage fund	Financial incentives fund
Total industry	88.23	11.77
Coal industry	93.57	6.43
Machine building industry	91.25	8.75
Machine building and metalworking industry	90.86	9.14

Source: Ukrainian Ministry of Statistics (1994: 24–7).

1993 and 24.1 per cent of enterprises made losses in the first quarter of 1994. They did not go bankrupt because the government subsidized them and, in addition, bankruptcy legislation, like that on privatization, is not well developed.

The social development fund can be considered as a means of avoiding the excess wage tax. It is sometimes possible to redistribute payments from the financial incentives fund to the social development fund because the notion of financial incentives is rather ambiguous and there are no precise rules on what is to be included in this fund.

The Ukrainian Ministry of Statistics (1994: 26–7) has published aggregate data on the consumption funds of state-owned enterprises by industry and by region. Some data derived from these sets of figures are reproduced in table 12.4. The table indicates that payments from the financial incentives fund comprise about 10 per cent of the consumption fund. These data suggest that the social wage in most enterprises exceeds 10 per cent of the consumption fund, if one takes into account social infrastructure expenditure. It also means that for large enterprises the ratio of the social wage to the monetary wage can significantly exceed 10 per cent depending on the size of the infrastructure.

Thus, whereas wage rises were strictly controlled by wage taxes and wage bracket regulations, funds providing social benefits were tax free and less rigidly regulated. In addition, tax legislation (i.e. legislation on personal income tax and enterprise income tax) may have led to a shift in total compensation packages towards an increase in benefits in kind. On the other hand, many enterprises were making losses and this may have led to their willingness to get rid of the social services infrastructure. Therefore, it is impossible to discover any clear trend in the social wage by considering wage and tax policy developments alone. Therefore, in order to substantiate our hypothesis about the level of social spending in enterprises, the following section will look at the enterprise level.

The social wage in enterprises: ten case-studies

This section presents data on the social spending of ten enterprises in 1993. It summarizes the main findings of enterprise case-studies on employee benefits that were carried out in 1994. The detailed results are published in Tratch and Wörgötter (1996).

Table 12.5 presents the basic characteristics of the enterprises: the number of employees, the employee distribution by sex, the date of establishment, branch of the economy, activities/products, ownership status, and region. The enterprises are classified according to the number of employees: four are large (24,792, 21,509, 10,321, and 9,143 employees, respectively); two are medium sized (2,600 and 2,171 employees); and four are small (fewer than 1,000 employees).

All the large enterprises operate in the machine building industry and each produces different products, which vary from consumer electrical goods to automobiles and military goods. They were established several decades ago and each is still state owned. Medium-sized and small enterprises belong to different economic sectors, including machine building, light industry, and the coal and transport industries. The medium-sized enterprises and one of the small ones were recently transformed into joint stock companies whereas the three other small enterprises are still state owned.

The following classification of labour cost components is used to analyse the social spending of enterprises:

(1) The monetary wage, or earnings, bonuses, and payments for days not worked (vacations, state holidays, and forced work breaks); these are paid from the wage fund.

(2) Statutory enterprise expenditures, that is, statutory contributions to the Pension, Employment, Social Insurance, and Chernobyl funds.

(3) The social wage, or customary expenditures; that is, the expenditures that enterprises make either voluntarily or because of contractual agreements with trade unions. These are expenditures paid from the financial incentives and social development funds.

Table 12.6 shows both the structure of total labour costs (comprising monetary wages, statutory contributions, and customary expenditures) and the structure of total compensation (the monetary wage plus the social wage). The share of wages in total labour costs varies from 46.68 to 62.25 per cent, the share of statutory contributions from 24.28 to 32.37 per cent, and the share of customary expenditures from 5.38 to 29.04 per cent. (The statutory contributions are proportional to enterprise wages since total contributions make up 52 per cent of the wage fund.)

Table 12.5. The basic characteristics of the case-study enterprises, 1993

Enterprise number & size	Number of employees	Distribution by sex		Date of establishment	Branch of economy	Activities/ products	Ownership status	City (town) & region
		Female	Male					
Large								
E1	24,792	12,892 (52%)	11,900 (48%)	NA	Machine building industry	Automobiles	State owned	Zaporizhzhia, East
E2	21,509	9,956 (46.29%)	11,553 (53.71%)	Between 1928 and 1933	Machine building industry	Tractors	State owned	Kharkiv, East
E3	10,321	4,644 (45%)	5,677 (55%)	December 1892	Aircraft industry and machine building	Military goods, electrical mechanisms, electrical goods	State owned	Kiev, Centre
E4	9,143	2,468 (26.99%)	6,675 (73.01%)	21 May 1945	Machine building industry	Buses	State owned	L'viv, West
Medium								
E5	2,600	963 (37.04%)	1,637 (62.96%)	1930	Machine building industry	Pistons	Joint stock company (since 1990)	Kharkiv, East
E6	2,171	1,590 (73.24%)	581 (26.76%)	NA	Light industry	Shoes	Joint stock company (since Aug. 1993)	Zaporizhzhia, East
Small								
E7	904	173 (19.14%)	731 (80.86%)	NA	Transport	Public transportation	State owned	Zaporizhzhia, East
E8	840	167 (19.88%)	673 (80.12%)	December 1959	Coal industry	Coal	State owned	Novovolinsk, West
E9	655	94 (14.35%)	561 (85.65%)	1961	Transport	Freight transportation	State owned	Zaporizhzhia, East
E10	621	430 (69.24%)	191 (30.76%)	1933	Light industry	Perfumes	Joint stock company (since Nov. 1992)	Kharkiv, East

Table 12.6. Total labour costs and total compensation, 1993 (monthly per person)

Enterprise number & size	Total compensation			Total labour costs							
	Wages	Customary expenditures	Total	Wages	Customary expenditures	PF	SIF	EF	CF	Total	Total
						Statutory contributions					
Large:											
E1 UKK	215,019	97,254	312,273	215,019	97,254	68,376	11,181	6,451	25,802	111,810	424,083
per cent	68.86	31.14	100.00	50.70	22.93	16.94	2.64	1.52	6.09	26.37	100.00
E2 UKK	123,312	44,000	167,312	123,312	44,000	39,213	6,412	3,699	14,797	64,121	231,433
per cent	73.70	26.30	100.00	53.28	19.01	16.94	2.77	1.60	6.40	27.71	100.00
E3 UKK	173,766	68,653	242,419	173,766	68,653	55,257	9,036	5,213	20,852	90,358	332,777
per cent	71.68	28.32	100.00	52.22	20.63	16.61	2.72	1.57	6.27	27.15	100.00
E4 UKK	163,778	45,496	209,274	163,778	45,496	52,082	8,516	4,913	19,653	85,164	294,438
per cent	78.26	21.74	100.00	55.62	15.45	17.69	2.89	1.67	6.67	28.93	100.00
Medium:											
E5 UKK	165,936	27,574	193,510	165,936	27,574	52,768	8,629	4,978	19,912	86,287	279,797
per cent	85.75	14.25	100.00	59.31	9.85	18.86	3.08	1.78	7.12	30.84	100.00
E6 UKK	193,892	28,931	222,823	193,892	28,931	61,658	10,082	5,817	23,267	100,824	323,647
per cent	87.02	12.98	100.00	59.91	8.94	19.05	3.11	1.80	7.19	31.15	100.00
Small:											
E7 UKK	174,585	15,076	189,661	174,585	15,076	55,518	9,078	5,238	20,950	90,784	280,445
per cent	92.05	7.95	100.00	62.25	5.38	19.79	3.24	1.87	7.47	32.37	100.00
E8 UKK	366,121	75,876	441,997	366,121	75,876	116,426	19,038	10,984	43,935	190,383	632,380
per cent	82.83	17.17	100.00	57.89	12.00	18.41	3.01	1.74	6.95	30.11	100.00
E9 UKK	145,969	19,263	165,232	145,969	19,263	46,418	7,591	4,379	17,516	75,904	241,136
per cent	88.34	11.66	100.00	60.53	7.99	19.25	3.15	1.82	7.26	31.48	100.00
E10 UKK	144,404	89,842	234,246	144,404	89,842	45,921	7,509	4,332	17,329	75,091	309,337
per cent	61.65	38.35	100.00	46.68	29.04	14.85	2.43	1.40	5.60	24.28	100.00

As regards the structure of total compensation, the monetary wage varies from 61.65 to 92.05 per cent and the social wage from 7.95 to 38.35 per cent. Thus, the average level of customary expenditures is rather high and represents approximately 20 per cent of the total compensation package.

In order to analyse the importance of the non-monetary wage for employees relative to the monetary wage, it is necessary to determine what part of customary expenditure is social. Following the approach suggested by Rein and Friedman (1994), the components excluded as not being social are: jubilee bonuses, free shares, and company cars. According to this approach, the term 'social benefit' suggests a role beyond business, i.e. it comprises not just business costs. There are several reasons for distinguishing between social benefits and other components of the social wage.

(1) Commodity subsidization. The rationales for commodity subsidies are shortages and high prices. In the first case, enterprises can perform a social function by ensuring that, for instance, food is available. In the second case, in a highly inflationary period enterprises can protect employees by subsidizing certain commodities such as food.
(2) Social services. These comprise benefits such as kindergartens, health and child care, housing, and holiday homes.
(3) Social protection; i.e. protection against risk. The most important risk is the risk of income loss. Sick pay and contributions to early retirement are examples of social protection.

There are two parts to the social wage: the social wage in kind and the social wage in cash.

The social wage in kind comprises: (1) benefits that require social infrastructure, (2) other social benefits, and (3) other components of the social wage (see table 12.7). Almost all enterprises own significant social infrastructure. Enterprise spending on infrastructure includes housing construction, the costs of maintaining houses, dormitories, cultural, sports, and sanatorium facilities, hospitals, kindergartens, holiday houses, canteens, and gardening cooperatives. Social infrastructure expenditures make up the largest part of the social wage. For large enterprises the share of expenses on infrastructure varies from 61.53 to 93.19 per cent. For medium-sized and small enterprises these shares are also very high, on average approximately 65 per cent. Other social benefits in kind include a housing rent, housing loans, funeral expenses, medical and sanatorium treatment, interest-free loans, subsidized canteen and food store, subsidies for kindergarten services, recreation

Table 12.7. Social wages in kind, 1993 (monthly per person, % total social wage)

	Large				Medium		Small			
	E1	E2	E3	E4	E5	E6	E7	E8	E9	E10
Social infrastructure investment	34.33	–	–	–	–	–	–	–	–	–
Housing:	14.42	7.68	33.55	46.92	–	42.83	73.37	38.66	4.47	–
– permanent housing	NA	NA	22.00	36.70	–	30.65	0.00	25.89	3.89	–
– temporary housing (dormitories)	NA	NA	11.55	10.22	–	12.18	73.37	12.77	0.58	–
Kindergartens	9.67	17.40	19.10	16.15	–	23.88	0.20	19.53	–	–
Cultural and educational establishments	0.03	6.50	7.27	–	–	–	–	–	–	0.06
Medical establishments	0.01	32.81	14.70	–	–	1.20	–	2.14	–	–
Sanatorium facilities	–	–	1.02	–	–	–	–	–	–	–
Recreation facilities	–	13.43	1.27	4.14	–	3.24	22.01	–	10.51	0.90
Sports facilities	3.07	0.73	6.18	6.90	–	–	1.25	–	–	–
Canteen facilities	–	1.90	10.10	–	–	–	–	–	1.15	–
Gardening cooperative	–	–	–	–	–	–	–	–	46.23	–
Subtotal: social infrastructure	*61.53*	*80.45*	*93.19*	*74.11*	*0.00*	*71.15*	*96.83*	*60.33*	*62.36*	*0.96*
Housing (rent, other expenses)	–	–	2.55	–	–	–	–	0.05	–	1.04
Medical care	0.01	–	–	–	–	0.13	–	6.08	–	–
Free food	0.44	6.95	0.17	1.15	–	9.87	–	–	–	–
Subsidized canteen and food store	–	0.10	–	3.91	53.23	–	–	–	–	–
Funeral expenses	0.04	–	–	0.04	–	–	–	–	–	–
Sanatorium access	–	1.96	0.03	1.24	0.72	–	–	0.44	9.18	–
Recreation access	–	–	0.05	–	–	–	–	0.31	0.42	–
Transportation expenses	–	–	–	4.37	–	0.13	–	8.69	–	–
Coal	0.02	–	–	–	–	0.20	–	11.40	–	–
Petrol	–	–	–	–	–	–	–	0.21	–	–
Cultural events subsidy	–	0.89	–	–	–	–	–	–	–	–

Gardening cooperative	—	—	—	—	—	0.76	0.12	—	—	—
Subtotal: social benefits in kind	0.51	9.90	2.80	10.71	53.95	11.09	0.12	27.18	9.60	1.04
Privatization fund	4.32	—	—	—	—	—	—	—	—	—
Free shares	6.91	—	—	4.01	—	—	—	—	—	—
Festive occasion	2.33	0.43	—	—	—	—	—	—	—	—
Company cars	—	—	—	—	—	—	—	—	—	—
Other	7.58	—	—	—	—	—	—	—	—	—
Subtotal: other social wage in kind	21.15	0.43	0.00	4.01	0.00	0.00	0.00	0.00	0.00	0.00
Total social wage in kind	83.19	90.78	95.99	88.83	53.95	82.24	96.95	87.51	71.96	2.00

and cultural events, transport to and from work, and commodities like petrol and coal that are either sold at a significant price discount or are distributed free of charge. The share of other social benefits in kind differs quite significantly across the enterprises (from 0.12 to 53.95 per cent of the total social wage). In all but one enterprise, total social benefits in kind make up a very high percentage of the social wage (from 53.95 to 96.95 per cent). Finally, only three enterprises contributed to other components of the social wage in kind. For two of them the share of these expenditures was low (0.43 and 4.01 per cent, respectively). These expenditures included benefits such as free shares, celebration of enterprise anniversary, and company cars.

The social wage in cash is subdivided into: (1) social benefits and (2) other components of the social wage (see table 12.8). Social benefits in cash include one-off payments to retiring employees, the reimbursement of the costs of commuting to work, student scholarships, and various kinds of monetary assistance. The shares of social benefits in cash vary significantly, from less than 1 per cent on average for large enterprises to approximately 20 per cent on average for small and medium-sized enterprises. One possible explanation of this is that the share of social infrastructure benefits is on average higher for large enterprises. Other components of the social wage in cash were paid in almost all enterprises and varied quite significantly across the enterprises.

Summary

The main findings on the structure of enterprise social wages can be summarized as follows (see table 12.9). First, the social wages of enterprises make up a quite significant proportion of total compensation packages, varying from 7.95 to 38.35 per cent and amounting on average to approximately 20 per cent. Second, the social wage in kind significantly exceeds the social wage in cash, the average share of the former amounting to approximately 70 per cent of the social wage. Third, social benefits make up the largest part of the social wage, with an average share of approximately 90 per cent. Fourth, benefits that require social infrastructure make up the largest part of social benefits. Finally, the enterprises have no social protection spending in the sense of early retirement and sick pay.

Thus, in contrast to market economies where firms pursue profits and pay wages accordingly, enterprises in the socialist economy of Ukraine were not just producers but fulfilled both economic and social functions. Enterprises provided social benefits mainly for political and ideological reasons no matter whether it was profitable or not. The data presented

Table 12.8. Social wages in cash, 1993 (monthly per person, % of total social wage)

	Large				Medium		Small			
	E1	E2	E3	E4	E5	E6	E7	E8	E9	E10
Pecuniary aid:										
– to disabled workers	15.49	0.03	–	7.01	4.15	0.07	1.59	11.64	–	8.81
– to the enterprise's veterans	0.01	–	–	0.14	NA	NA	–	–	–	NA
– to pensioned off workers	0.08	–	–	0.26	NA	NA	–	–	–	NA
– to pensioners	–	–	–	3.00	NA	NA	0.31	6.05	–	NA
– to ex-servicemen	0.00	–	–	1.58	NA	NA	–	–	–	NA
– to youth	0.03	–	–	–	NA	NA	–	–	–	NA
– to gardening cooperative members	0.00	0.03	–	–	NA	NA	–	–	–	NA
– other	15.37	–	–	2.03	NA	NA	1.28	5.59	–	NA
Funeral expenses	–	–	–	0.00	–	–	0.66	–	1.91	–
Transport allowances for commuting	0.66	0.00	0.05	0.02	–	–	–	–	–	–
Interest-free loans	–	–	0.02	–	–	–	–	–	0.33	–
Non-returnable loans	–	–	–	–	–	–	–	0.26	–	–
Canteen bonuses	–	–	–	–	41.29	–	–	–	–	–
Health payments	–	–	–	–	–	14.04	–	–	21.74	6.00
Subtotal: social benefits in cash	16.15	0.03	0.07	7.03	45.44	14.11	2.25	11.90	23.98	14.81
Jubilee bonuses	0.66	–	–	0.72	–	0.34	0.80	–	–	–
Additional annual leave premium	0.00	–	–	–	–	3.25	–	–	4.06	–
Student scholarships	–	–	0.52	–	–	0.06	–	–	–	–
Professional holiday payment	–	0.57	–	–	–	–	–	0.59	–	–
Other	–	8.62	3.42	3.42	0.61	–	–	–	–	83.19
Subtotal: other social wage in cash	0.66	9.19	3.94	4.14	0.61	3.65	0.80	0.59	4.06	83.19
Total social wage in cash	16.81	9.22	4.01	11.17	46.05	17.76	3.05	12.49	28.04	98.00

Table 12.9. The structure of the social wage

	Large				Medium		Small			
	E1	E2	E3	E4	E5	E6	E7	E8	E9	E10
Social wage in cash										
Social benefits	16.15	0.03	0.07	7.03	45.44	14.11	2.25	11.90	23.98	14.81
Other social wage	0.66	9.19	3.94	4.14	0.61	3.65	0.80	0.59	4.06	83.19
Total	16.81	9.22	4.01	11.17	46.05	17.76	3.05	12.49	28.04	98.00
Social wage in kind										
Social infrastructure benefits	61.53	80.45	93.19	74.11	0.00	71.15	96.83	60.33	62.36	0.96
Other social benefits	0.51	9.90	2.80	10.71	53.95	11.09	0.12	27.18	9.60	1.04
Subtotal	62.04	90.35	95.99	84.82	53.95	82.24	96.95	87.51	71.96	2.00
Other benefits in kind	21.15	0.43	0.00	4.01	0.00	0.00	0.00	0.00	0.00	0.00
Total	83.19	90.78	95.99	88.83	53.95	82.24	96.95	87.51	71.96	2.00
Total social benefits	78.19	90.38	96.06	91.85	99.39	96.35	99.20	99.41	95.94	16.81
Total other social wage	21.81	9.62	3.94	8.15	0.61	3.65	0.80	0.59	4.06	83.19
Social wage as % of total compensation	31.14	26.30	28.32	21.74	14.25	12.98	7.95	17.17	11.66	38.35

in the paper demonstrate that a significant social infrastructure is still attached to enterprises so that they take an active role in providing social services to their employees. Two main factors make the high share of social benefits possible: the incomes regulation policy and the policy of subsidizing loss-making enterprises. Such developments mean that enterprises in Ukraine have not been moving in the direction of adopting a more Western style of social protection system rather than just providing social benefits.

REFERENCES

Barr, N. (ed.) (1994), *Labor Markets, and Social Policy in Central and Eastern Europe: The Transition and beyond*, New York: Oxford University Press.

Chornobai, M. (1992), 'Social tension: measurement experience', *Sociological Studies*, No. 8 (in Russian).

Constitution of the Ukrainian SSR (1977), Kiev, Ukraine.

Ehrenberg, R. G. and S. S. Smith (1991), *Modern Labor Economics: Theory and Public Policy*, Glenview, Ill.: HarperCollins.

Fajth, G. and J. Lakatos (1994), 'Fringe benefits in transition in Hungary'. Paper presented to the CEPR/Institute for Advanced Studies Conference on Social Protection and the Enterprise in Transitional Economies, Vienna, 25–26 March.

Government Courier (1994), No. 62–63 (in Ukrainian).

ILO (1995), *The Ukrainian Challenge: Reforming Labour Market and Social Policy*, Budapest: Central University Press.

IMF (1992), *Economic Review: Ukraine*, Washington DC: International Monetary Fund.

— (1993), *Economic Review: Ukraine*, Washington DC: International Monetary Fund.

Programme of the Communist Party of the Soviet Union (1989), Moscow (in Russian).

Rein, M. and B. L. Friedman (1994), 'Policy implications of social protection in state enterprises'. Paper presented to the CEPR/Institute for Advanced Studies Conference on Social Protection and the Enterprise in Transitional Economies, Vienna, 25–26 March.

Tratch, I. and A. Wörgötter (1996), 'Employee benefits and social protection spending of enterprises in the transitional economy of Ukraine', Working Paper, Institute for Advanced Studies, Vienna, Austria.

Ukrainian Ministry of Statistics (1994), *Statistical Bulletin*, Kiev, Ukraine.

Vasylyk, O. (1992), 'Financial aspects of social guarantees', *Economy of Ukraine*, No. 11, 13–21 (in Ukrainian).

World Bank (1996), *Income, Inequality and Poverty during the Transition*, Research Paper No. 11, World Bank, Washington DC, March.

13 Social protection and enterprise reform

The case of China

ZULIU HU

Introduction

Ever since the establishment of a centrally planned economy in the 1950s, state-owned enterprises (SOEs) in China have assumed a central role in social protection. For decades, SOEs have provided their employees with lifetime job security, free medical care, pensions, and numerous other cash or in-kind benefits. All major social benefits are paid out through mandatory 'labour insurance and welfare' (LIW) funds. In 1978, the year when China started economic reforms, direct outlays by SOEs on labour insurance and welfare accounted for 70 per cent of China's total expenditure on social security, or 1.9 per cent of GDP. Since then, SOEs' expenditures on social security have been increasing steadily, as China's economy undertakes far-reaching structural changes. By 1993, SOEs' outlays on labour insurance and welfare had risen to 80 per cent of total social security payments, or 4.4 per cent of GDP (table 13.1).

In contrast to most of the other transitional economies, the system of social protection in China is built on individual employer liability programmes rather than on social insurance schemes. Whereas major benefits such as pensions and health insurance are typically provided directly by the state in many other countries, in China it is the SOEs that are primarily responsible for both the financing and administration of their own labour insurance and welfare funds, which constitute the principal pillar of China's social security system. Despite the fact that these labour insurance and welfare benefits are mandated by the state, financing from the central government budget has been insignificant.

With market-oriented reforms, the traditional system of social security has been under severe strain. Composed of employer liability programmes, it has placed a heavy financial burden on SOEs and adversely affected SOEs' economic performance. To assist loss-making SOEs in meeting medical and pension liabilities, the central government has

284

Table 13.1. China: social security expenditures, selected years, 1978–93

Item	1978	1980	1984	1986	1988	1990	1992	1993
In billions of yuan:								
LIW[1]	7.6	13.3	25.5	41.6	64.9	93.1	130.0	165.8
of which, SOEs[2]	6.7	11.6	21.0	34.0	53.3	77.0	108.7	137.5
Budget[3]	1.9	2.0	2.5	3.6	4.2	5.5	6.6	7.5
Total	9.5	15.3	28.0	45.2	69.1	98.6	136.6	173.3
As % of GDP:								
LIW[1]	2.1	3.0	3.7	4.3	4.6	5.3	5.4	5.3
of which, SOEs[2]	1.9	2.6	3.0	3.5	3.8	4.4	4.5	4.4
Budget[3]	0.5	0.5	0.4	0.4	0.3	0.3	0.3	0.2
Total	2.6	3.5	4.1	4.7	4.9	5.6	5.7	5.5
Memorandum: LIW by SOEs as % of the total	71	76	75	75	77	78	80	80

Sources: Ministry of Labour, Ministry of Finance, State Statistical Bureau, Beijing, and author's estimates.
1 Employer-financed labour insurance and welfare (LIW) benefits, including pensions and medical benefits paid by SOEs, urban collective enterprises, and other non-state enterprises.
2 Including LIW expenditures of non-enterprise state units.
3 State budget-financed social welfare expenditures, including natural disaster relief, special pensions for disabled military personnel and survivor benefits for military families, and social assistance to the poor.

pumped in massive subsidies, which in turn contributed to the budget deficit and inflationary pressure in recent years.

The system of enterprise-based, non-transferable social benefits has, by tying workers to their employers, hindered labour mobility. Many SOEs have found it difficult to trim the redundant workforce caused by the full employment policy inherited from the central planning era.

Moreover, because the traditional system of social protection was designed for an economy with a dominant state sector, lifetime job security, controlled prices, and rationing of goods, it is ill equipped to protect workers against new risks such as unemployment and open inflation emerging with market-oriented reforms.

To sustain public support for economic reforms and maintain social stability, the Chinese government has placed a high priority on strengthening social protection. Although it has followed a cautious, gradual approach to price liberalization and enterprise reforms, and relied heavily on budget subsidies and transfers to shield workers from the adverse impacts of structural reforms, the government has shifted its longer-term strategy for social protection from individual enterprise-based programmes to the establishment of more broadly based social safety nets. In 1986, the government began to overhaul the traditional system of labour insurance and welfare. More recently, social security reforms have been accelerated in order to facilitate enterprise restructuring in the state sector. This paper reviews China's past experience and present progress in social security reforms, with a focus on the changing role of SOEs in social protection, and explores the implications for the labour market, enterprise reform, and fiscal policies.

Enterprises as providers of social protection

The Chinese laws and regulations introduced since the early 1950s mandate state-owned enterprises and other state units to establish their own labour insurance and welfare funds, which consist of old age and disability pensions, medical care, and work injury, sickness, and maternity benefits. In addition, SOEs are obliged to provide wide-ranging social services to workers and their families, including day care, dining facilities, housing, recreation and sports, secondary education, and, in many cases, transportation. Many SOEs also give other cash or in-kind benefits to workers and retirees, such as living allowances and subsidized consumer goods.

Prior to the economic reforms initiated in 1978, the state sector dominated China's urban economy, employing more than half of the country's industrial labour force (table 13.2), and contributing 78 per cent of national industrial output (table 13.3). In 1978, the labour insurance and welfare system covered the entire working force of 75 million employed by SOEs.[1] While the economic importance of the state sector has substantially diminished since the reforms, the SOEs' role in social protection has become even more important. Labour insurance and welfare payments by state-owned units remain the bulk of the aggregate social security expenditures in China, with the share rising from 70 per cent in 1978 to 80 per cent in 1993 (table 13.1).[2]

By contrast, central government financing of social security benefits has been relatively insignificant. From 1978 to 1993, budgetary expenditures by the central government on social welfare, which also included natural disaster relief, averaged less than 0.4 per cent of GDP per year, compared with the annual spending of 4.6 per cent of GDP by SOEs. Out of total budgetary expenditures on social welfare, a tiny amount was actually spent on employment-related benefits such as pensions, while the biggest part was earmarked for natural disaster relief and social assistance for the poorest stratum of the population.[3]

Table 13.2. The changing distribution of the industrial labour force in the state and non-state sectors, 1978–93 (% of total industrial workers)

Year	State sector	Non-state sector
1978	51.5	48.5
1979	50.9	49.1
1980	49.7	50.3
1981	50.0	50.0
1982	49.7	50.3
1983	49.1	50.9
1984	46.3	53.7
1985	45.2	54.8
1986	44.0	56.0
1987	43.7	56.3
1988	43.8	56.2
1989	44.7	55.3
1990	45.0	55.0
1991	44.9	55.1
1992	44.2	55.8

Source: *China Statistical Yearbook, 1993.*

Table 13.3. The evolving role of the state and non-state sectors in industrial production, 1978–93 (% of total industrial output)

Year	State-owned sector	Non-state sector
1978	77.6	22.4
1979	78.5	21.5
1980	76.0	24.0
1981	74.8	25.2
1982	74.4	25.6
1983	73.4	26.6
1984	69.1	30.9
1985	64.9	35.1
1986	62.3	37.7
1987	59.7	40.3
1988	56.8	43.2
1989	56.1	43.9
1990	54.6	45.4
1991	52.9	47.1
1992	48.1	51.9
1993	43.1	56.9

Source: *China Statistical Yearbook, 1994.*

A very effective protection for workers took the form of permanent employment in the state sector. Until 1986, SOEs guaranteed a lifetime job for all employees. Since these enterprises faced soft budget constraints, with virtually no bankruptcy risk, the risk of workers losing their job and pay was non-existent. The practice of lifetime employment explains the conspicuous absence of unemployment insurance in the traditional labour insurance and welfare system in China.

The labour insurance and welfare funds are the principal building blocks of China's social security system. These funds cover pensions, medical care, and other benefits for active and retired workers at the enterprise level. Although in principle only SOEs are obliged to provide these benefits, in practice most urban collective enterprises are also required to establish LIW funds. In addition, the central government budget provides special pensions for disabled military personnel and survivor benefits to military families. In 1993, SOEs and non-state enterprises spent 137.5 billion and 23.9 billion yuan on labour insurance and welfare payments, accounting for 83 per cent and 14.3 per cent of total expenditures, respectively, while the central government budget contributed 1.2 billion as special pensions, accounting for 0.7 per cent of total expenditures on labour insurance and welfare for the year (table 13.4). These figures may understate the true magnitude of central government expenditure on social protection because, first, part of the LIW liability of loss-making SOEs was financed by budgetary subsidies for these enterprises; and second, the central and subnational governments have provided consumer subsidies and cash compensation for the urban population to mitigate the impact of increases in food prices and other consumer prices.

Table 13.4 also provides information for assessing the overall costs of labour insurance and welfare for enterprises. The aggregate expenditures on labour insurance and welfare as a ratio of the total wage bill for urban formal sectors have been rising over the reform period. In 1978, this ratio was 14 per cent. By 1993, however, labour insurance and welfare costs had climbed to 34 per cent of the total wage bill. This ratio could be considerably higher for SOEs because the levels of labour insurance and welfare benefits are generally higher in the state sector.

A detailed analysis of the composition of social benefits for SOE workers helps illustrate the fundamental role of enterprises in social protection. Medical care and pensions constitute the two largest categories of SOE expenditures on labour insurance and welfare. In 1993 they amounted to 38.8 billion and 41.1 billion yuan, respectively. Together they accounted for 58 per cent of total outlays by SOEs on labour insurance and welfare, or 2.5 per cent of GDP.

Among the labour insurance and welfare benefits paid to currently

Table 13.4. Labour insurance and welfare expenditures by sector, 1978–93 (yuan billion)

Year	State sector	Of which: SOEs	State budget	Urban collectives	Other	Total	Ratio[1]
1978	6.9	6.7	0.2	0.9	–	7.8	13.7
1979	9.5	9.2	0.3	1.2	–	10.7	16.6
1980	11.9	11.6	0.3	1.7	–	13.6	17.7
1981	13.6	13.2	0.3	1.9	–	15.5	18.9
1982	15.7	15.4	0.3	2.4	–	18.1	20.5
1983	18.3	18.0	0.3	3.0	–	21.3	22.7
1984	21.3	21.0	0.3	4.3	0.1	25.8	22.7
1985	27.4	27.0	0.4	5.7	0.1	33.2	24.0
1986	34.4	34.0	0.4	7.4	0.2	42.0	25.3
1987	41.6	41.2	0.4	9.0	0.3	50.9	27.0
1988	53.8	53.3	0.4	11.1	0.5	65.3	28.2
1989	63.6	62.8	0.8	12.7	0.6	76.8	29.3
1990	77.7	77.0	0.7	15.3	0.8	93.8	31.8
1991	91.3	90.5	0.8	17.2	1.0	109.5	32.9
1992	109.6	108.7	1.0	19.9	1.5	131.0	33.2
1993	138.7	137.5	1.2	23.9	4.5	167.0	34.0

Sources: Ministry of Labour, Ministry of Finance, State Statistical Bureau, Beijing, and author's estimates.
1 The ratio of total expenditures on labour insurance and welfare to the total wage bill for urban formal sectors.

active workers, medical care is the biggest item (table 13.5). In 1993, expenditures on medical care, including work-injury related benefits, amounted to 25.8 billion yuan, accounting for 41 per cent of the total benefits paid to active workers. Medical care covers the full costs for SOE employees and half of the medical expenses for their immediate family members. Workers on sick leave receive full pay for the first six months and 60 per cent of basic wages thereafter.

The second biggest item is collective welfare expenses, mainly those incurred in operating and maintaining enterprise-provided facilities for dining, laundry, child care, and other facilities. Expenditure on this item amounted to 10.8 billion yuan in 1993, accounting for 17 per cent of the total.

Another significant benefit paid by SOEs is allowances for barber and bath fees, with total expenditure being 8.7 billion yuan in 1993. Many SOEs either directly operate such facilities free of charge for employees or provide coupons to workers to cover such expenses.

Table 13.5. Expenditures on social services and cash benefits for current workers in the state sector (including non-enterprise state units), 1978–93 (yuan billion)

Item	1988	1989	1990	1991	1992	1993
Medical care	11.3	13.5	16.4	18.9	22.0	25.8
Collective welfare service	2.5	2.8	3.4	3.6	4.2	4.9
Collective welfare facility	2.8	3.0	3.5	3.8	4.6	5.9
Sports and cultural activities	0.7	0.9	1.1	1.2	1.4	1.7
Funeral allowances	0.4	0.5	0.7	0.7	0.8	1.0
Allowance for low-income families	0.8	0.9	0.9	0.9	1.0	1.0
Allowance for family planning	1.0	1.1	1.2	1.4	1.4	1.5
Allowance for transportation	1.4	1.7	2.2	2.5	3.1	4.2
Allowance for barber and bath fees	4.3	4.9	5.6	6.3	7.2	8.7
Allowance for heating in winter	–	–	–	–	–	2.4
Other	3.0	3.3	4.6	4.2	6.7	6.2
Total	28.1	32.6	39.5	43.5	52.4	63.4

Sources: Ministry of Finance, Ministry of Labour, State Statistical Bureau; and author's estimates.

Other miscellaneous enterprise-provided benefits include allowances for transportation, allowances for family planning (paid to eligible working parents with only one child), funeral allowances and survivor benefits, subsidies for heating,[4] subsidies for low-income workers, and so on.

The other major targeted group of beneficiaries under the labour insurance and welfare system is retired workers in the state sector. Total SOE outlays on labour insurance and welfare benefits paid to retired workers reached 74 billion yuan in 1993, or 2.4 per cent of GDP.

The principal benefit for retirees is old age and disability pensions, which amounted to 41 billion yuan in 1993 (table 13.6). Another major item is medical benefits, with total expenditures being 13 billion yuan in 1993. These two benefits together accounted for 73 per cent of SOEs' total outlays in 1993 on labour insurance and welfare for retirees. Retired workers also receive miscellaneous benefits such as allowances for barber and bath, transportation allowances, rent subsidies, subsidies for residential water and electricity, and funeral allowances and survivor benefits. Since there is no formal indexing of pension benefits to hedge against the risk of inflation, cash compensation for food price increases was introduced in 1993 to mitigate the impact on pensioners' living standards of rising urban inflation.

In addition to the above-mentioned social benefits, SOEs have another very important obligation – to provide housing for both current

Table 13.6. Expenditures by state units on pensions and other cash benefits for retirees (excluding payments by the Ministry of Civil Affairs), 1978–93 (yuan billion)

Item	1987	1988	1989	1990	1991	1992	1993
Pensions[1]	11.2	13.6	16.5	22.6	26.5	32.2	41.1
Medical care	1.6	2.3	3.8	6.3	7.9	9.8	13.0
Nursing fees	0.1	0.1	0.1	0.2	0.2	0.2	0.3
Funeral allowances	0.3	0.4	0.5	0.7	0.8	0.9	1.0
Allowance for living expenses	1.8	2.1	2.1	2.6	2.9	3.3	4.4
Allowance for transportation	0.1	0.1	0.2	0.3	0.4	0.5	0.8
Allowance for heating in winter	–	–	–	–	–	–	0.6
Cash compensation for food price increases	–	–	–	–	–	–	8.2
Other	0.8	1.1	2.0	5.0	2.9	9.4	4.8
Total	15.8	19.6	25.2	37.5	41.6	56.3	74.1

Sources: Ministry of Labour, Ministry of Finance, State Statistical Bureau; and author's estimates.
1 Pensions include retirement pensions, resignation pensions, and termination payments.

employees and retired workers. Although data on direct SOE outlays on housing are not available, capital spending on housing construction by SOEs can shed light on the role of SOEs in providing housing for employees. Table 13.7 shows that SOEs' annual residential investment for workers has been substantial, accounting for 3.3 per cent of GDP in 1993.

The limitations of the traditional system of social protection

The pre-reform system of social protection for the state sector has been characterized in the Chinese economic literature as the so-called 'three irons': (i) 'iron rice bowls' (guaranteed job assignment, pay, housing, pensions, medical care, and a host of other benefits; (ii) 'iron chairs' (permanent job positions in permanent state enterprises); and (iii) 'iron wages' (uniformly distributed, fixed wage payments that are unconnected to job performance and productivity). Although this system was effective in social protection in the pre-reform era, its rigidities and limitations have become important barriers to enterprise restructuring.

Since the market-oriented reforms, the Chinese government has gradually granted SOEs managerial autonomy and financial independence in the interests of promoting efficiency. The numerous social

Table 13.7. Residential housing investment in the state sector (including non-enterprise state units), 1981–92

Year	Investment (yuan billion)	As % of GDP
1981	13.2	2.8
1982	17.0	3.3
1983	16.7	2.3
1984	16.9	2.4
1985	24.9	2.9
1986	24.3	2.5
1987	25.7	2.3
1988	29.2	2.1
1989	25.3	1.6
1990	37.0	2.1
1991	49.5	2.5
1992	79.3	3.3

Source: China Statistical Yearbook, 1993.

responsibilities of SOEs, however, have hindered the process of transforming SOEs into fully autonomous, competitive, and profit-maximizing enterprises. Undertaking these social functions has diverted SOEs' resources away from pursuing their principal business objectives. Funding these social services has significantly pushed up SOEs' labour costs. With increasing competition from the rapidly growing non-state sector, particularly from rural industry and foreign-funded enterprises, SOEs have found it difficult to maintain the expensive system of labour insurance and welfare for their employees.

Because labour insurance and welfare benefits are financed out of SOEs' current revenue, rather than from past and current contributions, the level of benefits can no longer be fixed *ex ante*, but tends to fluctuate from year to year, depending on the particular SOE's actual financial performance.[5] For the past several years, approximately one-third of SOEs have been loss-making. Financially troubled SOEs have suddenly found themselves facing the threat of bankruptcy and reorganization because an automatic bail-out by the government has become less than a sure thing given the considerably weakened financial ties between SOEs and the government budget. They are struggling to shoulder social responsibilities for their workers and at the same time to survive the competition from a dynamic private sector. Although some better-performing SOEs have actually succeeded in raising welfare benefits for workers, others have been forced drastically to cut social benefits, causing anxiety and discontent among employees and reducing the effectiveness of social protection.

Under the existing labour insurance and welfare arrangements in China, the burden of social protection is unevenly distributed across enterprises and across regions. Separately financed and administered employer liability programmes for individual enterprises are ill equipped to cope with sectoral shocks, business cycle fluctuations, and demographic shifts. Such a system offers extremely limited pooling and sharing of risks.

As a result, many older industrial enterprises, established either in the pre-revolution era or during the first two five-year plan periods, have many more retired workers and, therefore, substantially greater pension liabilities, than younger enterprises. Those regions dominated economically by the traditional state sector, such as the northeastern provinces, generally have a heavier social burden than those regions having a larger non-state sector, such as the coastal provinces in the southeast, because the non-state sector – encompassing the traditional collectives as well as newly emerged rural township and village enterprises, joint ventures, wholly owned private or foreign businesses – tends to have a younger workforce and considerably fewer social obligations than the state sector. The differing demographic characteristics between provinces, such as divergent fertility rates, life expectancy, and age structure of the population and the workforce, also contribute to the uneven burden of social protection across regions.

Table 13.8 gives information on the number of retirees and the dependency ratios in China's 31 metropolises, provinces, and autonomous regions at the end of 1993. It can be seen that the ratio of active workers to retirees varies substantially across regions. Whereas there were 7.4 workers for every retiree in Inner Mongolia, there were only 2.8 current workers to support each retiree in Shanghai.

Some SOEs have attempted to bargain with the supervising ministries and tax authorities for tax exemptions or budgetary subsidies on the grounds that they are unable to meet their labour insurance and welfare obligations. Indeed it is concern about the SOEs' failure to honour major liabilities such as medical care and pensions that has prompted the government to increase subsidies and transfers to financially distressed SOEs. In 1989, such subsidies ballooned to 60 billion yuan, accounting for 20 per cent of total government expenditure. Thereafter, subsidies for loss-making SOEs declined slightly, to 41 billion yuan, or 9 per cent of total government expenditure in 1993. These subsidies contributed to the fiscal deficits and macroeconomic imbalances in China during the reform period.

One of the central features that distinguishes the Chinese system of

Table 13.8. Number of retirees and dependency ratio by region, end 1993

Region	Total retirees (millions)	Of which: state sector (millions)	Ratio of workers to pensioners
National	27.80	21.43	5.3
Beijing	1.04	0.85	4.5
Tianjin	0.71	0.54	4.2
Hebei	1.09	0.88	6.4
Shanxi	0.71	0.58	6.5
Inner Mongolia	0.53	0.49	7.4
Liaoning	2.31	1.56	4.4
Jilin	0.84	0.65	6.5
Heilongjiang	1.39	1.16	6.2
Shanghai	1.74	1.30	2.8
Jiangsu	1.76	1.07	5.2
Zhejiang	0.96	0.62	5.3
Anhui	0.83	0.63	6.0
Fujian	0.57	0.43	6.0
Jiangxi	0.68	0.60	6.1
Shandong	1.42	1.00	6.0
Henan	1.15	0.95	6.7
Hubei	1.22	0.94	6.1
Hunan	1.22	0.94	4.8
Guangdong	1.49	1.07	5.9
Guangxi	0.58	0.48	6.0
Hainan	0.24	0.24	4.3
Sichuan	2.19	1.67	4.5
Guizhou	0.41	0.37	5.4
Yunnan	0.63	0.55	4.9
Tibet	0.03	0.03	6.0
Shaanxi	0.71	0.57	5.6
Gansu	0.40	0.34	6.5
Qinghai	0.14	0.13	4.6
Ningxia	0.13	0.12	6.0
Xinjiang	0.73	0.69	4.4

Source: *China Statistical Yearbook, 1994.*

social protection from that in many developed market economies is that the Chinese system depends on individual employer liability programmes rather than on social insurance. The enterprise-based labour insurance and welfare system has important implications for the long-term financial viability of social security, particularly the provision of old-age pensions. The Chinese population has aged more rapidly than that in many comparable developing countries owing to declining fertility, induced by a strict population control policy, and rising life expectancy. As China

Table 13.9. Changing dependency ratios for old-age pensions, 1978–93

	Ratio of currently active workers to retirees			
Year	State units	Urban collectives	Other ownership units	Average ratio
1978	26.2	68.3	–	30.3
1979	16.3	18.5	–	16.7
1980	12.6	13.6	–	12.8
1981	11.3	12.2	–	11.5
1982	10.0	10.7	–	10.1
1983	8.6	9.9	–	8.9
1984	8.1	7.8	9.3	8.0
1985	7.7	7.1	8.8	7.5
1986	7.2	6.9	9.2	7.1
1987	6.8	6.5	12.0	6.7
1988	6.5	6.2	12.1	6.4
1989	6.2	6.2	13.2	6.2
1990	6.0	6.3	14.9	6.1
1991	5.8	6.2	17.3	6.0
1992	5.5	5.9	16.6	5.7
1993	5.1	5.7	13.1	5.4

Source: China Statistical Yearbook, 1993 and 1994.

enters an ageing society, the dependency ratio – the ratio of pensioners to workers – has been steadily climbing. The time-series data in table 13.9 clearly show a declining trend for the ratio of workers to pensioners – the inverse of the dependency ratio. In 1978, there were 30 workers supporting one retired worker. The number of workers per retiree fell sharply to 13 in 1980, and continued declining, albeit at a slower rate, throughout the following decade. By 1993, the number had fallen to only 5 workers per retiree. The rising dependency ratio poses special problems for meeting pensions liability by the pay-as-you-go pension schemes established at the enterprise level in the state sector. The variation across ownership units, on the other hand, suggests potential gains from pooling on a much wider basis than pension schemes established at the individual enterprise level.

Enterprise-based social protection also has major implications for labour market reforms. Because important benefits such as pensions and housing are not readily portable, the enterprise-based system of social protection has contributed to labour market rigidity by tying workers to their employers. The yearly job turnover rate in Chinese cities is less than 1 per cent, and mobility for non-agricultural households is estimated to be less than 4 per cent, compared with, for instance, an annual mobility rate of 10–20 per cent in Korea. Labour market inflexibility is an important obstacle to enterprise restructuring in the state sector, which is overstaffed and desperately needs to reduce its high costs to stay competitive against the more efficient rural industry and private enterprises. In 1993, about 21 million workers, or 20 per cent of the workforce in China's state sector, were estimated to be redundant. Even this figure may have understated the true extent of surplus labour in the state sector. Since involuntary layoffs were officially discouraged as socially undesirable, the only practical means via which SOEs can trim their redundant workforce is voluntary labour exit to the private sector. The non-transferable pension, medical care, and housing benefits, however, provide strong disincentives to such labour mobility.

The social benefits offered by state-owned enterprises to their workers were extensive and generous, but a critical feature was missing from the old system – there was no unemployment insurance programme. Therefore, the traditional system is ill equipped to cope with the relatively new problem of unemployment. Although unemployment protection was not needed with China's old system of guaranteed job security, the changes in the labour market and the legal environment since the economic reforms have introduced unemployment risks into the Chinese economy. First, with the bankruptcy law – the first such law in the history of the People's Republic – which came into effect in 1988, even state-owned enterprises, once regarded as permanent, can perish under market forces, and their employees may be confronted with the prospect of unemployment.[6] Second, the share of contract workers – whose job contracts are terminable as opposed to the traditional lifetime employment – in the urban labour force has been rising sharply since the mid-1980s. Third, temporary workers migrating from rural to urban areas, such as those employed in the booming construction sector, have also been rapidly increasing in recent years, and they are vulnerable to unemployment risks if China's overheated economy heads for a 'hard landing' and the demand for rural migrant labour falls. Without unemployment insurance as a component of the social protection system, market-oriented reforms would inflict poverty and human suffering on the jobless, whose number is expected to grow, and the reform programmes themselves could lose the general support of the people who, after all, are supposed to be the beneficiaries of these reforms.

Finally, the structural changes in the Chinese economy and labour market developments have substantially reduced the effective coverage of the traditional enterprise-based system of labour insurance and welfare. The traditional system of social protection, geared toward the state

Table 13.10. The share of contract workers in the total workforce, 1983–93 (%)

Year	In total urban labour force	State sector	Collectives	Individual & foreign businesses
1983	0.6	0.6	0.3	–
1984	1.8	2.0	1.0	8.1
1985	3.3	3.7	2.2	11.4
1986	4.9	5.6	2.7	14.5
1987	6.6	7.6	3.6	18.1
1988	9.1	10.1	5.8	20.7
1989	10.7	11.8	7.0	25.1
1990	12.1	13.3	8.1	26.3
1991	13.6	14.9	8.9	28.0
1992	17.2	18.9	11.0	29.8
1993	21.0	21.9	15.5	37.4

Source: Ministry of Labour and State Statistical Bureau, Beijing.

sector and targeted to permanent employees, is inadequate to protect workers in the fast-growing non-state sector.

One of the structural changes that has a bearing on social protection is the new job tenure system in the state sector. In 1986, China introduced the 'labour contracting system', under which all new employees in state-owned enterprises are hired on a contractual basis for a period of three to five years. The introduction of labour contracts marked a shift from the offer of a permanent job to more flexible 'contracting', breaking away from the tradition of lifetime tenure. In contrast to the obligatory permanent job offers of the past, these hiring contracts do not guarantee automatic contract renewal or job extension upon expiration. With employment contracts of a finite duration, workers face the risk of joblessness. By 1993, the number of contract workers in the state-owned sector had risen to 24 million, accounting for 22 per cent of the total workforce in the state-owned sector (table 13.10). In Shanghai, China's largest industrial city, contract workers accounted for 44 per cent of total workers in 1993. As can be seen from table 13.10, contract workers grew from less than 1 per cent of China's total urban workforce in 1983 to 21 per cent in 1993.

The traditional system of labour insurance and welfare, originally for permanent employees in the state sector, has extended protection to contract workers in SOEs as well.

Another significant structural change that affects social protection is the dramatic expansion of the non-state sector. After more than a decade of economic reforms, the Chinese economy has become a mixed economy with diverse ownership and control, labour contracts, and employment practices. The spectacular surge of the non-state sector has drastically changed the distribution of employment across sectors. With more than half of the industrial labour force now employed by the non-state sector, including the now extensive rural township and village enterprises, maintaining a system of labour insurance and welfare exclusively for the state sector would have left a great number of workers not covered by social safety nets. Employees of the non-state sector, including the self-employed, are arguably more vulnerable to uncertainty and risks in a market-oriented economy, and therefore must be brought into the formal system of social protection.

Chinese experiments with social security reforms

The traditional enterprise-based system of labour insurance and welfare has failed to accommodate the structural changes in the Chinese economy brought about by economic reforms, and therefore needs to be revamped to maintain adequate social protection. Proposals on social security reforms in China generally aim at shedding enterprises' social functions to facilitate enterprise restructuring and, at the same time, at improving the coverage and effectiveness of social safety nets.

Enhancing efficient risk pooling and sharing

A key objective of social security reform in China is to relieve individual enterprises of full direct responsibility for their workers' retirement pensions by establishing pension funds that pool resources and risks among enterprises.

Experimentation with pension pooling began in 1986 in several cities, including Shanghai and Shenzhen. By 1991, pension funds for SOE workers had been established at the city and county level across China except in several remote border regions. Pooled pension funds for state sector workers had been established at the provincial level in eight provinces or metropolises such as Beijing, Shanghai, Tianjin, Fujian, Jiangxi, and Jilin. Employers and employees are required to contribute a certain percentage of the payroll toward these funds.[7] More than half of China's cities and counties have also set up separate pension funds for workers employed in collective enterprises. Pension pooling has placed enterprise-based programmes under the supervision of local governments for the first time. Because of the diverse experiments in pension reforms conducted at the city and county level, however, contribution rates to pension plans vary across localities and sectors and apply to different bases, leading to a fragmented system with only a limited degree of risk pooling and sharing.

The modest progress made so far on pension pooling is nevertheless expected to ease enterprises' financial burden of supporting a growing number of retirees. Pension pooling also helps to maintain workers' retirement benefits from job to job and, hence, makes conditions more conducive to greater labour mobility.

In addition, to relieve individual enterprises' labour insurance and welfare responsibilities further, many local governments have established medical insurance and work injury insurance plans to cover workers in state and collective enterprises located in their respective jurisdictions.

Expanding the coverage of the labour insurance and welfare system

As pointed out in the preceding sections, the traditional labour insurance and welfare system was intended to cover permanent workers employed in the state sector and in urban collective enterprises. With the introduction of a parallel new tenure system in China's urban formal sectors, the share of contracting workers in the formally employed urban workforce has increased significantly. To bring these contract workers under the umbrella of social security, separate labour insurance and welfare funds were established at the local government level. Each participating enterprise contributes a certain percentage of its payroll for contract workers to the labour insurance and welfare funds, which are managed by the Labour Bureaus of local governments.

Although labour insurance and welfare benefits have been extended to contract workers, maintaining separate funds for contract and permanent workers does not appear to be an efficient scheme of social protection. One of the limitations is that this fragmented approach precludes risk pooling and sharing across age cohorts. Since most younger workers entering the formal urban labour market are contract workers, the rising number of retired permanent workers will have to be supported by a declining number of active permanent workers. In many cities, the spearate pools are being merged.

Even with the inclusion of contract workers in the system of labour insurance and welfare, the coverage of the social safety nets in China remains incomplete. China has to address the issue of social protection for workers currently employed in rural township and village enterprises, for employees of private and foreign businesses, for the self-employed, and for migrant labourers from rural areas. The number of such workers has been growing rapidly. By 1993, for example, the rural township and village enterprises already employed 35 million workers, accounting for 34 per cent of China's total industrial workforce.

Introducing unemployment insurance

To facilitate the necessary trimming of the redundant workforce in the state sector and the implementation of the bankruptcy law, the introduction of unemployment insurance has become a critical task.[8] The package of labour market reforms introduced in 1986 included the establishment of an unemployment insurance (UI) scheme as a natural complement to the labour contracting system. The main elements of the unemployment insurance legislation are closely linked with the proposed labour market reform measures. The legislation addresses eligibility criteria, benefit levels, funding, and administration. Workers eligible for unemployment benefits include: (a) workers in bankrupt enterprises; (b) workers made redundant by near-bankrupt enterprises during a process of reorganization; (c) contract workers on the expiration or cancellation of contracts; and (d) workers dismissed for disciplinary reasons. The eligibility criteria are thus compatible with the structural changes in China's labour market and overall economy. The UI legislation sets a two-year duration for benefits and a nominal replacement ratio of up to 75 per cent of standard earnings.[9] Enterprises are required to contribute 1 per cent of their payroll to UI funds. The UI scheme has the feature that the funds may be used to finance job training and job creation programmes administered by local Labour Bureaus and their affiliated labour service companies, which have a mandate to assist new entrants and, more recently, job losers in identifying employment opportunities.

Because the unemployment insurance has been established as a social insurance rather than an employer liability programme, it is mainly administered at the city and county government level, not at the enterprise level. There have been several attempts in China to establish pooled unemployment insurance programmes at the provincial level, further moving away from enterprise-based social protection. The regulations on Unemployment Insurance for State Enterprise Employees were enacted in April 1993, and provide for the establishment, management, and operation of unemployment insurance funds. The UI programme as contained in the existing regulations covers only the state-owned enterprise sector. In some cities, such as Shenzhen and Qingdao, which have moved furthest on the reform front, however, UI has been extended to cover temporary workers, the self-employed, and workers in joint ventures and foreign-funded enterprises. It is the goal of the government to expand the coverage of the unemployment insurance system in the near future. In particular, unemployment benefits will be provided to all involuntary unemployed regardless of cause, and coverage will be extended to employees in collectively owned and foreign enterprises nationwide. It remains a desirable goal for China to extend the UI coverage to employees of rural township and village enterprises and private businesses.

The timely introduction of unemployment insurance has added a crucial programme to China's social safety net, facilitated the release of 'excess workers' from the overstaffed state sector, and helped to contain the social and economic costs associated with transformation to a market economy. During the first three years after the inception of the UI programmes, an average of 30,000 workers annually claimed UI benefits. This number more than tripled in 1990 and 1991, with the deepening of labour market and enterprise reforms. About 200,000 SOE workers in 1992 benefited from UI programmes. The number of UI recipients has so far been quite small relative to the total workforce in China's state sector. But this number may start to rise sharply in the next decade, depending on the current extent of 'surplus labour' in the state sector, the proposed extension of UI coverage, and the growth prospects of the Chinese economy.

Embarking on housing reform

Transforming state-owned enterprises into autonomous economic entities also requires the development of alternative means of providing their employees with housing. The obligatory provision of employee housing by SOEs has not only created labour market rigidity, but also imposed a heavy social burden on SOEs in comparison with their private sector counterparts such as township and village enterprises, and foreign-funded enterprises. Since the late 1980s China has made some limited progress in housing reform. Consensus has been reached that the provision of housing is not an essential function of state enterprises or government and that it could be better carried out by the private markets. The initial reform measures mainly involved incremental upward rent adjustments aimed at reducing the housing subsidy in the state sector. More recently, the focus of reform has shifted to privatizing the public housing stock by selling housing units to state employees. Several legal developments, including the 1988 amendment of the

Chinese Constitution, the revision of the 1986 land law, and the national regulations concerning urban land use, land transfer, and property rights, have had a positive impact on the development of the real estate market in China. As is widely recognized, these legal developments are necessary to replace enterprise provision of housing for workers with market-based delivery of housing. Many real estate development companies have been rapidly formed in the past few years to construct and sell residential property to Hong Kong residents and Taiwan investors. Although the number of domestic customers purchasing residential housing has been growing, these buyers tend to be China's *nouveaux riches* – the prosperous private businessmen. Selling housing units at market prices to SOE employees has proved to be more difficult, because of their low wage income[10] and the lack of housing finance. In some cities municipal housing funds have been set up – to be funded from the issuance of savings bonds and the proceeds from selling existing state-owned housing stock – to construct affordable housing for urban residents in general and SOE employees in particular. Mortgage finance companies are also being established, whose primary source of funding is pension funds.

Conclusions

Historically, enterprises in China played a central role in social protection. After more than a decade of far-reaching economic reforms, however, the traditional enterprise-based labour insurance and welfare system has become outmoded. It prevents labour mobility, hinders enterprise restructuring, and is poorly equipped to protect workers against new risks.

The Chinese authorities have noted the necessity to transfer social responsibilities from enterprises to government. The new fiscal reform measures, introduced in 1994, aim at enhancing the role of government in social protection and other social services such as education and health care. However, the lack of clear allocation of fiscal responsibilities and revenues between different levels of government in China poses a risk in the transfer of government functions from enterprises to the appropriate level of government.[11] Currently, for instance, it is the subnational governments – provincial and, most importantly, municipal – that are responsible for the financing and administration of both retirement funds and unemployment funds. The stated goal, however, is to establish a unified national social security system encompassing old-age pensions and unemployment insurance at the central government level.

In the past decade, China has made some important progress in reforming its social security as well as the wage and employment system. These developments have substantially facilitated labour mobility, helped protect workers' well-being, and sustained social support for economic reforms. China still faces formidable risks and challenges, however. Much more remains to be done to restructure China's state-owned sector and to deal with the threat of massive open unemployment in rural as well as in urban areas. Nevertheless, with the emergence of a strong, dynamic private sector, and the gradual creation of conditions favourable to reforms, China should now be relatively better positioned than ever before to launch full-fledged enterprise reforms.

NOTES

I would like to thank Ke-young Chu, Barry Friedman, Martin Rein, and the conference participants for very helpful comments. The opinions expressed in this paper are strictly mine and do not necessarily reflect the official views of the International Monetary Fund.

1 Urban collective enterprises, particularly medium-sized and large ones, also established similar labour insurance and welfare funds for their employees. The vast rural population, however, was outside the formal system of social security, although people's communes were once fairly successful in operating cooperative medical care for rural people. A tiny percentage of rural people – the poorest of them – received social assistance from the government. To date no attempts have been made to include the rural population in provisions for old age and disability pensions.

2 Outlays on LIW by employers in the state sector, or state-owned units, include those of SOEs and government institutions. Since LIW expenditures of SOEs dominate those of non-enterprise government institutions, the rest of this paper makes no further distinctions between LIW outlays by SOEs and those by all employers in the state sector (state-owned units).

3 In addition to social assistance, the central government provided generalized food subsidies and cash compensation for food price increases for the urban population. In 1993, for example, food subsidies and cash compensation amounted to 30 billion yuan, or 1 per cent of GDP.

4 The heating allowance was introduced in 1993.

5 Hu (1994) argues that the contrasting financial performances between the lacklustre SOEs and the prosperous rural township and village enterprises can at least in part be explained by the substantial difference in labour costs, including labour insurance and welfare costs.

6 In 1992, the People's Courts handled 2,685 bankruptcy cases nationwide, involving some unprofitable and debt-ridden state-owned enterprises.

7 In Shanghai, for example, the contribution rates by both enterprises and workers are set at 5 per cent of the wage bill.

8 This subsection and the next draw heavily on Hu (1994).

9 Standard earnings are defined as the claimant's average monthly standard wage over two years prior to the date eligible for UI benefits.

10 The low monetary income of SOE workers reflects the payment of many subsidies in kind in China's state sector, including consumer goods and low-rent accommodation.

11 For a discussion of the issues and options for reforming social expenditure allocation in China, see Hu (1993).

BIBLIOGRAPHY

Ahmad, E. and A. Hussain (1990), 'Social security in China: A historical perspective', in E. Ahmad et al. (eds.), Social Security in Developing Countries, Oxford: Oxford University Press.

Bell, W. M., H. E. Khor, and K. Kochhar (1993), 'China at the threshold of a market economy', IMF Occasional Paper 107, Washington DC, September.

Blejer, M., D. Burton, S. Dunaway, and G. Szapary (1991), 'China: Economic reform and macroeconomic management', IMF Occasional Paper 76, Washington DC, January.

China Statistical Yearbook, various issues, State Statistical Bureau, Beijing.

Hu, Z. (1993), 'Social expenditure assignments in China: issues and options'. Paper presented at the International Symposium on Fiscal Federalism, Shanghai, 22–26 October 1993; forthcoming in V. Tanzi (ed.), Reforming Intergovernmental Fiscal Relations – An International Perspective, Washington DC: IMF.

 (1994), 'Social protection, labor market rigidity, and enterprise restructuring in China', IMF Paper on Policy Analysis and Assessment No. 22, Washington DC, October.

Lichtenstein, N. (1993), 'Enterprise reform in China: The evolving legal framework', World Bank Working Papers 1198, Washington DC, September.

Perkins, D. H. (1988), 'Reforming China's economic systems', Journal of Economic Literature 26, June, 601–645.

World Bank (1992), 'China: Implementation options for urban housing reform', Washington DC.

Index

Printed in the United States
By Bookmasters